Hanoi

Hanoi

City of the Rising Dragon

Georges Boudarel and Nguyen Van Ky

Foreword by William J. Duiker

Translated by Claire Duiker

ROWMAN & LITTLEFIELD PUBLISHERS, INC.

Lanham • Boulder • New York • Oxford

ROWMAN & LITTLEFIELD PUBLISHERS, INC.

Published in the United States of America
by Rowman & Littlefield Publishers, Inc.
An Imprint of the Rowman & Littlefield Publishing Group
4720 Boston Way, Lanham, Maryland 20706
www.rowmanlittlefield.com

12 Hid's Copse Road, Cumnor Hill, Oxford OX2 9JJ, England

British Library Cataloguing in Publication Information Available

Library of Congress Cataloging-in-Publication Data

Boudarel, Georges.
    [Hanoi 1936–1996, du drapeau rouge au billet vert. English]
    Hanoi: city of the rising dragon / Georges Boudarel and Nguyen Van Ky ; translated by Claire Duiker.
        p.   cm.
    Includes bibliographical references and index.
    ISBN 0-7425-1654-7 (alk. paper)—ISBN 0-7425-1655-5 (pbk. : alk. paper)
    1. Hanoi (Vietnam)—History.   2. Vietnam—History—20th century.
  I. Nguyên, Van Ky. II. Title.
  DS559.93.H36 B68   2002
  959.7—dc21   2001041790

Printed in the United States of America

♾ ™ The paper used in this publication meets the minimum requirements of American National Standard for Information Sciences—Permanence of Paper for Printed Library Materials, ANSI/NISO Z39.48–1992.

Contents

Part III: Toward Liberation

Part IV: Visions of the Future

Chronology

972:	Vietnamese independence recognized by China
980:	Foundation of Le dynasty (980–1009) by Le Hoan
1010:	Foundation of Ly dynasty (1010–1225) by Ly Thai To in Thang Long (now known as Hanoi), capital of the Dai Viet Kingdom
1070:	Construction of the Temple of Literature (Van Mieu) in Hanoi
1225:	Foundation of Tran dynasty (1225–1400) by Tran Thu Do
1257:	First Mongol attack on Vietnam
1400:	Foundation of Ho dynasty (1400–1407) by Ho Quy Ly
1407:	Conquest of Dai Viet Kingdom by Chinese Ming dynasty
1428:	Foundation of Le dynasty (1428–1788) by Le Loi
1627:	Civil war between the Trinh and the Nguyen (1627–72)
1771:	Eruption of Tay Son Rebellion
1787:	Treaty of Versailles between Nguyen Anh, Nguyen pretender to the Vietnamese throne, and the Kingdom of France
1788:	Defeat of the Trinh and foundation of Tay Son dynasty (1788–1802) by Nguyen Hue
1802:	Final defeat of the Tay Son and foundation of Nguyen dynasty (1802–1945) by Nguyen Anh. Unification of the kingdom under the name of Viet-nam
1858:	First French attack on Vietnamese territory in Da Nang Harbor
1883–85:	French conquest of Tonkin, including the establishment of the Treaty of the Protectorate (1884), confirming French control over all of Vietnam
1887:	Indochinese Union established over Vietnam and Cambodia

1893–1902:   Organization of French Indochina under Paul Doumer

1927:   Foundation of the Nationalist Party (Viet Nam Quoc Dan Dang) by Nguyen Thai Hoc in Hanoi

1930:   Foundation of the Indochinese Communist Party. Crises, revolts, and mutinies at Yen Bay; insurrection of Nghe Tinh

1935:   The Indochinese Communist Party holds its first national congress in Macao

1936:   Rise of the Popular Front in France and promulgation of a worker's code in Indochina

1937:   Halt to the reforms in Indochina

1938:   Conflict between Vietnamese Stalinists and Trotskyites

1940–45:   Japanese occupation of Indochina

1941:   Eighth Plenum of the Indochinese Communist Party sets up the League for the Independence of Vietnam (popularly known as the Vietminh)

1945:   Japanese coup d'état abolishes French rule in Indochina and offers Emperor Bao Dai independence under Japanese protection (March)

Vietnamese puppet government formed under Prime Minister Tran Trong Kim (April)

Ho Chi Minh sets up Communist Party headquarters at Tan Trao (May)

Japan surrenders (14 August)

Vietminh appeals for general uprising throughout Vietnam and declares Ho Chi Minh president of a provisional republic of Vietnam (16 August)

Declaration of independence of Vietnam by Ho Chi Minh (2 September)

Chinese occupation forces arrive in Hanoi, while British and French troops arrive in Saigon (September)

Vietminh forces retreat from Saigon and begin guerilla operations against French administration in Cochin China (October)

Indochinese Communist Party dissolved by Ho Chi Minh

Formation of a coalition government in Hanoi, including both Communist and Nationalist Parties, with Ho Chi Minh as president of the Democratic Republic of Vietnam

1946:   Fontainebleau Conference held between the French and the

Democratic Republic of Vietnam in Paris. Agreement is not reached, leading to a breakdown of relations

Coalition government reorganizes to exclude Nationalist factions

Beginning of the Franco-Vietminh war

1949: Victory of Mao Zedong in China

1950: The Soviet Union and the People's Republic of China officially recognize the independence of the Democratic Republic of Vietnam, while the United States and Britain recognize the Associated State of Vietnam under the leadership of Bao Dai, established as part of the French Union

Battles continue between the Vietminh and the French; President Truman approves $15 million in military aid to support the French

1954: The battle of Dien Bien Phu; French suffer devastating loss to Vietminh forces

Geneva Conference decrees a cease-fire and the partitioning of Vietnam

Formation of the Southeast Asia Treaty Organization in Manila

Departure of French troops from Hanoi

Ho Chi Minh returns to power in the North

1955: Ngo Dinh Diem defeats Bao Dai to become president of the Republic of Vietnam (South)

1956: Nikita Khrushchev's report against Stalin; movements in Poland and Hungary

Agrarian Reform Campaign established in the Democratic Republic of Vietnam

The revelation of excesses committed within the party lead to violence and antiestablishment activities

1957–58: Discontent rises against Ngo Dinh Diem in the South

1959: Central Committee of Vietnamese Workers' Party adopts program to resume revolutionary war in the South

U.S. advisers sent to aid the units of the southern army

1960: Third National Congress of the Vietnamese Worker's Party held in Hanoi. Le Duan elected first secretary of the party. Decision to escalate the struggle in the South

John F. Kennedy becomes president of the United States

Formation of the National Front for the Liberation of South Vietnam

1961: U.S. escalation, with special operations of sabotage in the North

1963: Assassination of Ngo Dinh Diem in the South and of Kennedy in Dallas

1964: Deterioration of the political situation in the South as several governments succeed each other in Saigon

Vote of the Central Committee on the Ninth Resolution against modern revisionism

1965: Attack by revolutionary forces on U.S. base at Pleiku provides Johnson administration with a pretext to launch bombing campaign in the North and begin dispatch of troops to the South

1967: Peace protests in the United States

Arrests in the North of several key figures in the Communist Party, including Hoang Minh Chinh and Vu Dinh Huynh

1968: The Tet Offensive against villages in the South

1969: Death of Ho Chi Minh

Peace talks open in Paris

1972: Nixon visits the People's Republic of China

1973: Paris Agreement signed, ending direct U.S. participation in the war

1975: Communist forces launch offensive in the South and occupy Saigon

The Khmer Rouge takes power in Cambodia

1976: Creation of the Socialist Republic of Vietnam, uniting North and South

Fourth Party Congress in Hanoi; the Indochinese Communist Party becomes the Vietnamese Communist Party

1978: Chinese refugees flee Vietnam claiming mistreatment; China cuts off aid to the Socialist Republic of Vietnam

Treaty of Friendship and Cooperation between Vietnam and the USSR

Membership of Vietnam in the Council for Mutual Economic Assistance

1979: Vietnamese forces invade and occupy Cambodia and set up pro-Vietnamese government, the People's Republic of Kampuchea

Chinese and Vietnamese forces clash over border disputes

Exodus of "boat people"

1982:   Fifth Congress of the Vietnamese Communist Party; Giap leaves the Politburo

1986:   Club of Resistance Fighters founded in Ho Chi Minh City, demand for free elections

Death of General Secretary Le Duan, replaced by Truong Chinh

Sixth Congress of the Vietnamese Communist Party; Truong Chinh and other veteran members are dismissed from the Politburo, and Nguyen Van Linh is elected secretary general

Decision to launch the campaign of Renovation (doi moi)

1987:   Adoption of economic reforms by the Central Committee

Truong Chinh and Pham Van Dong resign as head of state and prime minister and are replaced by Vo Chi Cong and Pham Hung

1988:   Death of Truong Chinh and Pham Hung; Vo Van Kiet becomes prime minister

1989:   Tiananmen Square massacre in Beijing

Fall of the Berlin Wall

Evacuation of Vietnamese forces from Cambodia

1990:   The Central Committee rejects a multiparty system and reaffirms its adhesion to socialism

The U.N. Security Council in agreement over a peace plan for Cambodia

Death of Le Duc Tho

1991:   First step toward a normalization of U.S.–Vietnamese relations

Collapse of the USSR

Seventh Congress of the Vietnamese Communist Party. Do Muoi is named secretary general

Paris accords end civil war in Cambodia

Normalization of Sino-Vietnamese relations

1992:   Revised constitution reduces the role of Marxism-Leninism in Vietnamese society

General Le Duc Anh is elected president; Vo Van Kiet is reelected prime minister

Vietnam and Laos gain entrance into the Treaty of Cooperation and Friendship in Bali, antechamber of the Association of Southeast Asian Nations

1993:   Influx of business people and foreign companies into Vietnam
               Visit of President François Mitterand of France to Vietnam
1994:   Development of a market economy and influx of foreign
                  investment
               Lifting of the U.S. embargo
               Intensification of the fight against corruption
1995:   United States and Vietnam establish diplomatic relations
               Vietnam joins the Association of Southeast Asian Nations
               Fiftieth anniversary of independence
1996:   Eighth Congress of the Vietnamese Communist Party
               Liberation of the dissident Ha Si Phu after one year of impris-
                  onment
               Le Kha Phieu replaces Do Muoi as secretary general of the
                  Communist Party, and Tran Duc Luong replaces Le Duc
                  Anh as head of state
1997:   Death of Tran Dan, one of the founders of the Hundred Flow-
                  ers movement
               Peasant revolts against corruption and abuse of power in Thai
                  Binh region
               Senator Lane Evans visits Vietnam
               Seventh Francophone Summit held in Hanoi
               Kim Phuc elected goodwill ambassador to UNESCO (she was
                  made famous by the 1972 photograph of her as a little girl
                  running down a Vietnamese street with napalm burns)
1998:   Senator John Kerry visits Vietnam
               Hanoi-to-Saigon bicycle race organized by U.S. war veterans,
                  including the participation of American and Vietnamese
                  veterans and cycling champion Greg Lemond
               Seattle and Hai Phong are linked as sister cities
               First International Conference on Vietnamese Studies orga-
                  nized in Hanoi with the support of the Ford Foundation and
                  Toyota
               Amnesty of 5,000 prisoners, including political prisoners Doan
                  Viet Hoat and Nguyen Dan Que and monks Thich Quand
                  Do and Thich Tue
               Vietnam enters Asian Pacific Economic Commission
               Korean President Kim Dae Jung apologizes for Korea's role in
                  the Vietnam War

1999:   Publication of *Mercury News* in Vietnamese, *Viet Mercury*, in San Jose

The Office of the High Commission on Refugees closes in Saigon after twenty-five years of activities

Liberation of biologist Nguyen Thanh Giang, arrested two months earlier for having "leaked documents sensitive to the regime"

Official visit to Vietnam by U.S. Secretary of State Madeleine Albright

U.S. consulate opens in Ho Chi Minh City on the site of the former embassy

End of the Orderly Departure Program, allowing Vietnamese in Vietnam to rejoin their families in the United States

The Cham towers of Quang Nam Province and the city of Hoi An are declared World Historical sites by UNESCO

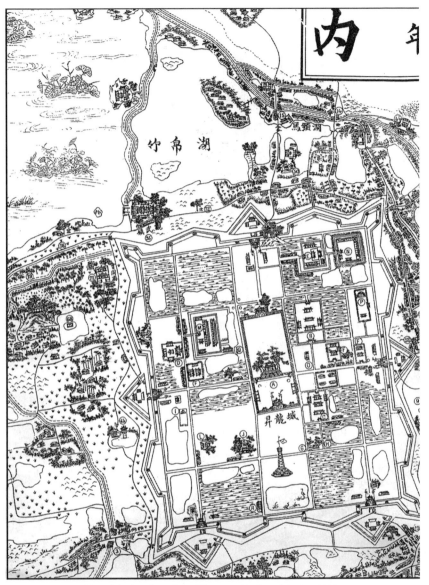

*Hanoi during the reign of Emperor Tu Duc (1848–1883),
with the rectangular imperial city located in the center.*

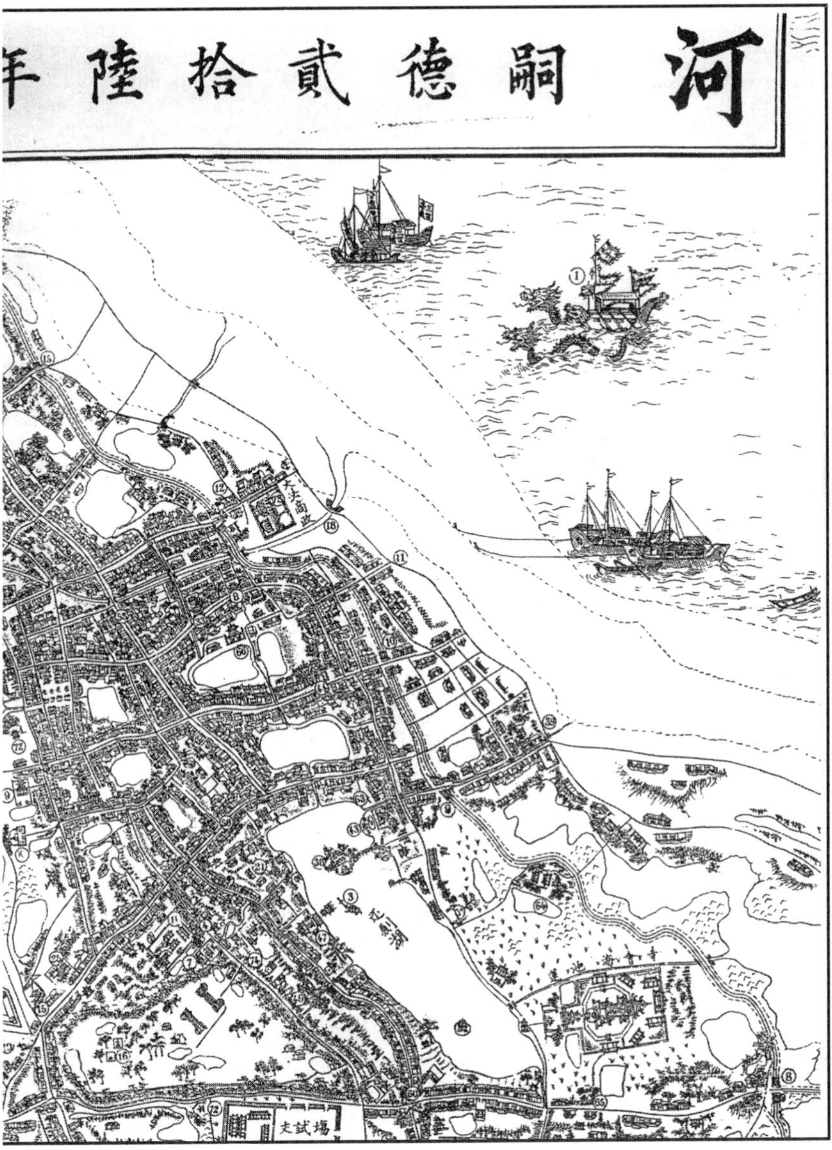
河 嗣德貳拾陸年
試場

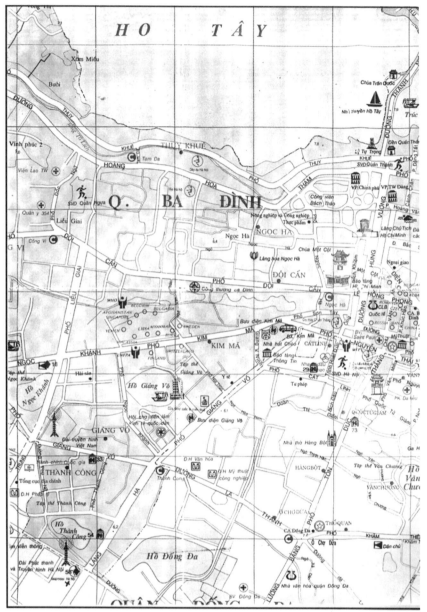

Hanoi today, showing major government installations and tourist sites.

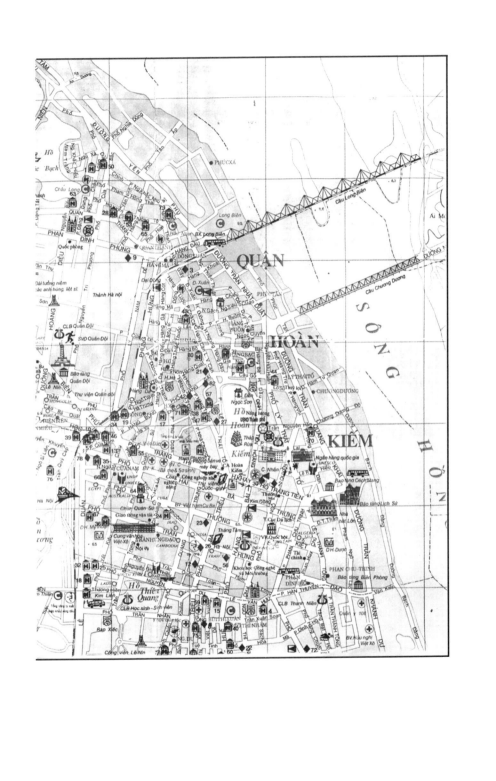

Translator's Note

Claire Duiker

To simplify the difficulties of rendering the tones of the Vietnamese language into English, accents and diacritical marks have been dropped. Vietnamese names are listed in the index by family name, which appears first (e.g., Vo Nguyen Giap is under Vo, Ho Chi Minh is under Ho).

Many of the works cited from the Vietnamese have not been translated into either French or English. If no translated source is given, the Vietnamese was translated into French by the authors and then rendered into English by the translator. Where translations are available, I have included them in the bibliography, leaving the original language text and page numbers in the notes.

The prologue from the French edition has been included in its entirety as it forms a part of the complete French text. Its author is a prominent scholar in Franco-Vietnamese studies who lives in Paris. He preferred, however, not to include his name given the rather controversial status of Georges Boudarel.

Last, I would like to thank my father, William Duiker, for his help and infinite patience.

Foreword

William J. Duiker

To most Americans old enough to recall the Vietnam War, mention of the name Hanoi conjures up recollections of a bitter period in the history of their country. To some, it conveys an image of waves of B-52s raining bombs on a defenseless city. To others, it evokes the memory of a faceless but implacable enemy scheming to subjugate the Vietnamese people under a tyrannical regime reminiscent of the Stalinist era in Russia. The reality, of course, is much more complex. What we now know as the bustling modern capital of Communist Vietnam has a history that dates back to the Bronze Age. It was then, in the first millennium B.C.E., that peoples living in the area first began to form an advanced civilization based on fishing, manufacturing, and the cultivation of wet rice.

In 111 B.C.E., the Red River Valley was conquered by the Han dynasty and subjected to 1,000 years of Chinese rule. After Vietnamese independence was restored in the eleventh century C.E., Hanoi, then called Thang Long, was named the capital of the independent state of Dai Co Viet, or Great Viet. Emperor Ly Thai To's decision to select Thang Long as the location of his new capital is understandable. Situated at the confluence of three rivers as they flow through the Red River delta toward the South China Sea, the site is located in the middle of the river valley and easy to defend against potential enemies. It is also surrounded by fertile soil suitable for the cultivation of wet rice, the prime staple on which the Vietnamese people rely for their subsistence. For the next several centuries, it was not only the administrative capital of the Vietnamese state but also its commercial and manufacturing hub, with its own outlet to the sea at the mouth of Red River as it flows into the Tonkin Gulf. Over the next several hundred years, Thang Long played an active part in the complex history of the Vietnamese nation. On several occasions the nation was occupied by hostile forces, notably during the early fifteenth century, when Chinese troops briefly occupied the delta and placed it under the control of the Ming Empire. In 1428 a new dynasty, known as the Le, drove out the Chinese, and during the ensuing centuries, Vietnam entered an era of rapid expansion. It extended its borders southward to the Mekong delta and ultimately to the Gulf of Siam, becoming in the process the most powerful state in the region. As the country grew, Thang Long took on the character of an imperial city on the Chinese model, with the Vietnamese emperor portraying himself as a smaller version of the Son of Heaven in imperial China.

But expansion brought problems, as the Le rulers encountered difficulties in managing their now enlarged empire. By the seventeenth century, the dynasty had declined in effectiveness, with political power dominated by two powerful noble families, one based in the North and the other in the South, each claiming the title of sponsor and protector of the figurehead emperor in Thang Long. As a frontier area with great expanses of cultivable land and a climate more favorable to the cultivation of crops, the South now began to take on a character of its own. Whereas the northern provinces remained highly traditional in outlook and inward-looking in their primary focus on the cultivation of wet rice, the South, with its profusion of tropical products, became increasingly linked to the regional trade network that passed through the South China Sea en route to China, Japan, and the Indian Ocean. The population in the southern provinces was thus less traditional and more entrepreneurial in nature, more prosperous, and more in touch with events taking place elsewhere in the world. The cultural rift between the two regions intensified as time passed and eventually would have a major impact on the country during the colonial era and the Cold War.

With the rise of a new Nguyen dynasty in 1802, Emperor Gia Long transferred the capital to Hue, several hundred miles to the south in central Vietnam, in order to symbolize the reunification of the country after two centuries of civil strife. Deprived of its symbolic power as an imperial capital, Thang Long was given the more prosaic name of Ha Noi—"amid the rivers." But the power of the new dynasty was not destined to last out the century. In the early 1860s, French troops defeated imperial armies near Saigon and transformed the Mekong River delta into the new colony of Cochin China. Two decades later France declared a protectorate over the remainder of the Vietnamese Empire. Under the French, Hanoi began to reclaim its central position in the destiny of the Vietnamese nation, as the country's new rulers selected the city as the administrative capital of their colonial empire in Southeast Asia. During World War II, Hanoi came briefly under Japanese military occupation. Then, at the moment of Japanese surrender in August 1945, Vietnamese troops led by the wily Communist leader Ho Chi Minh occupied the city, and Hanoi was quickly named the capital of an independent Democratic Republic of Vietnam (DRV), with Ho Chi Minh as its provisional president. But negotiations between representatives of the new state and the French failed to find a compromise solution between the restoration of French colonial rule and Vietnamese independence, and in December 1946 Ho's followers launched a surprise attack on French installations in the city. Then they retreated to the countryside, where they launched a guerrilla struggle to liberate their country from foreign control.

At the Geneva Conference of 1954, a cease-fire was signed, calling for the departure of the French and the temporary division of the country into a Communist North and a non-Communist South. Hanoi once again became the capital of the DRV. From there, Ho Chi Minh and his colleagues sought to create a socialist society in the North while formulating plans to complete the reunification of the entire country under their authority. When rising civil unrest in the South erupted into full-scale conflict in 1965, U.S. President Lyndon B. Johnson ordered B-52 raids over the North in a bid to force the DRV into submission. To keep the war from spiraling downward into a global confrontation, however, downtown Hanoi was not targeted, and it survived the war relatively unscathed. After the defeat of the South in spring 1975, the country was reunified under a new name—the Socialist Republic of Vietnam; Hanoi remained the capital of the country, and the socialist system that had already been put in place in the North during the long years of war was now extended to the southern part of the country.

The two authors who provide the reader with a guided tour of the history of this venerable city have excellent credentials. Nguyen Van Ky, an independent Vietnamese scholar who has resided in France for over two decades, is the author of the recently published *La Société vietnamienne face à la modernité*, which examines in fascinating detail the impact of modern Western institutions and ideas on traditional society in northern Vietnam during the seven decades of French colonial rule. In his sensitive hands, the old precolonial city, with its countless temples and numerous lakes, its poets and its Confucian scholars, comes to life. Later chapters trace the changes that took place after the French conquest, when the city underwent an architectural face-lift, with spacious new boulevards bordered by modern office buildings erected in the popular fin de siècle art nouveau style. There were also changes in the social character of the city, as Western-style cuisine and clothing styles gradually edged out their traditional counterparts. Still, in some ways the essential flavor of the city remained unchanged. It was still a city of culture, of poetry, and of love, whose numerous rivers and lakes inspired Western visitors to describe Hanoi as a "Venice of the Orient," more an urban village than a modern metropolis.

Georges Boudarel takes up the narrative as the post–World War II era begins. Boudarel, a professor at the University of Paris, is a scholar of long experience with modern Vietnam. He first went to French Indochina in 1948, an idealistic young man eager to see the world and prove his convictions for a worldwide Marxist revolution. He taught in a variety of schools in Saigon and in Dalat, where he was a firsthand witness to the oppression and racism inherent in the French colonial system. After struggling with his own conscience for two years, he deserted his post in 1950, joined the local revolutionary movement—popularly known as the Vietminh—and went off into the maquis. It is from these hiding places in the Vietnamese countryside that he learned the Vietnamese language and culture and became a fervent opponent of his own nation's colonial policies. He eventually became a political commissar at one of the Vietminh prison camps and was put in charge of educating French prisoners in the goals and aims of the revolution. These actions would later draw Boudarel into difficulties with the French government, and he was eventually accused of treason—charges from which he has only recently been acquitted.

Having experienced the horrors of war in Camp 113, including food shortages, unbearable heat, and rampant disease that would eventually wipe out one of every two French prisoners, Boudarel was eventually transferred to Hanoi, where he spent the next decade of his life. By now, the war against the French had come to an end, and the Communists had come to power in North Vietnam, now formally known as the Democratic Republic of Vietnam. It was during this period that he came into contact with some of Vietnam's brightest writers, thinkers, and artists, such as poet To Huu, pianist Thai Thi Lien, and philosopher Tran Duc Thao. He later used his knowledge of this period of relative artistic freedom to write his book *Cent fleurs écloses dans la nuit du Viêt-nam, 1954–56* [One hundred flowers in the night of Vietnam, 1954–56], which describes the frenetic intellectual activity that took place in the DRV during the mid-1950s and the brutal crackdown by the regime that brought it to an end.

During the next few years, Boudarel found himself growing increasingly disillusioned with the Marxist politics that he had supported as a youth. In 1964 he was offered a position in Prague and left Vietnam; in 1966, he returned to France following the declaration of a general amnesty. He then pursued an academic career and has become one of France's top experts on the history of modern Vietnam. He also wrote an autobiography that chronicles his long and controversial career as a participant in and observer of the Vietnamese revolution.

In keeping with his own background and the more ideological character of the postwar era, Boudarel adopts a more political approach to his task and seeks to describe how the city was affected by the dramatic events that took place during three decades of civil struggle and social revolution. As a one-time insider with years of personal experience within the movement, Boudarel takes the reader through the inner corridors of power in Hanoi and provides fascinating insights into the bitter struggles that took place within the Communist Party and the government leadership over the future direction of the Vietnamese revolution.

In his view, the regime that took power in Hanoi in 1954, far from being the monolith that it has sometimes been described as in the Western press, was bitterly divided over how to achieve the dual objectives of national reunification and socialist transformation. On the one hand was the humanistic side of the Vietnamese revolution, as symbolized by President Ho Chi Minh, while on the other were hard-line dogmatic elements represented by such senior party figures as Le Duc Tho, Truong Chinh, and First Secretary Le Duan. Ho Chi Minh is portrayed here as a man of infinite suppleness and subtlety, more a Gandhi than a Lenin or Stalin. A master practitioner of the politics of inclusion, Ho sought to win the support of virtually all strata of the Vietnamese population, including Catholics, intellectuals, and even progressive landlords and merchants. A profound student of Chinese military strategist Sun Tzu, he preferred to best his adversaries by artifice or seduction rather than to confront them head-on. In fall 1945, he ordered the release from prison of anti-Communist politician Ngo Dinh Diem (later, as president of the government of South Vietnam, to be Ho's chief competitor for the allegiance of the Vietnamese people) out of respect for Diem's father, who had been a patriot figure in the imperial court at the end of the nineteenth century. To win the support of the United States, he quoted from the American Declaration of Independence. He flattered Mao Zedong by citing Confucius and vocally praised Mao's unique ideas about waging revolution and people's war.

At the same time, as Boudarel admits, many cruelties were committed in Ho Chi Minh's name or in that of his creation, the DRV. During the August Revolution of 1945, many of the party's nationalist rivals, as well as a small but vocal band of Trotskyites, were executed as potential threats to the new regime. After the Geneva Conference of 1954, excesses committed by zealous cadres in carrying out the land reform program led to the deaths of thousands of individuals, many of them loyal supporters of Ho's Vietminh Front. When criticism of the party's policies began to proliferate during the late 1950s, the regime was pitiless in its response, arresting key dissidents and suppressing their publications. Although Ho Chi Minh expressed his disapproval of such actions in private, he failed to take decisive action to rectify the injustices committed, and the hard-liners had their way.

The reality of Ho Chi Minh's growing political impotence appeared in the mid-1960s, when key party leaders, rejecting the pleas of Soviet leader Nikita Khrushchev to avoid a confrontation with the United States, began to adopt a more active military role in the South, where discontent with the regime of Ngo Dinh Diem was on the rise. Ho Chi Minh had been wary of antagonizing his government's most powerful sponsor and preferred a more conciliatory approach that would avoid a confrontation with Moscow or provoke direct U.S. intervention in South Vietnam. By now, however, power in Hanoi had gravitated into the hands of militant elements around Le Duan and Le Duc Tho, who rejected Ho's appeals for caution and began to purge pro-Soviet elements gathered around Defense Minister Vo Nguyen Giap. According to some reports, they even considered a bid to force Ho Chi Minh's resignation as president. Once again, Ho remained silent.

In Washington, hawkish elements had also assumed command, and in 1965, both sides opted for military escalation in a bid to secure total victory. In Hanoi, militant elements around General Nguyen Chi Thanh wanted to confront the United States directly on the battlefield, despite the projected heavy cost in lives. In Washington, President Lyndon Johnson approved a policy of attrition to wear down the enemy and force Hanoi's submission. Under the circumstances, there was precious little room for compromise on either side. Only after the Tet Offensive in February 1968 had cooled the ardor of hotheads in both capitals did peace talks begin. By then, Ho Chi Minh's influence over policy had been marginalized by old age and bad health. Even his request to be cremated was ignored by his colleagues, who decided to erect a mausoleum enclosing his preserved body to provide a symbol for the future deification of the father of the Vietnamese revolution.

The Vietnam War imposed its own price on the city and people of Hanoi.

Although U.S. bombing raids, begun at the order of Lyndon Johnson in spring 1965, did not target the old administrative center of the city, air attacks on the industrial suburbs and on the transportation routes north and south of the city were commonplace. During the height of the war, many factories and government offices were relocated in the suburbs, while thousands of residents were evacuated to the countryside. Those who remained in the city were ordered to build primitive bomb shelters adjacent to their homes, their schools, or their work sites in case the enemy decided to launch a direct attack on the city.

In 1975, Hanoi was at peace for the first time in nearly two decades, and party leaders began to shift from war to peacetime reconstruction. As coauthor Nguyen Van Ky demonstrates, it has not been an easy transition. Ho Chi Minh's successors, still giddy from memories of their stunning triumph in the South, ignored his carefully laid plans for a gradual approach to national reunification and launched an ambitious plan to bring about socialist transformation throughout the country by the end of the decade. In a stunning display of hubris, they openly confronted their one-time ally China over the future of neighboring Laos and Cambodia. But it soon became clear that their self-confidence was misplaced. By 1979 the economic situation was in a state of crisis, and the regime was locked in a bitter dispute with neighboring China.

In 1986, the regime finally admitted its error and launched a new program of renovation, known in Vietnamese as *doi moi,* to bring about reforms in both domestic and foreign affairs. The consequences of this change in direction have been mixed. On the one hand, the pace of economic growth throughout the country perceptibly quickened, and the heavy hand of the state was loosened over many aspects of Vietnamese society. The impact on the city of Hanoi has been dramatic. Signs of prosperity are visible everywhere, from the proliferation of small privately owned shops to the appearance of modern office buildings. Despite these transformations, the old city center has retained much of its original character, and Hanoi is far from becoming a new Hong Kong.

But the regime's effort to create a socialist market economy on the foundation of the party's continuing domination over national affairs has not been without its problems. Rampant corruption and a growing gap in the division of wealth, along with rising unemployment and the removal of the safety net for the poor, have produced ominous signs of social malaise, including drug use, prostitution, and suicide. Beginning in the late 1990s, a slowdown in industrial production and a decline in exports and foreign investment have fueled fears of economic stagnation. Some of the difficulties could be assigned to the impact of the financial crisis that struck the region in 1997. But critics point out that much of the damage has been self-imposed by bureaucratic interference, foot-dragging by conservative leaders, and a primitive infrastructure. Domestic critics have been quick to seize on these problems as a consequence of the continuing dominance of the party over national affairs.

One of the other main components of *doi moi* is to encourage intellectuals to speak out about shortcomings in the system. As a result, a number of respected senior military and civilian figures have publicly called for political reforms to create a more democratic and pluralistic society. In the arts, authors such as Duong Thu Huong, Nguyen Huy Thiep, and Bao Ninh followed up by exposing the seamy underside of the Vietnamese revolution in novels and short stories. As had been the case during the 1950s, however, conservative leaders have shown little tolerance for such views that, in their opinion, threaten the very basis of party rule. In fact, the popular demonstrations in Tiananmen Square in 1989 and the collapse of the Soviet Union shortly after convinced many party leaders that only the maintenance of the traditional "dictatorship of the proletariat" could contain unrest. As a result, the regime persists in its crackdown on the "enfants terribles" of the literary renaissance, while dissidents within party ranks have been dismissed from office or even placed under house arrest. In the party's view, economic reform cannot be achieved without political stability. The recent visit to Vietnam by U.S. President Bill Clinton aroused some optimism that the regime would eventually adopt the path of comprehensive reform, but many senior officials remain deeply suspicious of the United States and its alleged efforts to undermine the socialist system. For the moment they will probably continue to resist the introduction of capitalist methods and bourgeois culture into Vietnamese society.

For Nguyen Van Ky, such concerns are understandable. Only in a few cases has the transition from a Marxist-Leninist to a pluralistic system worked successfully. For the most part, as in the former Soviet Union and the Balkans, it has led to social dislocation and civil war. Yet, he concludes, the price of domestic order is political suffocation. Vietnam is now at a crossroads and must decide whether short-term economic growth should take precedence over the long-term struggle to broaden the horizons of human freedom.

Prologue

The city of Hanoi has always been a symbol of Vietnam, even if it was sometimes eclipsed by the southern city of Saigon. During the war with the United States, voices of the South cried out, "If you bomb Hanoi, you bomb the heart of Vietnam!" Though currently the capital of Vietnamese Communism, Hanoi will always be remembered by the Vietnamese people as Thang Long, the city of the "rising dragon," as it was named by King Ly Thai To (r. 1009–28) following a vision.

The ancient city was rich in history, legends, and myths, thus assuring its role as guardian of the Vietnamese identity. Hanoi remained strong despite Vietnam's tumultuous contradictions: between rupture and continuity, revolt and submission, freedom of speech and operational secrets, human rights and totalitarian power, the intrusion of Western modernity and the preservation of tradition, and finally socialism and a market economy. Its ambivalence, as much as its topography, justifies the name Hanoi, which means "amid the rivers."

The Soul of the Dragon

The old city, built along the twists and turns of the Song Hong, or Red River, was considered by many to be the Venice of the Far East. Representative of a country that sometimes calls itself *dat nuoc* (earth water), Hanoi has always been centered around its "thirty-six neighborhoods," a name popularized by novelist Thach Lam in his book *Ha Noi 36 pho phuong* [The thirty-six neighborhoods of Hanoi]. In the neighborhoods is found the heart of Hanoi, beating with the bustling activity of its streets, where shopkeepers and artisans still make hemp, silk, furniture, and basketry and sell everything from brine to coal and white worms to noodles. Hanoi's soul thrives here, rich with pagodas, temples, monuments, memories, and a spiritual life pulsing with the mysteries of a supernatural universe. It is here that the city's senses come alive, in nocturnal pleasures that once lurked in opium dens and darkened rooms.

Rich with this vital energy, Hanoi also hosts a wealth of legends. Every area has its own story to tell: like Returned Sword Lake (Hoan Kiem Lake), where King Le Loi regained his magic sword with the help of a tortoise spirit; or West Lake, which sprang either from the footprints of a golden buffalo or from the imprints left by a fox with nine tails.

Hanoi is a royal city, shaped by the founding dynasty of the Ly. But it is also a great village, where immigrants from the countryside still retain their traditions. They live in neighborhoods called *phuong,* grouped together based on city of origin or profession. The city is thus a product of ancient majesty, legendary splendor, and rustic simplicity. It also boasts a vibrant sensuality that it hides well beneath an exterior of sobriety and reserve. Its streets are animated by the flux of constant activity and tempt the passer-by with the rich aromas of its famous cuisine, such as the popular noodle dish *pho.*

Women, such as the Trung sisters (first century) and Dame Trieu (third century), have also played an important role in Hanoi's history. Of course, Confucian reserve has reigned for centuries, imposing its resistance to the advance of modernity. Despite this resistance, however, love has always been praised by romantic poets of both sexes, and elegance is held in high esteem. And finally, the famous long tunic, the *ao dai,* which caused a veritable revolution in women's fashion in the 1930s, was created by a Hanoi designer, Nguyen Cat Tuong (alias Lemur).

The "City amid the Rivers" is also famous for its arts and literature, remaining true to a long tradition symbolized by the Van Mieu (Temple of Literature) and sustained by generations of educated civil servant–scholars. Hanoi has always fostered the seeds of literary creativity, which remained strong and vibrant throughout the years. In 1934, the Tu Luc Van Doan (Self-Reliant Literary Group) rose up as a new intellectual landmark under the impetus of writer Nhat Linh and led to a blossoming of poets and novelists. And the Thang Long School channeled the discontent and rebellion of a generation into art.

The City amid the Rivers

This rich and varied history explains why Hanoi has inspired both fascination and mistrust in the conquerors of yesterday and the visitors of today. As current and historical capital of Vietnam, Hanoi has seen much hardship, symbolized by the ever changing colors of the flags that have waved above its rooftops. The blue, white, and red of the French Republic held sway from 1885 until 1945, interrupted briefly by the red rising sun of the Japanese. Pro-Japanese nationalists chose three bands of red on a yellow background before Ho Chi Minh established the golden star against a red field. These contrasting hues have created different facets of the city, which reveal the impact of each successive regime.

For centuries the Vietnamese people forcefully resisted Chinese domination. They finally accepted Chinese culture, going so far as to adopt China's sociopolitical system, based on a rather rigid interpretation of Confucian thought. Then, like many Asian countries, Vietnam was subjected to domination by the West, which came armed with superior technology. The French took over in 1885 after the success of the Tonkin campaign and ruled in Indochina until 1954. This caused an unprecedented fracture in Hanoi, most concretely felt in the city's structure itself: ancient buildings were destroyed, whole neighborhoods of straw huts disappeared, and the French model of building design was imposed as the standard. Paul Doumer, first governor-general of Indochina, was the architect of this transformation, guided by two forces: mutual incomprehension, which pushed the Vietnamese inhabitants back toward the periphery, and modernity, one of whose legacies would be a school of revolt.

Hanoi had then become the administrative capital of the colony of Indochina and the seat of Western learning. The French hoped to use Western knowledge to educate the Vietnamese, but it eventually turned against the French once their "subjects" started demanding their freedom. Franco-Vietnamese education was developed at the beginning of the century, and its public and private schools became a breeding ground for modern intellectuals. Some worked for cultural emancipation, notably through the propagation of *quoc ngu* (the alphabetized transliteration of Vietnamese characters), such as Pham Quynh, writer and director of the Imperial Cabinet who collaborated with the French. Others, in association with the famous private school Thang Long, became involved in the political struggle for independence, for example, Nguyen Tuong Tam with the Nationalists and Vo Nguyen Giap, future victor of Dien Bien Phu, with the Communists.

Throughout the world the advance of modernization has been revolutionary, but its effects are often on the superficial level. In Vietnam, only a small minority has been affected, leaving the basic core of daily life intact. We see its influence mostly in the so-called urban elite, who now copy Western modes of behavior, cinema, and fashion. French culinary practices have also gained acceptance, with the popularity of foods such as milk, butter, wine, and champagne, but they still have not completely replaced traditional cuisine.

In fact, colonization may have made Indochina into the "pearl of the French Empire" through economic development (which came at the high cost of social injustice), and it may have sparked a wave of modernity, but it was not able to create a fusion of cultures. Two forms of life, of architecture, of society, were juxtaposed rather than harmonized and often even contradicted each other.

Of course, some ethnic fusion took place through mixed marriages. And in certain cultural domains, for example, theater, we can find a play called *Monsieur Franco-Annamite*, a satire in the style of Molière written by Vietnamese author Nam Xuong that pokes fun at Franco-Vietnamese society. However, because the least liberal trend was destined to fail—like the one extolled by Governor-General Varenne in the 1920s and especially those of the reforms envisaged by the Popular Front in 1937—it was the authoritarian and repressive tendencies that definitively won out and led to violent confrontation.

Combat and Secrecy

Hanoi was also a place of combat. The 1930s began with two explosive events: in February 1930, the mutiny of the garrison of Yen Bay under the flag of the Nationalist Party Viet Nam Quoc Dan Dang; and in the fall, the Communist uprising of the so-called Soviets of Nghe Tinh. The ensuing repression provoked the dismantling of many organizations and the dispersion of their members, either to hideouts in Hanoi or in villages, to prison cells, or to exile in far-off points of refuge: Moscow, Shanghai, Nanjing, Paris—in short, anywhere the struggle could be continued in secret.

The liberal détente established by the French government as a result of the Popular Front in 1937 permitted a reappearance of some of these groups, under different names and of a variety of political affiliations. Shortly thereafter, however, the return of repression following World War II forced them to go back into hiding, either in the old city of Hanoi or in the new colonial city. Although Saigon and the South had seen the nationalist resistance grow and take its first steps, the capital of the North soon turned into a battleground. It became the birthplace of the 1945 revolution and saw the emergence of a leader shaped by village life—who took the name Ho Chi Minh.

A glimpse into the life of this emblematic figure is given to us by Vu Dinh Huynh, the revolutionary and master of clandestine operations, who wrote down his memories of Ho before his death in 1991. The account was curiously censored, probably because it shed light on the arcane aspects of the revolution and created an "Uncle Ho" who was as familiar and human as he was cunning and shrewd.

It is through the writings of another author, Nhat Linh, that we learn about one of the deplorable consequences of history: that the repressive violence of colonialism, incarnated by the manipulative and terrorist activities of the Sûreté (the French Ministry of State Security), provoked extremist tendencies in the Nationalists that would later lead to destructive totalitarianism.

The war of independence, fought from 1946 to 1954, shattered the City of the Rising Dragon, a city just barely reawakening from years of foreign domination. Hanoi was thrust back into the secrets of its labyrinths. As history has shown, most revolutionary struggles begin in silence, shrouded in secrecy to protect their fragile roots. And so it began, in hideouts abroad and hidden in the limestone hills of the highlands, where plans were made to take power after the great strategic campaigns of Dien Bien Phu. This practice of secrecy was then adopted by those who came to power in Hanoi, a city that had once again become the official capital of the Vietnamese nation. The debates that raged in the circles of power proceeded behind closed doors, and decisions could only be carried out through secret networks. Meanwhile, a sort of Manichean propaganda was being sent to the outside world—but in a language so floridly red that, by contrast and in fatigue, the people of Hanoi could only see in gray and black.

A Time of Renovation

The secret networks that developed during wartime were based on and around a core group, but they could not keep dissidents from speaking out when inspired by hope. Like the group of the "Hundred Flowers," they were trampled before they had time to see the spring. Those few months of open debate only resulted in recriminations and crackdowns, as the government proceeded from purges—or "reeducation"—to trials for treason.

In the absence of archives, we rely on various eyewitness accounts that shed light on the dissension that was carefully hidden among the secrets of the inner circle. It seems that the clear and pragmatic realism of Ho Chi Minh was attacked by Maoist ideologues, who chose the path of violent confrontation and harshly put an end to all democratic expression. We learn from these accounts how, in the course of a terrible battle against the American Goliath, Le Duc Tho, in charge of organization at the heart of the party, tried to get rid of Uncle Ho. We learn that General Vo Nguyen Giap, the master strategist, was opposed to the Tet Offensive of 1968. And we learn about the indictment of a loyal Communist like Hoang Minh Chinh, director of the Institute of Philosophy, which marked a radical departure from the pragmatic politics of Ho Chi Minh—whose personal secretary, Vu Dinh Huynh, was arrested and ended his days in obscurity.

Hanoi lives according to this rhythm of paradox, from the falsification of Ho's last will and testament to the building of a mausoleum that he never wanted, from the empty reassurances of Marxist jargon to the continued repression of the intellectual world. Fixed in its dignified role as noble and ancient political capital, Hanoi today resembles a ship sailing more or less happily between two currents.

Despite the repression of the hard-liners and the difficulties of war, the spirit behind many of these protests was never destroyed. To the contrary, the repercussions of Soviet perestroika and the 1986 decision to embark on the new policy of openness, *doi moi* (renovation), allowed certain writers to speak out against the ills of the past. Some evoked the disasters of the war, others denounced the injustices of the Agrarian Reform Campaign, and still others critiqued the contradictions within the system and the corrupting of minds. These writers included Duong Thu Huong, Nguyen Huy Thiep, and Bao Ninh.

But this renovation, if it is genuine and characterized by an openness to a market economy, still has a long way to go. The ideologues have not had their last word yet, and the countless survivors of Vietnam's many battles may well question the ambiguity of liberation, of national unification, of a socialist system that offers no prospects for the popular majority, and of economic development that only aggravates inequality. But it could not be otherwise in a system that encourages opportunist business people and foreign investment but does not resolve problems like overpopulation, dilapidated housing, poor sanitation, or schools that are deserted because of high tuition and low teacher salaries. Moreover, there is a new crisis among the youth: cut off from their past, young people have become depoliticized. In this new society that is taking shape, they create their own value system, one based on the dollar bill. Unemployment is rampant, and karaoke and motorcycle drag races are the new favorite pastimes.

Hanoi itself has kept its charm, of course, and has always maintained its personality through the fluctuations of history, even under the pressure of colonial domination. Much of its charm comes from the character of its inhabitants and what is left of the old architecture. It was nearly disfigured by development projects that would have turned the ancient city and the areas surrounding West Lake into a jumble of cement and glass. But the authorities were smart enough to change their plans, following protests and in consideration of a disturbing reality: the population is already up to two million people and strains the city's limits. A new city of the twenty-first century will now be built some fifty kilometers from present-day Hanoi. The old neighborhoods will be preserved by virtue of their status as historical monuments.

Despite Hanoi's problems, one can still have hope for the city in the dawn of the third millennium. It is now visited by both tourists and Vietnamese émigrés driven by nostalgia or business. Let us hope that it will one day become the capital of a reconciled Vietnamese people.

PART ONE

THE SPIRIT OF THE CITY

CHAPTER ONE

A City That Remembers

Nguyen Van Ky

In the year 2010 the city of Hanoi will celebrate its millennium, making it one of the oldest capitals in Southeast Asia. The monarchs of the Ly dynasty (1010–1275) founded the city after having regained their country's independence from the Chinese, abandoning the old capital of Hoa Lu. The city would change its name several times in the course of its long history. It was first called Thang Long (the rising dragon), a name given to it by King Ly Thai To (r. 1009–28). It then became Dong Do (capital of the east); then, in the fifteenth century, it was renamed Dong Kinh (royal capital of the east).[1] When the Nguyen established its capital at Hue in the nineteenth century, the city became Ha Noi (the city amid the waters). From the seventeenth century until the beginning of the twentieth, many Vietnamese still referred to Hanoi by its more popular name, Ke Cho (the market).

Hanoi has always been the center of the country's political, economic, and cultural activity, earning it the title "land of a 1,000-year-old culture" (*dat nghin nam van vat*). It is physically located in a very vulnerable spot, on the Red River delta and just south of the powerful Chinese Empire. When the French chose Hanoi instead of Saigon as the capital of the new Indochinese Union in 1887, they were affirming their power and determination in the face of the Chinese Middle Kingdom, which was always ready to proclaim its sovereignty over the region. At the same time, North Vietnam has always served as the cornerstone of any attempt by the Chinese to influence or dominate Southeast Asia. This strategically sensitive location has proven to be the source of many of the city's conflicts and difficulties. In order to physically protect itself, Hanoi had to surround itself with fortifications. It protected itself culturally by establishing its own identity, one that grew out of a wealth of myths and legends.

The City under the Waters

The city of today was built, literally and figuratively, along the bends of the Song Hong, or Red River, which cuts across Hanoi from the northwest to the southeast. A high iron content gives the river its brick-red color and its name. It has its source in the mountains of southwest China and around Mount Ba Vi is joined by several tributaries, one of which is the Black River (Song Da).

The region around Hanoi was originally swampy and riddled with lakes, which remained as vestiges of the river's previous paths. The current configuration of the city was carved out in part by the sea and the powerful Red River—whose floods sometimes altered the shape of the city overnight—and in part by the lush vegetation, whose traces can still be found in certain place-names, such as Gia Lam (forest of banyans) and Mai Lam (forest of plum trees). As a result, the inhabitants of this floodplain area have always maintained a high concern for the construction and integrity of the dikes that protect them. Even today, the city lies below the water level in times of flooding.

In centuries past, Hanoi was in a sense the Venice of the Far East, as people traveled from place to place by boat along a complex network of lakes, streams, and canals. The presence of water shaped the material and cultural life of the city, carrying with it both life and death, to the point at which the word *country* in popular language is *dat nuoc* (earth water). The Vietnamese people have always lived this duality. Because they could not definitively master the water, they learned to make it their ally and an integral part of their nation. Once again, language provides a key for understanding the importance of water to the people of Hanoi: the term for "our country" (*nuoc nha*) literally means "water home," and the word for "the state" (*nha nuoc*) means "home water."

From its founding in 1010 until the eighteenth century, Hanoi was composed of two distinct parts. The Imperial City was in the center, ringed by the fortified walls of the citadel, and included the Forbidden City. Surrounding this was a group of neighborhoods that housed merchants, artisans, and the imperial servants. Writings such as Nguyen Trai's *Dia du chi* [Treatise on geography] describe the scope of the city in the fifteenth century. The Imperial City underwent many changes throughout history, as best illustrated by

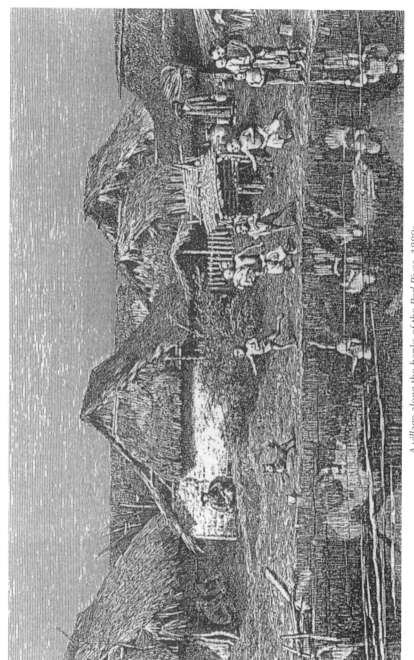

A village along the banks of the Red River, 1880s.

the successive constructions of its citadel: the old fortress of Dai La (great citadel), built in the ninth century, was replaced by the citadel of Thang Long in the eleventh century; this, in turn, was then enlarged by Olivier du Puymanel in 1805 under the Nguyen dynasty to emulate the French style of Vauban.

As the seat of power, the Imperial City was laid out in the form of a square, a reference to Confucian cosmology, which holds that the square symbolizes the earth while the sky is represented by a circle. It was delimited in the north by West Lake, in the south by what is now the Street of the Bridge of Paper, in the east by what is now called Ba Dinh Square, and in the west by the To Lich River. Outside of this square lay old Hanoi, with its thirty-six commercial neighborhoods. The capital was thus protected by natural defenses: on the north and northeast by the Red River, separated from West Lake by a dike, and on the west by the To Lich River. Moreover, the fertility of the alluvial soil was undoubtedly one of the reasons that successive Vietnamese dynasties remained in Hanoi until the nineteenth century, taking advantage of the richness of the soil to develop and prosper.

A City of Legend

One of Hanoi's most famous legends is that of Returned Sword Lake. It is said that a mythical tortoise gave its sacred sword to King Le Loi (r. 1428–33),[2] allowing him to expel the occupying forces of the Chinese Ming dynasty in the fifteenth century after ten years of resistance. The people from Hanoi also love to tell stories about the etymological origins of Thang Long, the city's first name. When the boats of Ly Cong Uan, the founder of the eleventh-century Ly dynasty, arrived on the site from Hoa Lu, a golden dragon appeared to welcome them and then flew off into the sky. This good omen convinced the king to build the capital there, calling it Thang Long, which means "the rising dragon."

The dragon is an important symbol for the Vietnamese. One of their national legends tells of the city's ancestors, the mythical couple Lac Long Quan and Au Co, the former a descendant of dragons, and the latter, of fairies. Popular belief also contends that dragons can cause rain, which is indispensable for growing rice. Last, the dragon is a symbol of imperial power in Chinese ideography, a writing system adopted by the Vietnamese court. The name Thang Long thus brought together the monarchy and the common people, a meaning that was ruptured in the nineteenth century by the trans-

Returned Sword Lake (Ho Hoan Kiem) before colonization by the French.

fer of the capital to Hue. The Nguyen dynasty then emptied the city of its symbolic role by renaming it Ha Noi.

West Lake can claim two origin legends. One goes back to the founding of the country and tells of how the region of Hanoi was terrorized by a fox with nine tails. Lac Long Quan, the dragon god, entered into battle with the fox to drive it from the area. The fox fled and left behind him the tracks of his many tails, which then collapsed and gave birth to West Lake. Some older storytellers offer another version: there once was a giant named Khong Minh Khong who went to China to find a cure for a princess who had fallen ill. Out of gratitude, the king offered him a piece of black bronze from the royal coffers. Khong Minh Khong transformed the bronze into a bell, whose peals could be heard all the way to China. A golden buffalo heard the bell, thought he recognized the lowing of his mother, and so traveled from China to Vietnam, following the sounds of the bell. His tracks became the river Kim Nguu (golden buffalo), a former arm of the river To Lich; and the forest of lim,[3] which was now trampled and flattened, became West Lake.

Temples: The Guardians of History

Hanoi has more than 1,000 historical buildings, with some 579 communal houses,[4] 676 pagodas, and 261 temples spread out across the city. Since 1954, more than 200 have been classified as historical sites. During the Ly dynasty, a number of Buddhist religious structures were built. One of the most famous, the One Pillar Pagoda, was built in 1049 in the shape of a lotus, a symbol of Buddha's enlightenment. The pagoda was built in the middle of a pond on the east side of the Imperial City and has been destroyed and rebuilt many times. It was completely demolished by the French Army during the Franco-Vietminh War and was entirely rebuilt. Then, in the 1970s, a senior government official suggested that it be torn down because it did not conform with the new mausoleum being built to house the remains of Ho Chi Minh. Outspoken historian Tran Quoc Vuong dared to protest against the proposal and was reprimanded by ignorant opportunists hoping to impress key leaders. Fortunately, however, other protests followed, and the idea was finally abandoned.

A short distance away to the south stands the Temple of Literature (Van Mieu), built in 1076 in homage to Confucius and his disciples. The site also served as an academy where court-appointed scholars could meet to discuss classical literature. Shortly afterward, the Imperial Academy (Quoc Tu Giam) was built. Considered to be the country's first university, it attracted hundreds of students who moved into the surrounding areas in order to profit from its prestige. In 1442, graduates of the Mandarin examinations were celebrated in inscriptions on stone tablets that were erected upon the back of a sculpted tortoise, the symbol of longevity. The first tablets were erected in 1484 under the reign of Le Thanh Tong (1460–97), a ruler known for his humanism and erudition.

On the shores of West Lake in the extreme northeast of the city, at the beginning of what is now Thanh Nien Street (the Avenue of the Grand Buddha in colonial times), is the Quan Thanh Temple. This Taoist structure was built under the Ly in the eleventh century and was originally dedicated to an ancient protector spirit. It also served as one of the sixteen gateways to the city. In 1677 a bronze statue of the spirit, four meters (thirteen feet) high, was erected inside. On the shores of Bay Mau Lake (Lake of Seven Mau),[5] another temple was built in the twelfth century, dedicated to the two Trung sisters. These two heroines tried in vain to evict Chinese occupying

A pavilion at the Temple of Literature (Van Mieu).

forces in the first century. They committed suicide by plunging into a river in order to escape humiliation.

To the west of the Imperial City are two other historical monuments dating from the twelfth century: the Temple of the Reclining Elephants, now located in a zoological park, and the Lang Pagoda, situated a bit farther south. The former was erected to protect the western side of the capital, whereas the latter is known for its picturesque location and ancient statuary, some of which date back to the seventeenth century. It is still in use today and is the site of one of Hanoi's most popular annual festivals.

We can see that the Hanoi of today was shaped by the dynasty that founded it. The dynasties that followed did little but preserve it, renovate it, and construct palaces for various dignitaries. None of these other buildings, however, could withstand the violence of history. In 1216, the struggle between rival factions of the declining Ly dynasty provoked a fire and the destruction of the Imperial City, which later had to be rebuilt by the Tran dynasty (1225–1400). From the sixteenth to the eighteenth century, royal palaces were built outside of the old Imperial City because of the fighting between the reigning dynasty of the Le, reduced to a nominal function, and the Trinh lords (an aristocratic clan that had seized power at court) who held real power. This infighting between the ruling classes led to chaos and political instability, including the assassinations of several Le kings by the Trinh lords. In 1623, one of the latter burned down the Imperial City. In 1787, the last reigning Le ruler called for assistance from the Qing dynasty in Beijing, but the Tay Son brothers, leaders of a rebel faction that had taken control in the South, took advantage of the instability to intervene and liberate the capital from its Chinese occupiers. In 1789, the battle of Dong Da (named for a hill situated several kilometers to the south of Hanoi) put an end to the Chinese intervention.[6]

Invasion upon Invasion

Throughout its history Hanoi has been plagued by foreign invasions and was ravaged by bitter power struggles between the thirteenth and nineteenth centuries: the Mongols invaded twice in the thirteenth century (in 1285 and 1287) before being definitively pushed back by the Tran, which won a decisive naval victory on the river Bach Dang;[7] the Chams made two incursions toward the end of the fourteenth century; then the Ming came in 1406; and finally the French took power in 1882. Once the colonial authorities were well established, they razed the citadel, which had been rebuilt only fifty years earlier. The Imperial City was thus reduced to a simple watchtower (*cot co*). Such actions incurred the lasting enmity of the local inhabitants: "Hanoi is not a holy land in the religious sense of the term, but a sacred land," wrote Nguyen Tuan. "Any foreigner who offends it must pay for it with his life."[8]

Francis Garnier and Henri Rivière were two Frenchmen who paid with their lives for their transgressions. Garnier, a young French military officer who seized Hanoi with a small detachment in the early 1870s, was killed in a skirmish with Vietnamese forces on the Bridge of Paper. Ten years later, during a second assault of the city, Rivière met the same fate in the same place. But the fate of the citadel's defenders was not any less dramatic: Hoang Dieu and Nguyen Tri Phuong both committed suicide before the advancing colonial French forces. The event was memorialized in a poem by an anonymous author (see sidebar, "Homage to Henri Rivière").

Rural City or Urban Village?

The 1,000-year-old city was also shaped by its people, who gave it a soul and a cultural richness that softened the more austere contributions of the scholarly community. Western travelers in the seventeenth century estimated the number of homes in the city at 20,000, which corresponds to a population of around 100,000 inhabitants. By the nineteenth century, though, there were no more than 60,000 people living in Hanoi. This is undoubtedly due to the transfer of the capital to Hue, which emptied the city of a substantial part of its population.

The French loved to repeat that "Hanoi was a big village," a remark that actually has some truth to it. There has always been a constant influx of people from rural areas into the city, the numbers varying over the centuries according to political, economic, and social conditions. This steady migration, however, never became an exodus, for the countryside always remained a place of security and refuge in case of war or social strife. But the city exercised a powerful pull on surrounding villages because of its reputation as an active place of commerce. During the colonial era, the influx of destitute villagers was so great that the municipality of Hanoi had to pick them up every month by the hundreds and place them in a shelter for the homeless at Bach Mai, on the outskirts of town. This trend continues today as poor peasants arrive daily from the Red River delta, exacerbating an already heavy population density. On the outskirts of the city one still finds many beggars from Thai Binh, a delta province that has been overpopulated for centuries.

Homage to Henri Rivière

Anonymous

I remember him[a]
He had curly hair
He had a long nose
Sitting on a donkey
He whistled for his dog
His home was decorated with bottles
In his garden, he grew nothing but grass
He came to the village of Mat Do
To fight the Black Flags[b]
In order to restore tranquility to the people
Who would have thought they would cut his head off?
And take it with them
Leaving his body there
We obey the decisions of the court. . . .
To venerate you: a diet of bananas
A round of alcohol, a basket of eggs
Bon appétit, Sir
Let nothing trouble your tranquility
What misery is your lot!
Shit on them!

Notes

[a]Translator's note: Henri Rivière was a captain in the French Army who was instrumental in the seizure of North Vietnam in the 1880s.

[b]Translator's note: The Black Flags was a group of bandits and pirates who preyed on local villagers and merchants in the hills of North Vietnam in the nineteenth century. They fought with Vietnamese imperialist troops against the French and were responsible for the death of Captain Henri Rivière in 1883.

The rural people who moved into the city did not, however, abandon their customs, traditions, or ways of life. They brought with them a whole host of social and spiritual practices from their native regions that helped them to preserve the past while confronting the future. Many came to the city accompanied by their families, sometimes even their whole clans, and sought employment as artisans or merchants, without ever abandoning their habits of daily village life. Many have retained the physical mannerisms of their regions, revealing an entire state of mind in a simple gesture. The way in which some recent arrivals squat, for example, with their feet planted on low stools or on chairs at a theater, reveals a certain nonchalance and carefree attitude toward the future that is characteristic of their particular region.

Street Life in Hanoi: The *Phuong*

If the village is the heart of rural life, its urban counterpart is the *phuong*—a word that is usually translated as "neighborhood" and whose origin dates to the thirteenth century. The *phuong* was much more than an administrative zone, however, as each one included one or more trade associations that usually came from the same village. They were a kind of multidimensional space that, like the village, had their own customs, festivals, cults, spirits, and territory. These *phuong* sprang up and flourished outside of the imperial walls. One of the more classic examples is old Hanoi itself, bordered to the east by the Red River, to the south by the southern border of Returned Sword Lake—the old Petit Lac (small lake) of colonial times, which used to be much larger than it is now—and to the west by the fortifications of the Imperial City.

The growth and development of these working-class neighborhoods in Hanoi were based mainly on two factors: family ties and professional skills. Hang Dao Street, for example, known since colonial times as the Street of Silk, is occupied by silk merchants who sell merchandise bought in neighboring areas specialized in the making of silk.[9] It is the same for many other streets in Hanoi.

The origin of the *phuong* also had a social dimension. In order to combat isolation and marginalization, immigrants from the countryside worked together in an effort to constitute an economic and social force. Without ever severing ties with their native regions, these neighborhoods served as a kind of relay point between the two worlds. In this way, immigrants lived a sort of double life: their social life revolved around the city, while their hearts remained in the countryside. The countryside served as a meeting place for families where life was organized according to the rhythm of major holidays like Tet (the lunar new year) or the anniversary of an ancestor's death. It was also used as a kind of haven, whereby the scholar who was in disagreement with those in power could always return to the native village in order to avoid confrontation.

These city streets are much more than addresses for the people of Hanoi; they also carry with them traces of the city's history. Take 10 Pho Hang Dao, for example: In 1907 it housed the seat of the Dong Kinh Nghia Thuc move-

Hang Dao Street, 1926.

ment (Tonkin Free School), run by Luong Van Can and other scholars who were at odds with traditional teaching methods. Using *quoc ngu* as a new vehicle of instruction,[10] they offered free courses, day and night, to anyone who wanted to learn about the modern spirit. This school also served as a cover for anti-French political activities and was forced by the local authorities to close its doors after several months of operation. Like Pho Hang Dao, just about every street in Hanoi bears witness to elements of the city's history.

The Spirit of the Streets
The names of streets tell us a lot about the past, especially about the importance of water to the city. Thus, we find Hang Be Street (Street of Rafts), situated on a pier, and Hang Buom Street (Street of Sails), devoted to the business of boating sails. Until the thirteenth century there were canoe races on the lakes and rivers of the city much like those that still take place in Laos, Cambodia, and Thailand. These boats probably navigated through heavy river traffic up the Red River to old Thang Long, which even then was an important crossroads for trade and commerce.

From the nineteenth century until the Sino-Vietnamese conflict in 1979, the Street of Sails was especially known for its Chinese restaurants, which had set up there in the seventeenth century. Chinese residents were also grouped on the old Phuc Kien Street, named for their home province of Fujian. It is now called Lan Ong Street, after an eighteenth-century pharmacist who specialized in traditional medicine, and shares with nearby Thuoc Bac Street (Street of Chinese Medicine) the specialty of traditional medicines. With the outbreak of hostilities at the Vietnamese border, the Chinese community of Hanoi was taken hostage, and its people were forced to pack their bags and move out.

The Street of Sails is famous for an edifice that is older than the city itself, Bach Ma Temple (Temple of the White Horse), which dates back to the ninth century. According to legend, when Ly Cong Uan, founder of the Ly dynasty, transferred the capital from Hoa Lu to Thang Long, he decided to build a fortress to protect the city and its inhabitants; but the fortress periodically collapsed. The young monarch called for a solemn ceremony to invoke protector spirits who could help him in his enterprise. A white horse then emerged from the temple, made one circle around the fortress, and returned inside. The emperor understood the message and ordered the fortifications to be erected along the tracks left by the spirit animal, and the temple thereupon remained standing. To show his thanks, he elevated the horse to the rank of protector spirit of the capital.

The Temple of the White Horse also had a second function, serving as the eastern gate of the city. Abandoned and left in ruins for decades as part of the fight against superstition, the temple has recently been renovated and given back to the people of the neighborhood who are once again bringing it back to life.

Hang Trong Street (Street of Drums, renamed Avenue Jules Ferry by the French) presents a different case, in which the shopkeeper was also the artisan. The street was once inhabited by three guilds: the drum makers from Hai Hung Province fifty kilometers (thirty-one miles) to the east of Hanoi; the parasol makers from the village of Dao Xa, in Ha Tay Province, some thirty kilometers (nineteen miles) to the south of the capital; and the printers and designers of popular engravings, from Ha Bac Province, which borders Hanoi on the northeast.[11] Today all of these guilds have moved elsewhere, thereby altering the appearance of the neighborhood. In 1954, *Nhan dan* [The people], the official organ of the Communist Party, set up its seat in this neighborhood along Returned Sword Lake. Nowadays one must go to the village of Dong Ho, still in the province of Ha Bac, to find the engravers and printers; it is one of the rare places that has preserved this tradition. At the approach of Tet, the market there comes alive with traditional engravings marking the beginning of festivities in vivid colors.

Other streets have kept their names from days gone by. There is Hang Bac, or Street of Silver (renamed Street of the Money Changers by the French), which contained three separate guilds (for coin casters, money changers, and gold and silver smiths), all from neighboring provinces. The first group built a temple there to venerate the founder of their profession, but they ceased their activities in the nineteenth century after the transfer of the capital to Hue. The second guild continued its operations during the colonial era, and the third erected a temple on a neighboring street in homage to the founder of that trade.

Hang Gai (Street of Hemp) has a slightly more complex history. In olden times, local artisans made and sold rope made of braided hemp. Later, engraving and printing workshops were set up there in the nineteenth century. It was here that the imperial viceroy lived, across from the residence of the French *résident supérieur,* the seat of the new colonial power. As for Hang Chieu (Street of Mats), the French renamed it in honor of the merchant and arms dealer Jean Dupuis—instigator of the colonial conquest of the North—

Hang Bac Street, 1883.

who had opened a shop there in 1872. Hang Non (Street of Hats) was marked by another memory, that of the "Red" labor union that held its first congress there in 1929 at the house at number 15. Revolutionary memories also enliven Hang Ruoi (Street of the Beetle Grub)—so named because every year in the ninth lunar month a market was held to sell this popular delicacy. In 1930, the house at number 4 on this street harbored the office of the newly founded Central Committee of the Communist Party.

Other streets of old Hanoi had less political destinies. Hang Than (Street of Coal) was originally a pier where limestone was delivered to ovens set up along the river; then it became a coal market. Then there is Hang Giay (Street of Paper), where shopkeepers sold paper that they had bought from the artisans who lived in the village of Buoi, situated at the extreme western edge of West Lake. At the beginning of the colonial era, the street housed many *maisons des chanteuses*,[12] before they were moved to the outskirts of town during the 1920s.

Curiously, today there is no street in Hanoi called the Street of Rice. Previously, all trade dealing with this important grain took place either in the central market, where the consumers usually dealt directly with the producers, or on the docks along the river. During colonial times there was a Street of Rice (Hang Gao), which passed in front of Dong Xuan market. The street eventually took the name of the market after independence and following the collectivization of the agricultural sector that brought about the disappearance of the rice trade.

People often speak of the "thirty-six neighborhoods of Hanoi," an expression that has been in use since the fifteenth century and which underscores the importance of the *phuong* in Hanoi's history. Each of these neighborhoods has been shaped by history, by the complex forces of immigration, trade, and political changes. The expression took on even greater popularity in the 1940s after writer Thach Lam used it as a title for one of his stories.

Villages and Labyrinths

Throughout its history, the city has been assaulted and infiltrated by the countryside. In 1946, one year after independence, legislative elections had expanded to include the participation of 118 villages within the Hanoi region. Even today there are parts of Hanoi that are still called "village" *(lang)*. After innumerable administrative changes and repartitioning since 1954, central Hanoi is currently divided into five areas, which are themselves subdivided into *phuong*. The outskirts are divided into five districts that are split into communes of one or two villages.

An itinerant merchant sells his wares.

The houses of Hanoi, most of which look modest from the outside judging by the size of their façades, nonetheless hold many surprises for those who enter for the first time. Many of them are up to fifty meters (160 feet) long. This is why they are called *nha ong* (tube houses). This way of occupying space is actually Chinese in origin and was adopted by the Vietnamese only after long domination by the Middle Kingdom. Traditionally, the Vietnamese prefer rather wider constructions that are less deep, like the houses found in the countryside.

In the summer, storms and torrential rains inundate the streets and refresh the city when it is overwhelmed by the heat. In the winter, on the other hand, the leaden sky and melancholic mist plunge the city into a kind of depression. The paintings of Bui Xuan Phai are dominated by gray and illustrate the type of architecture that one finds in old Hanoi: small houses pressed together with roofs of unequal height that form a jagged skyline.[13] Years ago, the roofs were of thatch and the walls were of clay. Only rich people had the means to build permanent structures with wooden frames, tiled roofs, and paved floors. When the French arrived in the nineteenth century, a good part of the houses in these working-class neighborhoods were just thatched huts.

These many neighborhoods are linked together by innumerable little alleyways (*ngo*) that accentuate the depth of the houses and their chaotic placement. Kham Thien Street, known for its *maisons des chanteuses* in the 1930s and bombed in December 1972 by an American B-52, has no less than twenty-six of these little alleys. It was a veritable labyrinth, which became a real advantage in colonial times with the creation of opium dens and brothels: this construction allowed the inhabitants to escape from the control of the authorities.

The picturesque charm of these old houses has helped to shape the city's identity. If Hanoi bristled with gigantic high-rises, it would lose its soul. There is great concern today about protecting the old city, which is now confronted by new economic pressures. Many Hanoi residents, for example, complain about the number of new building complexes erected in recent years around West Lake. Some progress has been made, like when authorities gave in to public protest and changed a height restriction on a new hotel near Returned Sword Lake from twelve stories to five. In fact, old Hanoi has just been classified as a historical monument by the city, thanks to the efforts of some concerned citizens and the support of a Swedish organization.

As a result of this new sensitivity to Hanoi's historical importance, the extension of the capital will take place out toward the west. According to a recent urban plan, the Hanoi of the twenty-first century (business center, industrial zone, university, lodging for some 200,000 people) will be built in the region of Xuan Mai, some fifty kilometers (thirty miles) from Hanoi. There is a greater problem, however, that faces the city now, one that goes beyond the picturesque: Hanoi already has more than two million people and continues to grow, straining the city's limits.

The City and Its Cuisine

One cannot speak about Hanoi without mentioning one of its most appreciated pleasures: extraordinary cuisine. In fact, the city first entered into Vietnamese literature because of its reputation as a city of gourmets. Thach Lam dedicated many pages to it in his *Hanoi 36 pho phuong* [The thirty-six neighborhoods of Hanoi]. And more recently, Vu Bang wrote a long tale called *Mieng ngon Ha Noi* [Gastronomy in Hanoi] when seized by nostalgia for his native North while he lived in the South in the 1960s. More recently still, Duong Thu Huong has also paid homage to this aspect of the city in her novel *Paradise of the Blind*.

The cuisine in Hanoi is famous not only for its diversity but also for the

The cuisine of Hanoi: something for every taste.

subtlety and richness of its flavors. There are specific drinks and dishes that correspond to almost any moment of the day and night, to every season, to each sex, and to practically every age. The city also benefits from having a wide variety of shops: the shopkeeper from Hanoi knows how to focus on his or her own specialty while working in tacit solidarity with neighboring shopkeepers, even though they may be competitors. For example, a stall that specializes in the famous Tonkin-style soup called *pho* (see sidebar, "Pho") usually does not serve any drinks. If a client is thirsty, the owner of the stall simply orders something from a neighboring stall that does serve drinks. If the client desires to drink tea or smoke a water pipe, perhaps an old woman sitting close by will serve it. Undoubtedly, the charm of these open-air restaurants is not enough to stave off the invasion of foreign ways, especially now during these times of economic openness. In Vietnam, as in all of Southeast Asia, whiskey is now served as a mark of social distinction. This Westernization, however, is only a slight alteration of a Vietnamese tradition. In Southeast Asia, guests at a banquet used to drink rice wine, but now with the introduction of European goods wealthier individuals substitute whiskey as a sign of modern savoir faire.

Another popular drink is made from the juice of sugarcane. In the summer it is squeezed and lightly scented with the juice and zest of a lemon, making a great thirst quencher. In the winter it is steamed or roasted over a fire, sending out a tantalizing aroma that tempts many a customer. On the way to school and throughout the day, children chew on long pieces of sugarcane that have been peeled and cut into round slices.

The most popular alcoholic drink in Hanoi is beer. Introduced by the West in the nineteenth century, the famous "33" from the French brewery of colonial times is back again, under the new brand name "333." The Vietnamese call it "three-three" and drink it with ice cubes. Groups of men love to get together around glasses of "three-three" in the stalls offering dishes prepared with goat meat—whose Vietnamese name (de) in slang means "lecherous." A certain ritual presides at these get-togethers. The men generally start with small glasses of rice wine mixed with goat's blood, a mixture that supposedly aids virility. To celebrate an exceptional occasion, they prefer snake; one drinks the blood diluted in alcohol, a potion that is reputed to relieve backaches. After that, they enjoy an order of the "seven dishes"—all snake—and, in good spirits, they invite the guests of honor to drink a fermented mixture of snake and traditional herbs "100 percent" (to the last drop).

One of Hanoi's most famous local specialties is cha ca: pieces of fish grilled on a wood fire, served over a plate warmer, and accompanied by noodles, herbs (chives, dill, coriander), and shrimp sauce (man tom). The dish was so popular that in 1954 a street was named after the restaurant La Vong, which up until very recently was the only place that would serve it.[14] Doan Xuan Phuc, founder of the restaurant, came from peasant stock from the Bac Ninh region. He was a friend of De Tham, a resistance fighter who led a difficult life in the French forces and was considered a pirate. When the latter was tracked down, Phuc had to retreat to Hanoi. He then opened the restaurant, which became a meeting place for secret contacts among partisans. After the capture of De Tham and his execution in 1913, Phuc settled permanently in Hanoi as a restaurateur. His descendants have continued the family business and are thriving.

With the new open economy, the little alley called Cam chi regained its reputation as the site of one million flavors. From early morning until late at night the merchants work in shifts to provide their various specialties to a

Pho

Nguyen Tuan

Pho is also a very popular dish. . . . Many of our fellow citizens have been eating *pho* since they were children, at that tender young age when one hasn't yet tasted life's disappointments or known need; unlike adults, who are well acquainted with problems that taste of onion and spice, of bitter lemons, or of hot peppers. Even poor children can make do with meatless *pho*.

You can eat *pho* at any time of the day: early in the morning, at noon, in the evening, or late at night. . . . No one would dare to refuse the invitation of an acquaintance to go have a bowl of *pho*. It permits those of modest means to be able to express their sincerity towards their friends. It is also great because it has a different meaning in every season. In the summer, a bowl of *pho* makes you sweat, and when you feel a gentle breeze brush your face and back you feel like the sky is airing you out. In winter, a nice hot bowl of *pho* brings color to pale and cold lips, and warms up poor people like an overcoat. . . .

Pho has rules all its own, like in the names of the stalls. The name of a *pho* vendor's stall usually only has one syllable—its "popular" name—or is sometimes named after the vendor's son: for example Pho Phuc [the Pho of Happiness], Pho Loc [Pho of Generosity], Pho Tho [Pho of Longevity]. . . . Sometimes they are named after the vendor's physical deformity: Pho Gu [Pho of the Hunchback], Pho Lap [Pho of the Stammerer], Pho Sut [Pho of the Hare-Lip]. . . . Sometimes people give the vendors nicknames based on where they usually set up: Mister Pho from the Hospital, Mister Pho of the Gate, the Young Pho under the Bridge. . . . Sometimes the name is taken from a distinctive way that the vendor dresses. One vendor became known for the hat that he wore during the French colonial period, called a *calot*, and has since enjoyed an unparalleled reputation in the whole capital as Pho Calot.

One of the best things about *pho* is that you can transgress the rules while still remaining true to this special dish. I think that this principle rests on the fact that it must be prepared with beef. Maybe *pho* would be better with the meat of other animals (four-legged, winged, etc.), but if it is *pho*, it must be prepared with beef. Is it then a transgression of the rules when it is prepared with duck, with Chinese-style pork, or with rat? . . . The working classes are attached to classic *pho*. Today, some people experiment by seasoning it with soy sauce and Chinese ingredients; this is the privilege of the rich. . . . In reality, the true flavor of *pho* for a connoisseur is that of cooked beef, which is more aromatic than boiled beef and has an odor that carries the spirit of *pho*. Moreover, artists find that cooked beef presents itself better aesthetically than boiled beef. In general, vendors without respect for their craft first cut the cooked beef into small formless pieces, and when the clients arrive they just toss them into the bowls; this isn't important for those who are just trying to fill their stomachs as quickly as they can. But when a finicky customer arrives (a vendor can always tell when a client is demanding, even if he has never seen him before), the vendor places his knife on a nice piece of cooked beef and slices it into thin, wide pieces, with the pleasure of someone who takes pride in his work.

One intellectual who was worried about the future once wondered "if one day, when the nation's economy reaches the ultimate stage of socialism, our national *pho* will be in danger of disappearing, and if we will eat canned *pho* that you have to heat up in boiling water before opening it, which would make the noodles soggy." He was harshly answered by one of the clients in a stall: "Go to hell! Quit speculating about the day when the sky will fall on our heads. . . . As long as there are Vietnamese, there will be *pho*. In the future *pho* will be as hot as it is today, and maybe even more delicious. Our bowl of *pho* will never be put into a can, American style; as a true native of Hanoi, I can assure you that this bastardization will never happen."

Whenever I start talking about *pho*, I always end up thinking of a good friend with whom I used to eat *pho* and talk for hours about everything and nothing. Like many people, she left for the South out of pride. Now each time I discover a clean little stall that makes good *pho* I can't help thinking of her, since she loved really hot peppers. Out of superstition, she even attributed her ability to make a living to the areas where they have hot peppers which make your lips swell up. Every time I eat a spicy *pho* that burns my lips, my affection for this friend who left for the South also grows stronger. . . . I know that there is *pho* in the South, and even a southern style *pho*, but the *pho* that you find on the sidewalk as an émigré is never as good as the one you find in Hanoi—prepared in the traditional way, eaten around a fire in the middle of downtown, in this "city of a thousand-year-old culture."

Note

This article by Nguyen Tuan first appeared in the first and second issues of the literary magazine *Van* [Letters], on 10 and 17 May 1957. It was translated into French by Nguyen Van Ky.

busy clientele. One may find everything there: from cheap rice cakes to the most gourmet meals, such as chicken, pigeon, or duck sautéed with traditional herbs, as well as a wide variety of noodle soups. The alleys are also a common place for getting together with friends. This is where the young motorcyclists who race through town during the day, provoking both terror and fascination, meet each other to elude the police who have been sent out after them.

Rituals of the Table

Like many other Asian cities, Hanoi is a morning city. Long before the loud-speakers begin to broadcast official announcements, one can hear the cries of the itinerant merchants ringing out in the alleyways to wake the taste buds. Each merchant has his or her own neighborhood and clientele. They proffer a whole range of "sticky rice": plain, with soy sauce, with sesame, with peanuts, with grilled shallots, and so on. Between errands, many Hanoi residents seek out these ambulant merchants for a bowl of noodles with crab (*bun rieu cua*) or with snails (*bun oc*); these are two dishes typically eaten by women and equally appreciated by men. In his book *Hanoi 36 pho phuong*, Thach Lam writes:

> If you pass by the *Maisons des Chanteuses* or brothels during the afternoon lull or late in the evening, you can see women eating this dish *[bun oc]* with great care and attention. The acidic broth makes their tired and heavily made-up faces contort, and the hot peppers make their withered lips murmur and whisper. The peppers some-times even make tears roll down their faces, tears that are more sincere than tears of love. The woman who sells this dish has a tool, with a hammer at one end and a point at the other. With one quick flick of this useful tool, the whole snail falls into a bowl of bouillon. And yet even the quickest pace cannot keep up with demand. As she watches her customers eat, she also wants to have a bowl, she told me.[15]

The morning is also the best time to savor *banh cuon*, a kind of ravioli served with grilled shallots and thin slices of pork pâté (*gio*); one dunks the whole thing in fish sauce (*nuoc mam*). The afternoon is generally reserved for indulging in good food. Between two meals many people snack on duck eggs, eaten with salt, pepper, and sprigs of aromatic knotgrass. They also go in search of *che*, a candy made from soy or black bean, lotus grains, or sticky rice. This typically Vietnamese dessert is served in small bowls and perfumed with banana flavoring.

Autumn is the nicest season in Hanoi and the best loved. It too has its special dishes. Early in the season, farmers harvest a kind of sticky rice to make *com*, identifiable by its green color, the color of the leaves of the banana tree. This delicacy can be prepared in a number of ways: some prefer it fried and lightly sweetened; others eat it plain. Rich or poor, cultivated or not, no self-respecting person from Hanoi can say no to this delight, which has almost become a symbol of cultural identity.

Contrary to Chinese cuisine, which is very rich and complicated, Viet-namese cuisine—at least that of the common people—is prepared with com-pletely ordinary ingredients. People from Hanoi use their ingenuity in the art of making the most out of the ingredients at hand. For example, another typical dish from Hanoi is called *bun cha*. It is prepared with simple ingredients and small pieces of grilled pork and is served with noodles, lettuce, herbs, and the ubiquitous fish sauce, but it has an incomparable flavor. As in all Vietnamese dishes, meat is an indispensable element, but it does not play the same role or occupy the same space as it does in Western dishes. Its primary function is to give flavor, while the base remains the rice: it is no surprise that in Hanoi (as in the rest of Asia) they say "to eat" as "to eat rice" (*an com*). *Bun cha*, for example, is made of vermicelli—but the noodles are made from sticky rice. Passing by the Street of Chickens (Hang Ga), clients can savor the aroma of this succulent dish coming from a small shop run by an elderly couple. Out on the sidewalk, the husband keeps an eye on the grill and from time to time plugs in his little fan to stoke the fire; inside the stall his wife serves the clients, who call her *chi* (big sister) or *co* (little paternal aunt). This division of labor is quite rare in Hanoi, where traditionally women work hard throughout the day, while men pass their time in the drink stalls. This couple has even declined the offer of a businessman who wanted to transform their little stall into a mini hotel, and they are content to live off of their small business.

Traditional "fast food" served by an itinerant merchant.

A Flowering of Poets and Novelists

Hanoi is also a land of culture, and in the 1930s it experienced an incredible blossoming of poets, novelists, and journalists. There is now renewed interest in and appreciation for these writers who, for decades, were ignored or suppressed. Paradoxically, their rise was made possible by their anticolonialist ideas, which were hidden for a time so that they could devote themselves to literary creation and the reexamination of the cultural traditions of the past. They used two newspapers as a forum for their ideas, *Phong hoa* [Manners], created in 1932, and *Ngay nay* [Today], which was created in 1934 and reached a circulation of more than 10,000—a considerable number at the time. The figurehead of these progressive writers was without contest Nguyen Tuong Tam, also known under his pseudonym Nhat Linh (see sidebar, "The Intellectual, Nguyen Tuong Tam"). He took over as head of an editorial committee made up of his two younger brothers, Nguyen Tuong Long and Nguyen Tuong Lan,[16] and Tran Khanh Giu (alias Khai Hung), poet Tu Mo, the artists Nguyen Gia Tri and Nguyen Cat Tuong (alias Lemur), and poet The Lu. Together they elaborated an ambitious plan of action and formulated simple and daring mottoes in order to develop a literature in *quoc ngu*— written by Vietnamese, for Vietnamese, and nourished by themes taken from Vietnamese society:

- the search for a new ideal
- refusal to accept preconceived notions
- refusal to serve anyone or to give one's allegiance to any power
- guides for action: conscience, justice, and honesty
- humor as means, laughter as weapon

The newspaper *Phong hoa* aimed its criticism at old-fashioned cultural traditions and the outdated customs of society. It also published press reviews, international and local news, stories, poetry, and theater, all illustrated by caricatures, a first for the Vietnamese press of the time. The success of the paper encouraged the principal editors to form the group Tu Luc Van Doan (Self-Reliant Literary Group) in 1934, which became the driving force behind literary creation both in Hanoi and in the whole country.

Determined to break with classical forms weighed down by Chinese philosophical and literary allusions, these writers fashioned a new, forceful style marked by realism. Because they could not carry out a political revolution, they set their sights on profound reforms regarding modes of thinking, behav-

The Intellectual, Nguyen Tuong Tam

Nguyen Tuong Tam was born on 25 July 1906 in the Cam Giang district, between Hanoi and Hai Duong, from a long line of educated civil servants and scholars. He was the third in a family of seven children from the central Vietnamese city of Hoi An who came to settle in the North. One of his ancestors had been minister of the Army in Gia Long. His father was a modest secretary in the provincial colonial government. After his father's premature death, Tam's mother had to raise the children by herself.

Tam began his studies in an apprenticeship of Chinese characters. A gifted student, he continued Franco-Vietnamese education at the School of the Protectorate.[a] His family's modest financial situation forced him to take a job as an employee at the Financial Office in 1924. It is at that time that he met Ho Trong Hieu, the satirical poet who would become known by the pseudonym Tu Mo. Their friendship was built around discussions on literature and the importance of *quoc ngu*.[b] His first novel, *Nho phong* [Confucian manners], was published in 1925; then a second, *Nguoi quay to* [The spinning woman] was published some time later.

In 1925 he enrolled at the Indochinese University, first as a student of medicine before abandoning that for the School of Arts, created that very year by Victor Tardieu. Finally, he interrupted his studies and began to make a living in Saigon and then in Laos as a designer of film posters. But his dream lay elsewhere. After getting married, he left for France in 1927 with the help of his family and an association that promoted studies abroad. He enrolled in the Department of Sciences in Toulouse and graduated two years later. According to his younger brother Nguyen Tuong Bach,[c] he was impressed by the French social system, by the development of democratic ideas, and by journalism, especially *Le Canard enchaîné*.[d]

Upon his return to Vietnam in 1930, he taught at the private school Thang Long, an institution that attracted a fringe group of intellectuals involved in a variety of political movements. Among these intellectuals, the most well known are Dang Thai Mai, a scholar interested in Marxist theories; Hoang Minh Giam, an influential leader in the Vietminh in 1945; Ton That Binh; and the Communist Vo Nguyen Giap, future victor of Dien Bien Phu.

This was in the days following the Yen Bay uprising of 1930, led by Viet Nam Quoc Dan Dang (the Nationalist Party), and the formation of the "Soviets" of Nghe Tinh orchestrated by the nascent Communist Party, two insurrectional movements that were suppressed with brutality by the French. Fed on progressive ideas, Nguyen Tuong Tam planned to launch a Vietnamese-language newspaper called *Tieng cuoi* [Laughter] with his brothers and friends. Authorization being slow to come, he found a job as head of the journal *Phong hoa* [Manners], which was near bankruptcy. Completely redone, *Phong hoa* appeared in July 1932 and is credited with being the first satirical journal illustrated with caricatures. Despite threats, cuts, or suspensions imposed by the censors, *Phong hoa* aimed its criticism at those Vietnamese who collaborated with the colonial power—in the absence of any capacity to undermine the latter. The newspaper served as a reflection of the social and cultural situation of the times and made history by proposing the creation of a modern society. In May 1935, after having attained a circulation of 10,500 over a period of four years, it was finally pulled out of circulation.

At the same time, Nguyen Tuong Tam's literary output flourished and grew in importance. He often wrote in collaboration with his friend Khai Hung. In 1934, he also published with his friends another newspaper, *Ngay nay* [Today], which was similar in content to *Phong hoa*, in case the latter was shut down. This group then founded the Tu Luc Van Doan (Self-Reliant Literary Group), whose objective was to promote a national literature in the Vietnamese language which focused on Vietnamese society. They made up the only group to have its own independent publishing house, Doi nay (Our Times), which allowed them to publish a large number of novels and short stories.

It is natural that someone involved in so many intellectual pursuits would eventually turn to politics, but Nguyen Tuong Tam was just waiting for his time to come. When World War II broke out, he was present at the foundation of the nationalist Dai Viet Party, which rejected all forms of collaboration with foreign forces. In 1941, he rejoined survivors from the abortive Viet Nam Quoc Dan Dang uprising who had withdrawn to China. Firmly opposed to shedding any more blood in the name of politics, he sought support from the Americans—the only ones he thought capable of facing up to the Communists, who were committed to armed struggle. When the Vietminh took power in 1945 after the surrender of Japan, he returned to his country to reinforce the Nationalist ranks.

The political situation was then awash in total confusion. The rival nationalist factions made deals with the Vietminh in order to have representation in the new government. At the same time, the Chinese nationalist army of General Lu Han had been sent by the allies to disarm the Japanese forces and occupied Tonkin under the benevolent watch of the Americans. In an atmosphere of secret operations and intrigue, each party tried to take what it could get, but the different nationalist factions could at least agree on one thing: they had to beat the French in setting up an independent state.

After the August Revolution of 1945, the declaration of independence of 2 September, and the elections of January 1946, Nguyen Tuong Tam was named minister of Foreign Affairs in the new coalition government. His assistant was Pham Van Dong, a member of the Communist Party and future prime minister of the Democratic Republic of Vietnam. Tam led the Vietnamese delegation at the Dalat Conference in April–May of the same year, but his disagreement with the Communists convinced him to flee again to China. There he found his two younger brothers, Nguyen Tuong Long and Nguyen Tuong Bach.

After five years in exile, he returned secretly to his country in 1951 and took refuge in Dalat. In 1956, he returned to Saigon and to his career as a publisher and writer. In 1960 he launched the political movement Mat tran quoc dan doan ket (National Solidarity Front) to oppose the dictatorship of Ngo Dinh Diem. Accused of subversive activities, he was called before a tribunal on 8 July 1963. On the eve of his trial, after having summoned his family and friends, he put an end to his life. In a brief press communiqué, he wrote: "I offer my life to History, which will be the judge. I don't leave the task to anyone else. The arrests and condemnations of the opposition are serious crimes, which will end up handing the country over to the Communists."

Notes

^aTranslator's note: In French, the school is called the Lycée du Protectorat. It is more widely known to Vietnamese as Truong Buoi (Grapefruit School), after the name of the town Buoi.

^bAt the time, all courses were taught in French, so Vietnamese was taught as a language in its *quoc ngu* form.

^cBach is currently most probably in China. A group of Vietnamese historians based in Canada has published his memoirs: Nguyen Tuong Bach, *Viet Nam nhung ngay lich su* [Vietnam, historical days] (Montreal: Groupe vietnamien de recherche sur l'histoire et la géographie, 1981).

^dTranslator's note: *The Chained Duck* is a weekly paper that began publishing satirical articles on French society and politics in 1918 and is still popular today.

ior, and beliefs. They attacked the constraints of a society that suffocated individual aspirations in the name of tradition. The characters of their novels became the spokespeople for their thoughts. In *Doan tuyet* [Rupture], Nhat Linh liberates women from the weight of oppression of the family. Nguyen Cong Hoan ridicules the mandarinate and village notables in *Buoc duong cung* [The last attempt],[17] a work that was immediately banned as soon as it appeared in print. Ngo Tat To denounces outdated traditions in his many journalistic writings and criticizes rigid literary competitions in his novel *Leu chong* [The tent and the cot]. Vu Trong Phung writes about youth faced with the problems of life in his novel *Vo de* [The dikes burst] while introducing a perfume of eroticism in *Giong to* [The storm]. There were also exposés on the slums of Hanoi by young journalists. Some of these books have since become classics, and others have been made into movies.

This generation wanted to go beyond mere denunciation or criticism of

cultural traditions; their works advocate alternative solutions. For some, the
key to happiness was liberation from the yoke of colonialism. Others advocate Westernization but in a limited fashion and only as a catalyst for change,
by which Vietnam would become a truly modern society. In this manner, the
political revolution would begin from a cultural base. And it was in this context of cultural change that modern poetry found a fertile soil for its expression. Marked by the Romanticism of such French poets as Baudelaire,
Rimbaud, and Verlaine, young authors discovered the solitude of the individual in conflict with the community, the latter representing constraint and
anonymity. They thus usurped the position once held by their elders, who
were steeped in the strict rules of classical poetry that went back to the Chinese literature of the Tang dynasty. The famous literary competitions, now
considered antiquated in that era of profound change, were abolished in
1915 by the colonizers, under the guise of a royal decree. What remained of
the past was now not much more than a faint glow of nostalgia. Some of
these old scholars had to become public scribes on the sidewalks of the city
just in order to survive. This climate of confusion and reversal of norms is
illustrated in a poem written in 1935 by Vu Dinh Lien:[18]

"Ong do" [The scholar]

Each year when the peach trees blossom[19]
We see the old scholar
Spread out the ink and the red paper
On the sidewalk of well-traveled streets
Those who come by ask him to write[20]
Compliment him on his talent
His fine touch sketches out the strokes
One would say a dancing phoenix,
Or dragons in flight
But year after year
What has become of the clients of yesteryear?
Saddened, the red paper hides its sheen
The ink confines itself to the morose inkwell
The scholar is always there
Though no one notices him
The yellowed leaves fall on his paper
Outside the rain and dust pass by
This year the peach trees blossom
But the scholar has not returned
What has become of the souls
Of the people of days gone by?

The Women of Hanoi

During this same period, women were encouraged by the success of their sisters in China and in the West and began to break taboos and demand their proper place in the family and in society. Taking advantage of the new freedom of the press, they began to put into question backward and oppressive customs, such as the commercial exploitation of feminine virginity, early marriage in which children were regarded solely as objects of exchange, perpetual widowhood, injustice, and the discrimination found in everyday life. In short, they demanded equal rights and denounced ancestral practices that affected them. Free love also made an appearance, and young couples began to assume a European air and go to the movies to see Western films. They could be seen holding hands, strolling around Returned Sword Lake, and then slipping into a hotel to spend their first night of love together.

These new freedoms had their price, however. Hanoi saw a dramatic

1930s cartoon: "Autumn rain: surprising how useful it can be."

increase in female suicide: women who threw themselves into the river after a first heartbreak, taking with them their secrets and lost loves. The phenomenon reached such a height that men in Hanoi cynically began to call local lakes Mo hong nhan, "Tombs of Beauty." Still other women, led in a different direction, ran aground in brothels or in dance halls.

Women also began rejecting traditional constraints placed on fashion. Vietnamese women had previously bound their breasts with pieces of cloth (yem) to hide them from the concupiscent gaze of men. Modern women rejected what they considered to be a both physical and moral constriction, provoking a reform in women's fashion. It was designer Nguyen Cat Tuong (also known as Lemur) who invented the tunic (ao dai), which then became the national dress of Vietnamese women. He took inspiration from the traditional tunic with four panels, the two front ones knotted at the waist; the new one only had two panels, open at both sides from the waist down and fastened at the right shoulder with snaps. His creation met with enormous success, and is still seen today.

This emancipation of Vietnamese women and their revolt against the traditional moral order were due to two factors: changes in the educational system, which began to accept female students, and especially a change in mentality. In the 1920s, colonization brought with it the establishment of Franco-Vietnamese education, which, though not a perfect system, still allowed women the opportunity to obtain even the highest university degrees. In 1924, eleven women from the schools of medicine, law, and literature were rewarded by a class trip to France. In 1935, it was, ironically, a woman from Hanoi, Hoang Thi Nga, who was the first Vietnamese to obtain a doctorate in science in Paris after having finished secondary school in Vietnam.

In the time of the emperors, only men studied Chinese characters in the hopes of passing the literary competitions, which were the doorway to respectability and prestige. Most women, with the exception of singers and a few individual cases, were raised to become either housewives or, at most, shopkeepers. For this reason there is not one woman's name inscribed on the eighty-two stone tablets erected at the Temple of Literature which, since 1442, celebrate the memory and glory of the valedictorians of each session of the Mandarin examinations. The educational system was solely a machine for producing scholars imbued with Confucian doctrine, an edifice raised by men against women, with women forever excluded. Along these same lines, in the first half of this century it was often said that "women don't need much education." If by chance a rebellious woman was discovered trying to learn to read in secret by the light of the hearth, her family would simply tear up her books. What bothered parents the most was not the fact that their daughter could read; rather, that they feared they would find her exchanging love letters with a young man. It was of ultimate importance that their progeny did not escape their control in matters of love.

In the more popular quarters, however, Confucian principles could not be observed to the letter, for they ran contrary to many native beliefs and traditions. Among the beliefs of the common people, for example, half of all popular spirits are female.[21] One of the "four immortals" (*tu bat tu*) is a goddess, Lieu Hanh. This pantheon still remains important in the countryside, having survived the campaign against superstition from 1945 to 1985. On the shores of West Lake, the Phu Tay Ho Temple is dedicated to this goddess and is the site of a yearly pilgrimage that attracts worshipers from around the country. Recent years have seen the return of religious festivities, and the weeks preceding Tet are often animated by the spirit of times gone by.

During the war with America, Vietnamese women showed to the world that they, too, could fight and defend their country. In a way, they were just carrying on the tradition of their ancestors. History reveals that some of the first recorded historical figures in Vietnam are women, for example, the Trung sisters. Throughout the North one can find temples dedicated to these two national heroines, like the one in Hanoi mentioned above. In recent years, novelist Duong Thu Huong has become the bête noire of the regime, which is of course run by men. But she has done nothing other than dare to say openly what her sisters thought in silence.

Secret Loves

Despite its history of combat, Hanoi is also a city of love. The city's parks and riverbanks are now swarming with young couples who are no longer afraid to show their affection in public. This open display has reached such a pitch that the street sweepers refrain from working near places conducive to intimate encounters. In a sense, love has been forced outside into the streets, by promiscuity, housing problems, nosy neighbors, and a certain sense of tradition. The mores advocated by the Stalinist-Maoist reign were those of a very prudish Confucian tradition whereby rules of conduct were dictated by the leaders, under threat of severe punishment in case of transgression. But the public saw that those who advocated this decent behavior clearly felt above the law themselves. For example, the former party Secretary General Le Duan soon earned the reputation of being a ladies' man and a sensualist. He did not have a harem, but the nurses assigned to give him daily massages understood the situation clearly. So, while such dignitaries—clearly disciples of Mao—could indulge in any pleasure they liked, the common person had to hide any scandal for fear of being accused of criminal licentiousness. In this moral universe, women only had two options: to be "virtuous," that is, live in denial of their bodies and their passions; or to act on their impulses and be considered as no better than common prostitutes.

In Vietnam, as in the West, prostitution tends to reflect the society in which it develops—including persecution under repressive regimes. In the past, male scholars often took female singers as lovers, just as some young men today find love with hostesses who work in bars called *bia om*, or "love cafés." As a direct consequence of social taboos, many live out their romantic adventures in secret, outside of the traditional family circles. The most cautious meet their lovers in cafés that are set up precisely to facilitate discreet, amorous encounters. In general, behavior has changed radically. It is no longer surprising to see couples holding hands or walking arm in arm in public, something that would have been unimaginable just ten years ago.

The city of Hanoi itself is loved by its citizens, especially those who have had to flee persecution (see sidebar, "Vu Bang and *Thuong nho muoi hai*"). From books, to poetry, to songs, the Vietnamese sing the praises of their capital city. As testimonial to this city of love, there are many songs that celebrate Hanoi's spirit of romance. The following excerpt, for example, evokes the good-byes of a young couple from Hanoi whom destiny has separated:

"GIAC MO HOI HUONG" [THE DREAM OF THE RETURN]
by Vu Thanh

He left his dear city one morning
When the autumn winds returned
The heart of the traveler was smitten with melancholy
He watched as his beloved
Disappeared into the smoky haze
Retreating into the distance with uncertain steps
Tears in her eyes, tears of bitterness.
Good-bye. . . .
One day, even if I am lost in the four corners of the world,
I will return towards the horizon
To find once more my dreams of springtime
And forget the days, the months which fade
In sobs I think of her
Oh Hanoi!

Vu Bang and *Thuong nho muoi hai*
[The twelve nostalgias]

Like many of his generation, Vu Bang made his literary debut in the world of journalism in Hanoi and Saigon in the 1930s. He then left Hanoi in 1954, part of the
exodus toward Saigon, where he resided for the rest of his life. The following tale,[a]
in homage to Hanoi and the North, was begun in 1960. He finished it eleven years
later, at the height of the Vietnam War:

At first, no one could believe it. Why should it matter whether you're here or somewhere else—it's all the same country, what's the difference? Don't you find everywhere,
from the North to the Center, eyes that speak with a sea of emotion and affection;
and from the Center to the South, laughter which is held back but still reveals ardent
charms?

But no, when you are far from home you feel like a piece of rotten and worm-eaten
wood as old as time immemorial. . . .

The wind in the night made you cold, water pounded the shore in squalls; it is always
sad to be on the docks. We loved each other and we wanted to encourage each other,
but we didn't dare or didn't know how to say it. The woman only knew how to bow her
head with a long sigh, while the man stood silent and looked with sad eyes, like the
eyes of a ghost, the black night cradled by the song of crickets and the tears of earth-
worms. Sadness, and lassitude persisted thus. Until the day . . . when the first rains of
the season inundated the streets, while we were in a little shop tucked away by the edge
of the river Tan Thuan.[b] Sitting beside us, clients from the North felt dazed and lost.
As if this atmosphere were intolerable to them, to the point where they had to find a
pretext to speak.

One of them said:

—In the North, it's probably the beginning of the rainy season.

Another:

—But, Madame, the rain in the North is different.

And the third:

—Everything is different. Stop talking about it. It makes me want to cry.

The fellow adventurer looked at his friend standing next to him; they were both
silent for they couldn't manage to utter a single word, yet they felt a kind of electricity
which ran through their bodies.

They didn't need much, just the exchange of banalities amidst the rain of a desolate
afternoon, to reawaken the melancholic impressions of a worm-eaten heart. . . .

The more nostalgic it is, the more one loves Hanoi, and the more passion one feels
for the North. This nostalgia is disproportionate, inexplicable! When you miss Hanoi
and the North, it is as if you miss your beloved: anyone at all can make you start thinking of her, and she is, of course, the most beautiful of all. . . .

I love Hanoi so much, and think so often of the North, that I cannot appreciate all
of the magnificent things that are presented to me here. This is surely a grand injustice.

And I end up loving this injustice, and the twelve months and their climatic changes, the harmonious vibrations of passing time, of birds, of beauty, of the leaves, of sentiments, of love; I thank this injustice which has allowed me to become aware of my ardent love for Hanoi. Oh Hanoi, you hear me!

Notes

ᵃThe following is an extract from Vu Bang, *Thuong nho muoi hai* [The twelve nostalgias] (reissued in Saigon in 1989, translated into French by Nguyen Van Ky).
ᵇTan Thuan is a small river in the outskirts of Saigon.

Notes

1. Dong Kinh and Tokyo are two "readings" or transcriptions of Chinese characters, one Vietnamese, one Japanese.

2. King Le Loi was the founder of the later Le dynasty (1428–1527).

3. *Lim* is a tree with a very hard wood used to make columns or beams to support roofs.

4. *Translator's note:* Communal houses were public buildings in a village center that served as both religious and civic hub.

5. *Translator's note:* A *mau* is a unit of measurement equivalent to 3,600 square meters. The area of this lake is thus about six acres.

6. The Tay Son brothers managed to unify the country, which had been divided since the sixteenth century by two rival families: the Trinh in the North and the Nguyen in the South. However, they were eliminated soon after by the founder of the Nguyen dynasty (1802–1945), with the help of the French, who began their own conquest of the South in 1858.

7. This is one of the arms of the Red River, which flows into the China Sea near Haiphong.

8. Nguyen Tuan (a writer from Hanoi, 1910–87), "Mot it lich su Ha Noi" [Some stories about Hanoi], in *Canh sac va huong vi dat nuoc* [Landscape and flavor of the land] (Hanoi: Editions "Tac pham moi," 1983), 170.

9. *Hang* means "merchandise," and *dao* means "peach." This does not seem to fit the convention whereby the name of the street reflects the products sold there. However, the *peach* in this case refers not to the fruit but to the color of the dye most commonly used on the raw silk made in the area.

10. *Quoc ngu* is a romanized transcription of the Vietnamese language devised by the Jesuit Alexandre de Rhodes and other missionaries of the seventeenth century.

11. On 1 January 1997, Ha Bac Province was split in two—Bac Ninh and Bac Giang—returning to the old provincial borders from colonial times.

12. *Translator's note:* Centuries ago, these houses were places where women would sing

and recite poetry for scholars and refined gentlemen. As a result of modernization and colonization, however, the women became less popular for their voices than for their "easy virtue." Over the years, this tradition has died out, and today they no longer exist.

13. Phai (1921–88) is a painter from Hanoi whose works are now much respected.

14. For more details on this dish, see the article by Nguyen Thi Huong Lien, "Nha hang La Vong va mon dac san cha ca" [The restaurant La Vong and its specialty *cha ca*], in *Van hoa dan gian* [Popular culture], no. 2 (1990): 30–32.

15. Thach Lam, *Ha Noi 36 pho phuong* [The thirty-six neighborhoods of Hanoi] (Hanoi: Doi nay, 1943).

16. Lan's alias was Thach Lam, the author of, among other things, *Hanoi 36 pho phuong* [The thirty-six neighborhoods of Hanoi].

17. *Translator's note: Mandarinat* was a French term for the imperial bureaucracy, composed of officials trained in the Confucian classics.

Buoc duong cung was translated into French by Georges Boudarel as *L'Impasse* (2nd ed., Hanoi: ELE, 1983).

18. Lien (1913–96) was a poet from Hanoi who began his literary career in the 1930s.

19. This is an allusion to Tet, the Vietnamese New Year, which takes place at the time of year when the peach trees bloom.

20. As Tet approached, public scribes composed sentences at the request of clients.

21. *Translator's note:* See the article by Georges Boudarel, "L'Insertion du pouvoir central dans les cultes villageois au Vietnam," in *Cultes populaires et sociétés asiatiques: Appareils culturels et appareils de pouvoir* (Paris: L'Harmattan, 1991), 87–146.

CHAPTER TWO

The French Model

Nguyen Van Ky

An imperial decree, dated 1 October 1888, accorded a small territorial con-cession to the French conquerors. Located near where the Municipal The-ater is now,[1] it progressively grew as the colonial regime consolidated its hold on the territory and became a real municipality. Hanoi enjoyed special status as a French city and even had its own budget. It had a certain autonomy, at least in principle, with respect to the Protectorate of Tonkin. The difference between this Vietnamese city and France was nevertheless considerable: the French resident-mayor was not elected but appointed, an "anomaly" that was denounced even by the colonists themselves.

From the Concession to the
Colonial Municipality

That anomaly was resolved by an order of 31 December 1891, relating to the organization of the cities of Hanoi and Haiphong, which gave French resi-dents and certain Vietnamese the right to elect council members. In January 1892, Hanoi thus got its own municipal council, made up of sixteen French members and two Vietnamese (increased to six in 1928). Out of 475 regis-tered colonists, 320 voted. This assembly decided to extend the borders of the city, against the advice of Resident-Mayor Beauchamps, claiming that all the land situated within the urban perimeter and not claimed by individual owners should belong to the municipality. Delegates wanted to construct an infrastructure that would be more conducive to economic development.

Main Street in the French concession, 1890s.

Plans were drafted to fill in the numerous small lakes that stood in the way of modern urbanization and were a "perpetual source of infection with each temperature change." Trees were also cut down to open up new roads and build housing.

The evolution of the city during the French colonial period had two main phases. The first stretched from the French conquest to World War I, reaching its peak with the Doumer years (1897–1902),[2] and the second was from 1919 to World War II. Before the leadership of Paul Doumer, the construction followed no particular plan. The projects of clearing and reclaiming land brought in their wake the destruction of many important sites, some of them endowed with great historical significance.

The Bao Thien Pagoda, which dated from the Ly dynasty (1009–1225), was razed to allow the construction of a new cathedral. The latter, a "masterpiece of size and ugliness," in the words of colonial writer Alfred de Pouvourville, was built under the direction of Monsignor Puginier, bishop of Hanoi, with the support of his Vietnamese flock and was consecrated on 24 December 1886. Other important religious structures met the same fate, like the eighteenth-century temple that was destroyed in 1883 to make room for the new City Hall, now the headquarters of the Municipal People's Committee. The next to fall were the Bao An and Ba Danh Pagodas. The former was destroyed in 1892 and was replaced by the main post office, whereas the latter was replaced by the print shop of the Schneider brothers and then later still by the College of the Protectorate.

The French police barracks were erected on the site of the former Scholars' Camp, near the Imperial Academy, where the traditional civil service examinations administered by the imperial court had taken place. The citadel met a paradoxical fate. Built in 1805 according to the plans of a Frenchman in the service of Prince Nguyen Anh (future emperor Gia Long), after the fall of Hanoi it was converted into a simple barracks for French forces, but curiously it eventually became dreaded by its new owners. In an editorial dated 21 January 1892, Alfred Le Vasseur, editor-in-chief of *L'Indépendance tonkinoise*, ardently demanded nothing less than its demolition. The municipal council then made the same decision one year later, on 23 July 1893. The work lasted four years (1894–97); only the watchtower (*cot co*) was spared.

Colonial urbanization also brought with it the destruction of a great number of thatch huts, the traditional housing of the Vietnamese—an act that was welcomed "with pleasure" by the colonial press. During the years 1891–92, these working-class quarters were ravaged by incessant fires, an event that

*The watchtower (cot co), all that remains
of the imperial city.*

L'Indépendance tonkinoise covered diligently every week. The most spectacular of these fires took place on the night of 22 January 1891: more than 200 houses and four pagodas fell prey to the flames, all located in the area described by the Street of Chalk, Street of Rafts, Street of Bamboo, and the dike. The origin of these fires is still unknown, and they mysteriously all took place at night. The French attributed them to the carelessness of the locals, and the colonial press denounced the ill will of these "natives who shut themselves up in their homes or ran away when the Europeans called out to them." The few firemen who came to help were poorly equipped and usually arrived too late to save these fragile structures. Literally, then, the new French city was built upon the ashes of Vietnamese lives.

"Hanoi is an old city," reported *L'Éveil économique de l'Indochine* [The economic awakening of Indochina] in 1927: "The most venerable antiquities may not be so old, but it is regrettable that they have been respected so little; that we have destroyed, for example, the Pagoda of Torments" (see page 52).

But old symbols are not destroyed without new .ones immediately taking their place. The statue *Liberty Illuminating the World*, a modest replica of the one in New York, had been sent to Hanoi during the World's Fair of 1887. It was placed on top of a pagoda located on a small island in Returned Sword Lake,[3] a preposterous decision that was denounced by the colonists themselves. "*Liberty* on top of the pagoda is the victory of light over obscurity. And why don't we put the Grand Buddha on top of one of the spires of the cathedral?" wrote *L'Avenir du Tonkin* [The future of Tonkin], an anticlerical newspaper that had been accused by its rival, *L'Indépendance tonkinoise*, of having been "sold out to the Chinese of Hong Kong." *Liberty* finally was transferred to another park, before disappearing from view entirely. As for the statue of Paul Bert (former governor-general), inaugurated on 14 July 1890, it had been placed in the square of the same name, a few steps from the City Hall and across from Returned Sword Lake and the Statue of Liberty. Vietnamese critics said that Bert was in love with the "Lady of the Lake" and thus stood guard day and night for fear that she would get away. The Vietnamese were meant to understand that only the colonizers were capable of interpreting this symbol of freedom and giving it meaning. They would soon understand, if they did not know already, that freedom is never given freely; to get it, one has to pay a price.

Colonial Urbanization

In the early years of French rule, the main French road in Hanoi was Rue Jean Dupuis. By the end of the nineteenth century, the center of gravity had moved toward the Rue Paul Bert (currently Trang Tien Street), the most commercial, most animated, and oldest street of the French Quarter. At that time there were two cafés, the Café de la Paix and the Café Alexandre, three butcher shops, a hotel, and a host of other shops specializing in everything from liquor to furniture. Though not an actual fortress, Paul Bert Square was surrounded by four buildings built between 1887 and 1888 (the office of the French *résident supérieur*,[4] the Post and Telegraph Office, the Treasury, and City Hall); in a sense it was the heart of the colonial headquarters. In the same period, a garden was built on the shores of West Lake; it later became the Botanical Gardens, whose surface area grew from one to forty acres after expropriations. The racetrack opened along the Avenue Gambetta, which had just been traced out (currently Tran Hung Dao Street), before being transferred to a location adjacent to the Botanical Gardens.

The face of Hanoi, which became the capital of the new Indochinese

The Pagoda of Torments, which was destroyed by the French.

Union created in 1887, was transformed under the direction of Paul Doumer. Doumer carried out several ambitious projects designed by architect August-Henri Vildieu, head of the new Office of Civic Construction: the palace of the governor-general, the new buildings of the *résident supérieur*, the post office, City Hall, and the Court House—all of them in the massive neoclassical style symbolizing both power and perpetuity[5]—and last the bridge that bears Doumer's name.

The building of this bridge, in Doumer's own words, "the most remarkable work which has ever been executed in the Far East," had a political dimension: it was to show "the strength of the French civilization in the interests of peace." These projects were run by the company Daydé and Pillé and lasted just over three years (1898–1901), costing the Indochinese budget six million piasters. It was a sort of colonial answer to the Eiffel Tower. The latter had been built some fifteen years earlier in the height of the renaissance of the iron age, inspired by the development of a new means of transport: the train. The new bridge was reserved for trains, "two-wheelers," and pedestrians, with a second bridge to be added upstream for automobiles. It was also under Paul Doumer that the large-scale train projects were begun, though only a few sections were in service. With the construction of the

The Long Bien Bridge, formerly Paul Doumer Bridge, 1925.

railway from Yunnan, Hanoi became the necessary transit point for travelers coming from the south and heading to China.

Electricity was introduced in 1892, but a power plant would not be built until 1914 (on the shores of Returned Sword Lake), and it only produced 700 kilowatts of energy. This was just enough to provide energy for the lighting of the wide avenues, the official buildings, and the houses of French residents. Access was thus out of reach for the local population, with the exception of a few Chinese shopkeepers. Working-class neighborhoods would not get electricity until after the financial crisis of 1929, when the electric company put into place its new power plant, built this time on the shores of Truc Bach Lake. It was still inadequate, however, to satisfy growing demand, and during the winter months the citizens of Hanoi had to undergo daily power cuts while energy went to satisfy industrial needs. The situation was only rectified in the 1930s.

In 1911 the centerpiece of Hanoi's high society—the Municipal Theater—was inaugurated. Built by the French in a very ornate, late classical style, it welcomed performances from French acting troupes every year in November and December. Paradoxically, it would later become center stage for the Vietnamese struggle for independence as site of the patriotic demonstrations of August 1945, as well as becoming the seat of the National Assembly of the Democratic Republic of Vietnam.

Hanoi also had an architect who played the role of Haussmann in the colonies:[6] Ernest Hébrard. His plans for development were strongly supported by Governor-General Martial Merlin (1921–24), who followed the lead originally provided by Paul Doumer. Government offices were located in one area specifically set aside for this purpose. The imposing Finance Building was completed in 1927, after just two years, while work on the Indochinese University was virtually brought to a halt.

In the same period, an annex was built to the École française d'Extrême-Orient (est. December 1898),[7] whose architectural style was a successful marriage of local and Western styles. After independence it was transformed into a museum of history. Under the impetus of the Association for the Intellectual and Moral Formation of the Annamites,[8] led by Pham Quynh,[9] young Vietnamese architects were called on to get involved in new projects. The award-winning projects were published in L'Éveil économique de l'Indochine, a weekly created by Henri Cucherousset in 1917, whose main offices were on Paul Bert Street.

This second phase of the city's development was made possible because of its gradual extension toward the west and south. This new land was taken by force by both the administration and local French residents, who pushed the Vietnamese back toward the periphery. This process led to the establishment of several working-class neighborhoods in the south of Hanoi, situated between Mandarin Street and Hue Street, the most famous of which was Kham Thien, the "neighborhood of the singers."

In 1925, one part of the Hébrard plan elicited protests from some of the more enlightened colonists, at least those who knew the city and its history. The architect planned to destroy the Cemetery of the Grand Buddha by razing rows of tombs along the shores of Truc Bach Lake. This cemetery contained, among other historical figures, the body of Sergeant Bobillot.[10] The plan was deemed a "sacrilege" by *L'Éveil économique de l'Indochine*, which condemned it as irrational. The newspaper claimed that the plan was only conceived "to please a princess who was afraid of the dead" and because the tombs bothered people (presumably French) out on their Sunday strolls. The plan was nevertheless approved by a municipal decision and put into action, but it was mercifully stopped because of a lack of funds. Two years later the administration resumed the attack, this time without Hébrard, and again ran into opposition from *L'Éveil économique de l'Indochine*. The newspaper called for "a solution that would not offend Hanoi public opinion and render the French odious to the Annamites," but its appeal was to be in vain.

Education and Society: The School of Revolt

Hanoi was not only an administrative center but an intellectual and cultural metropolis as well. It had a well-established infrastructure and famous institutions such as the Rabies Institute, modeled after the Pasteur Institute, the École française d'Extrême-Orient, the École supérieure de pédagogie, the University of Hanoi, and the School of Fine Arts, as well as many libraries.

In 1904, Governor-General Paul Beau introduced a new Franco-Vietnamese educational system. It was revised by his successor Albert Sarraut in 1917 and gave rise in the 1930s to a new generation of modern Vietnamese intellectuals. Some became spokespeople for cultural emancipation, while others devoted themselves to political causes. This new intellectual openness also led to the creation of the famous Thang Long School. It was established in 1919 by Pham Huu Ninh, secretary of finance, to come to the aid of public schools, which were too few in number. Fifteen years later, this private institution had weathered difficulty to become a beacon for the younger generation. At its height, it had laboratories for physics, chemistry, and the natural sciences, and the students had their own library. Between

1928 and 1935, there was a dramatic rise in enrollment, from twenty-nine students to more than 1,000. This success was due to the reputation of its teaching faculty: the school had about thirty professors and teachers, some of whom, in the course of the following decade, became leaders in the national struggle for independence.

Secondary education was taught by a team with solid training in modern methods, including seven graduates of the École supérieure de pédagogie, three with university degrees, one architect, and a British professor who taught English courses. Primary school courses were taught by teachers with high school degrees. Among the latter was Vu Dinh Lien, author of the famous poem "Ong do" [The scholar] cited in chapter 1. It is worth noting that before hiring its personnel, the director of the school had to present the applicant's file to the *résidence supérieure* of Tonkin, which then tasked the Sûreté with a preliminary investigation of the candidate's "morality." We learn thus that Commissioner Fleutot found Vo Nguyen Giap's 1934 application "unacceptable" for reasons of "political involvement." To justify his decision, Fleutot recalled that Giap had been condemned in 1930 to two years of prison and two years of government surveillance by the court of Thua Thien and was "then liberated conditionally in 1931, before being pardoned by His Majesty Bao Dai." But the administration disregarded this recommendation and gave Giap the job.

Dang Thai Mai, a confirmed Marxist and future father-in-law of Giap, had also been condemned to two years in prison and two years of government surveillance for "affiliation with the Indochinese Communist Party," before being pardoned by the minister of the Colonies. In 1931, he had been fired from his job as a teacher in a Franco-Vietnamese primary school by a decree by the governor-general. His candidacy, presented to the administration in 1932, still received a favorable reception. Hoang Minh Giam, former student-teacher in the higher Franco-Vietnamese primary school system in Cambodia, was removed from his post for disciplinary reasons. He got involved in journalism and wrote tendentious articles. But without legal precedent known in the personnel files of the Tonkin Sûreté, his application was accepted in 1934. He appeared again in 1945 as part of Ho Chi Minh's entourage and the following year became Ho's minister of Foreign Affairs.

In 1934, the administration refused the candidacy of Nguyen Cao Luyen, a recent graduate from the School of Fine Arts, because "an architecture degree is not on the list of titles required to be authorized to teach." He was not able to join the teaching faculty until the following year. Also among the teachers at the school was Nguyen Tuong Tam, a writer who, upon his return to France, founded the newspaper *Phong hoa* [Manners] while still contributing to the school's fame between 1932 and 1934. Another famous pupil was the lawyer Phan Anh, future minister of Youth and Sports for the Tran Trong Kim government in 1945 and later a nonparty minister of National Defense in the coalition government of Ho Chi Minh the following year.[11]

In 1936, a group of alumni from the school founded an association that became one of the components of the Indochinese Congress of that year.[12] One can easily draw parallels between this school and the first independent university of the country: Thang Long University, created in Hanoi in 1988 on the initiative of Hoang Xuan Sinh, a mathematician and professor at the University of Hanoi.

This rapid progress in education, taken in hand by the Vietnamese themselves, was given added support by the creation in March 1938 of the Association for the Propagation of *Quoc Ngu*, which rallied all the big names of the intelligentsia of the time. At its head was Nguyen Van To, secretary at the École française d'Extrême-Orient and future minister in charge of Social Welfare in Ho Chi Minh's first government. Among its members were Tran Trong Kim, Nguyen Van Huyen, and Hoang Xuan Han.[13] Vo Nguyen Giap and Dang Thai Mai were also founding members. The association obtained the support of Yves Chatel, then *résident supérieur* of Tonkin, who agreed to be the honorary president. With the approach of war, however, Vo Nguyen Giap and Dang Thai Mai abandoned this intellectual battle for armed resistance.

Between a Rock and Hard Place: The Interpreter

The Vietnamese love to tell the anecdote of a French resident who had just arrived in Indochina and, discovering the existence of an unknown cat, called for his interpreter. The latter did not know the French name for the cat. Confronted with this problem, which put his prestige and credibility at risk, the interpreter used his imagination to describe the animal: "Kitty black kitty yellow, him eat me, him eat *monsieur*. . . ." Seeing that the Frenchman had trouble understanding him, he added: "Five minutes, him eat the whole world." He was describing a tiger.

Interpreters were part of a world that was still relatively unknown but was characteristic of the colony. They were subdivided into five main classes, with the most "prestigious" working at the *résidence supérieure*. Next came those who worked in the government offices of the capital; finally there were the employees of the provincial administration. In the eyes of the colonists, they were all no more than subalterns who owed them full respect.

The unfortunate story of Nguyen Dinh Cau illustrates the tense relationship that existed between the French and the Vietnamese during the colonial era: while working as an interpreter at the *résidence supérieure*, he was arrested and then condemned by the court of Hanoi to three months of prison for "insult and rebellion" against a police brigadier. With respect to their compatriots, interpreters had a position that was at the very least ambiguous. Bon Mat (the pseudonym of a French journalist) painted an instructive portrait of this phenomenon in *L'Indépendance tonkinoise* on 25 July 1891 (see sidebar, "Our Interpreters").

Race Relations: Incomprehension and Suspicion

Colonial society lived well within its ivory tower, condemning anything that lay outside of its own known realm. The colonists' arrogance and disdain were reflected in the language that they used to refer to their Vietnamese subordinates. Common people were referred to as "flea-ridden Annamites"; beggars were likened to a "foul horde"; and then there is the term *nha que* (peasant), which was on the tip of nearly every colonist's tongue. Incomprehension and misunderstanding were complete, exacerbated by the linguistic barrier. What is more, no one tried to overcome these barriers. This only made it more difficult for those back in France to get an accurate portrait of the colonies. A Parisian baroness who wanted to find out about Vietnamese women wrote to *L'Indépendance tonkinoise* to ask if they were "capable of feelings, these little *congaïs* with ebony teeth."[14] The question was deemed "quite embarrassing" by the newspaper.

In the street, Vietnamese could be arrested if they so much as addressed a French bureaucrat sharply in a way judged disrespectful. Incidents of this type were common, especially on the streets, where some people got around in cars and others were on foot. *L'Éveil économique de l'Indochine* could not help voicing certain opinions: "On one side there are those who ride in cars, on the other those who are run over by them. . . . One of these days we will see

Our Interpreters

Bon Mat (French journalist)

What pests!

Like the jockeys in France, they are the uncontested kings of the Tonkin streets. The interpreter from Saigon is the most pedantic of all of them, he whose knowledge of the Annamite language led us to bring him here as interpreter from the beginning of the Conquest. Then there is the interpreter from Tonkin properly speaking—the little *nha que* [peasant] still green and fresh out of school, in front of whom a correct page of writing flung open the doors of the presidential coterie of the capital—they are like administrative confidants of both important and petty government officials, draped in their pride as new-comers. They both, however, put on insolent and high airs in front of Europeans like someone who thinks himself indispensable and feels himself highly favored.

And why wouldn't they become vain about this? Just the night before, they were only *nha que*, and now they find themselves in this unexpected situation which brings them so markedly close to us? Why wouldn't they try to show off in front of this European, a simple employee like themselves, who has made them what they are? Isn't their salary equal to the European's—or even higher considering the fact that they are in their own homes and can live on nothing, in true Annamite fashion?

How many employees and bureaucrats in France, even the most highly paid, earn the healthy amount of fifty or sixty dollars—money that here is not even counted before it is thrown in the face of these simple copyists who merely sketch out words like one traces a drawing? An infinite number of variables and social classes limits what each of them is allowed to do, and marks the limits of how far they can go in their way of dressing and living, in their secret desire to become Europeans.

The interpreter of Saigon, like a Frenchman of 1860, perfectly exemplifies this gradual transformation. It is he who prepares the chrysalis and watches over it as it blossoms, he who finally sets the fashion!

Let us begin with his feet: that is where the transformation started. It is between the ankle and the toe that we first saw signs of this creeping infection, which spread into the spirit of a people who lag behind our protective and invading civilization.

Contrary to all native habits, there are no more Saigon interpreters without socks. This one item borrowed from our wardrobe distinguishes them more than all of their expertise from the crowd of Mandarins who have all, without exception, remained faithful to the sacred traditions of their barefoot ancestors.

The addition of these white socks has brought about the wearing of cloth shoes, and the slim, flared trousers of France then complete the metamorphosis. The transformation is so complete that today the only things left of their national accoutrements are the ample *cai ao* of shimmering silk which is also disappearing, and the monumental and feminine hairstyle which to all appearances will remain with them.

It is a poem in itself, this hairstyle!

Their hair is piled up in a bun, and is always conscientiously greased. A large tortoise-shell comb makes it look like a wedding cake just waiting for the pastry chef to come plant his shiny-handled knife into the middle of it. Atop this whole scaffolding sits the legendary green turban, uniformly arranged.

You are obsessed by this "green turban" because you encounter it everywhere and all the time! Always correct and worthy, the trousers that are shiny with wear and well-worn, the silver-handled riding crop at the small of the back, the hand laden with enormous rings which he makes glitter at each new encounter, the cigar holder, a real *kummer*, at his lips, and his green spectacles at his eye (another poem, these spectacles), the interpreter from Saigon walks with small steps with the automatic movements of a rhetorician in the flesh, in the middle of the gray smoke from the *condrès* he inhales with small breaths, his head lightly tilted to the side, his lips pursed with disdain.

On foot or on horseback, in a rickshaw or in an automobile, alone or with his better half—a plump little doll who is at least as radiant as he, whom he prome-nades through town to show off her glitter, like a sacred relic—he is always there, just steps away from us, almost brushing up against us, looking for a parallel which flatters him, a comparison which aggrandizes him, where he triumphs.

The interpreter from Tonkin, on the other hand, has fearful feelings of inferior-ity which generally subordinate him to his brothers in Cochin China. But beneath this indifferent exterior he hides a ferment of profound jealousy for these "trans-planted foreigners" in his backyard who look at him as if he were a savage and chip away at his prestige.

He still copies the various transformations of these kings of the streets, but at a distance; and their noisy life overwhelms him.

Like them, he already has his own rickshaw and his *kummer*, which is authentic as well. It is true that he usually shares the expenses for these purchases and the up-keep of the rickshaw with a classmate, and that, from what is left of his tact—and for this we can only be grateful—he usually substitutes in place of the cigar-holder in *bout-dehors* of his majestic rival a cigarette holder, which is more modest, from our "pchutteux" of the boulevards.

No socks yet, for example!

No white cloth shoes in the French style!

While the Saigon interpreter no longer withdraws at our approach, as a result of our over-eager enthusiasm, the Tonkin interpreter is more modest. Though he already dreams of his own independence, he consoles himself at home in the eve-ning about this inferiority which torments him everywhere.

There on the family mat, in the obscure and limited milieu where his title of "interpreter" rings with magical consonances and allows him to reign as master, a whole horde of natives come to place their petitions.

It is his hour of triumph.

Sure in advance of his effects, he composes a serious expression and blinds his over-confident visitors with illusory promises, as their belts stuffed with sonorous and tempting coins come unknotted at his feet, amidst discreet encouragement from the *baïa*, his mother. She, whose voice is filled with honey and with her hand outstretched, raises the stakes again on this impoverished protector.

On that count, at least, the understanding is perfect between the parties involved. Interpreters from both Saigon and Tonkin swim in the same troubled seas, side by side despite the hatred, hands joined before common interest.

Here as everywhere else, naïveté opens the door for deception.

They all know it, at heart, these poor *nha que* who end up spending the fruit of so many years of labor most often on the gemstone of a ring; and all incessantly come back to the attack, head lowered, to this luminous home which attracts them—poor emeralds stunned by the bright lights of an inn.

In sum, in this venal country, as in so many others, everything is subjected to an inevitable tariff of influence or friendship: charges, protection, council, etc.

But here influence is often only apparent and friendship never counts for anything.

In all of Tonkin there is no sacrament that is solemn enough, no moral profound enough, to resist the bewitching shine of a new piaster.

---

public opinion—i.e., those who ride in cars—demand that the law create posthumous punishment for those who have been run over."[15]

In 1928 Governor-General Pierre Pasquier sent a memo to colonial administrators regarding "French bureaucrats, employees, and agents in their relationships with the native personnel" and asked that they stop addressing the natives as *tu* (the informal "you" in French). He was, however, ridiculed by an editor of the same newspaper, who wrote in June 1932: "[He] is not going to say to a ferryman: 'If it please my respected colleagues, could you row a bit faster?' Instead: 'You say coolies the oars make *mao len*': this is how the fine scholar Pierre Pasquier would express himself in that circumstance."[16] To appreciate the gulf separating the two worlds, one only has to read Philippe Franchini's *Continental Saigon*—a book that describes Saigon society but applies equally well to Hanoi. Incomprehension, disdain, and injustice were the mothers of the revolt that was to shatter the colonial system.

Pastimes and Pleasures

In 1942 Hoai Thanh and Hoai Chan wrote a book consecrated to modern poets wherein they claim that

> the meeting with the West caused the greatest upheaval in centuries in the history of Vietnam. . . . We live in French housing, we wear French hats and French shoes, we dress in French fashions; not to mention our use of commodities like electricity, the watch, the car, the train, and the bicycle. It is difficult even to enumerate all of the products of Western origin. . . . It is exactly these new material possessions which drive us toward new ideas. . . . all in the space of only fifty or sixty years, but which seems like centuries and centuries. However, westernization doesn't stop there. After having passed through two stages, one formal and one ideal, we have begun on a third. It has changed our manners and customs in daily life, and also our way of thinking, but it will end up changing our sensibilities. These new ways of life, new ideas, and especially the progressive influence of French literature are the agents of a third phase of westernization. The West has penetrated to the very depths of our soul.[17]

The French were obviously the principle agents of this modernization. In Hanoi in 1936 there were about 5,000 French out of a total population of 150,000: just over 3 percent. This small percentage was amplified by their privileged status and the fact that their pastimes and lifestyle had a great effect on the Vietnamese. With the introduction of dance halls and cinemas, Vietnamese society followed closely behind its colonizers. Of course, we are speaking about a small but advanced stratum of society, for the social barrier, dictated by economic and financial conditions, prohibited most Vietnamese from enjoying this new wave of modern life.

One official report stated that about two-thirds of all moviegoers in Hanoi were French and the remaining "one third [were] natives belonging to the bourgeois class (secretaries, employees, shopkeepers, and especially young scholars and students)." The French had a preference for "The Palace" on Paul Bert Street, which was the most luxurious, the most modern, and the most expensive of the seven existing cinemas in the 1930s. Most Vietnamese, on the other hand, went to the "Trung Quoc" [China], on the Street of the Fans, which was the least expensive and was Chinese owned. And finally, the poorest Vietnamese had to make do with a place standing up on the other side of the screen. In 1937–38, more than 500 films were shown in the theaters of Hanoi. This rapid rise was encouraged by the reviews appearing regularly in the Vietnamese-language newspapers. They were, of course, commercial films produced in Europe or the United States, most of which have now been completely forgotten. But the images that flickered on the screens of Hanoi helped to reinforce the dominant role of the West, which infiltrated world cultures through superior technology.

Dancing was a particularly novel addition to Hanoi society, for the Vietnamese do not have any particular dance traditions of their own as do many other Southeast Asian nations. The art of dance had been judged unworthy of Mandarin manners and was banned in the thirteenth century by the reigning Vietnamese monarchs. The latter were not, however, completely immune to its charms: some of them took advantage of certain occasions, like wars with the Champa, to capture several dancers and bring them back to the Forbidden City where they could be admired in private. It was modern dance steps that finally got the Vietnamese out on the floor. The creation of dance halls in the 1930s provoked a proliferation of dance classes. But still, it was only the well-to-do who had the luxury of following this European trend.

There are two principal reasons behind this cultural phenomenon. The first is of a moral nature: traditional Vietnamese society was impregnated with Confucian doctrine and so forbade all social contact between men and

The Palace cinema, 1924.

women outside of marriage. Pleasure was taboo, except for court dignitaries. In urban centers, however, these constraints weakened under the pressures of the new modern lifestyle. The quest for pleasure, even if it was only dancing with a partner, became a new preoccupation for the young, liberated generation. The second reason stems from the first. The dance halls took the place of the *maisons des chanteuses*, which offered rather old-fashioned entertainment. In fact, the French and the Vietnamese did not frequent the same establishments. With the exception of the Legionnaires, the French went to dance halls, most often accompanied by their dance partners; meanwhile, Vietnamese men went out alone, finding hostesses once they got to wherever they were going. Most Vietnamese still remained, thus, under the hold of tradition.

The Europeans Call Them *Congaïs*

Public opinion was not gentle with Vietnamese women who, for one reason or another, took French companions—a situation that was worse still if the latter was of high social standing. The Vietnamese created a special term for these cursed women, one that is saddled with heavy innuendo: *me tây*, "concubines of Westerners." A survey conducted in 1934 by Vu Trong Phung in a village close to a French barracks and published in 1936 under the title *Ky nghe lay Tây* [The industry of marriage with the French] describes this sort of relationship—one that was distorted from the beginning by the inequality of colonial society. To shake off the boredom and loneliness of the barracks or else in search of exoticism, many young French bachelors spent their salaries on a few moments of love with Vietnamese women. As for the women themselves, many had no other prospects and were in search of material security. Often, however, these relationships were fraught with brutality and deceit and could be broken at any time on the initiative of either party. Both the meeting and the separation usually went without ceremony.

One excerpt from Vu Trong Phung's survey says a lot about the nature of these relationships:

>   —You no have right sleep again my house! You leave me no pay, so finished wife, finished husband. So leave.
>   After a few moments of silence, the woman's voice rose up again:
>   —No, it over! Get out! . . .
>   The soldier—was it her husband or a client?—remained without uttering a

sound, as if he first wanted to see the effect of his silence. So the woman got angry and showed him the street with her outstretched finger:

—Get out! Right now!

It was only at that moment that the rejected husband reacted:

—Repeat what you just said!

The woman looked him straight in the eye and told him:

—Get out! I no afraid you! If you do something, I tell commander put you prison and you court martial!

Pow! The slap punctuated the insulting and threatening words of the insolent woman.[18]

Another "partner" of a Western man explains the reasons behind this type of conflict:

Everybody knows that it's money and not love which binds us to these men. But sometimes they're impossible. When their pockets are full, they go look for younger women just for laughs. And when they've got nothing left, they come back to see us. We shouldn't stand for that! . . . Some of them are very faithful. But it's destiny. I seem to find only good-for-nothings. But what can I do? The last one was a German. A criminal who had fled his country. It's terrible! We must be really suicidal! To sleep with criminals even! Physically he is handsome, but his soul is very ugly. . . . If I ever admitted this, he would kill me. Since I only married him for money, he should forgive me. But if I ever admitted it, he would consider me a whore. . . . People like us are society's rejects. Even if society doesn't look down on us, we are aware of our condition. I scoff at the teasing of others about my poverty and my humble situation; I only want to get rich so that one day I can get my revenge on those who despise me now.

Here is another testimonial collected by Vu Trong Phung:

—Yes, I have French nationality but I don't think I will marry a Frenchman. If I do, it's because I had no choice; because I know them too well now. My mother got married four times, and when my father returned to France I saw what happened afterwards. My situation is quite embarrassing. If I marry a Frenchman, one day he will have to go back to France; will I have to follow him and leave my mother to die of hunger?

—What about marrying an Annamite?

—That's also difficult. Anyone who dares to ask for my hand risks the veto of my parents, who would never accept such a union. . . . So they really have to be brave. As for the others, the conformists, they wouldn't have the guts to ask for the hand of a half-breed. To be a half-breed is a misfortune. The French don't really appreciate us, and the Annamites don't like us much either. In the eyes of Western high society, mixed blood is shameful, and it brings no glory in Annamite society either. My God, in reality I am without a country.

The fate of children born from this type of union was not an easy one. Justin Godart, who had been sent by the Popular Front government in France to inspect the situation in Indochina, says as much in his 1937 mission report (recently published in 1994). Such children, he says, were victims of prejudice and of social segregation, treated as second-class citizens; and their salaries were closer to those of the "natives" than those of the French, for the same work.

Monsieur Franco-Annamite

Cultural mixing also took place at other levels, however. In everyday life as in formal occasions, the European influence made itself felt in ways of dress, which differed depending on one's social class and condition. Many young people from well-to-do families were great fans of modernism and dressed from head to toe in European style. Most city dwellers, however, made do

*The Godard Department Store, on the corner of Tran Tien street
(formerly the Rue Paul Bert), 1924.*

with half measures by either adopting the Western trousers and keeping their long tunics over top or by wearing shirts over the traditional loose and flowing pants.

A photo taken in 1946 after the formation of the coalition government of Ho Chi Minh shows that a good number of ministers still kept their traditional garb. This was the case with Nguyen Van To, former secretary at the École française d'Extrême-Orient and president of the Association for the Propagation of *Quoc Ngu*; and of Huynh Thuc Khang, former inmate of Poulo Condore,[19] condemned for having participated in the antiestablishment movement of 1907, and ex–editor-in-chief of the newspaper *Tieng dan* [Voice of the people], edited in Hue. On the other hand, during General Leclerc's reception in Hanoi of the same year, Vo Nguyen Giap was wearing a helmet and white colonial uniform. As for hairstyles, although most city dwellers traded their hair buns for the square haircut and abandoned their turbans for hats, the purists still kept their traditional hairstyles until the end of World War II.

Some, of course, took the assimilation of Western culture to an extreme—even to the point of denying of their origins. This theme is dealt with in a play by Nam Xuong, called *Ong Tay An Nam* [Monsieur Franco-Annamite]. At first, Vietnamese theater in the colonial era was inspired by French plays that had been translated at the beginning of the century by Nguyen Van Vinh, notably the comedies of Molière. It reached its maturity in the 1930s and was considered by the Vietnamese as being in a "period of transition." Young playwrights, all amateurs, took their material from social realities of the time: families in trouble, the emancipation of women, and free love were the principle themes put on stage before a public that at first was uncomfortable with the newness of this style. Nevertheless, this new art form contributed, along with literature and modern poetry, to fostering the beginnings of a cultural revolution.

In this way, playwright Nam Xuong was first inspired by Molière and then wrote *Monsieur Franco-Annamite* (1930) as a critique of Vietnamese society with his own particular brand of humor. The main character is Cu Lan, a young graduate who returns from France and is representative of the urban microcosm of Hanoi. The play opens with his return to Vietnam, but he has changed dramatically: he no longer speaks Vietnamese, he acts like a European by kissing his father on both cheeks, he knows nothing about Confucius, and he has no desire to learn about this figure who is venerated by his father. He only addresses his father in French through the help of his servant, who serves as interpreter:

—He is my father, and I don't deny it; but on the other hand, I am European and
I shall remain that way, tell him. . . . Tell him to be quiet! I must speak first. . . . I
cannot, in consequence, abide to be treated like a dirty native, to be seen together
with natives, or to call "father" a man who smells like a native from twenty feet
away. . . . I wish he would stop being Annamite. . . . It is not as difficult as one
might think. He must simply get rid of this hideous outfit and dress like a European,
cut back his beard, cut his hair, put some liner on his eyes so they look larger, put
on creams and powders to have a whiter skin, that's a first step. . . . Then, he must
show a categorical disdain for all that is Annamite, even for the language, the
height of Annamosity in this Annamizing Annam, and which is idiotically called
a "mother" tongue. Finally, so as not to mix with these swarms of *nha que*, who are
not even of the same race, he must sell all of his possessions, follow me to France,
and settle there permanently; then he would be a Frenchman in race just as I am
now.[20]

The author goes beyond caricature and describes a world whose moral order
has been reversed. For a Vietnamese son to demand that his father be quiet
was nothing less than blasphemous in the Confucian tradition.

As slight as its role was in the world of arts, the theater already contested
the role of its classical rival of Chinese origin, the *tuong*. In 1936, a group of
friends asked at the mayor's office in Hanoi if the city could let them use the
Municipal Theater to put on a commemorative performance. They wanted
to celebrate the memory of Nguyen Van Vinh, who a decade earlier had
been the father of Vietnamese theater. Vinh later tried to make his career in
journalism but eventually went bankrupt; he died shortly after in Laos during
an adventurous search for gold. Their request was refused. This was, however,
during the time of the Popular Front, which had raised Vietnamese hopes of
seeing real understanding on the part of the French, of regaining their dignity, and of obtaining a minimum of material comfort.

Hopes for a Day

In 1926, the colony's hopes were raised again with the arrival of Alexandre
Varenne, a new governor-general from the ranks of the French Socialist
Party. His most spectacular gesture was to order the amnesty of Phan Boi
Chau, who had been condemned to death in absentia.[21] The conservative
colonial milieu saw this act of clemency as a sign of the end of white rule in
the area and protested vehemently against any interference. These new
hopes for change were short-lived, however, for Varenne eventually let himself get caught up by the dominant current.

In many ways, the colonial microcosm was but a reflection of political life back in France, with its conservatives and liberals, its contradictions and good intentions. In 1891, *L'Indépendance tonkinoise* printed the results of a poll taken in France by the newspaper *La France* on the subject of the eventual departure of the French from Tonkin. The 10,000 responses give the following results:

For Evacuation	2,700
Full evacuation	500
Maintain present forces	1,200
Other	1,000
Remain in Tonkin	7,300
For reasons of pride	1,000
Strike hard and finish it off	3,000
Put a general at the head of Tonkin	2,000
Send Jules Ferry	1,000
Other	300

In sum, three-quarters of those surveyed wanted to maintain the current state of affairs. Among them, Le Myre de Villers, first civilian governor of Indochina, declared in an interview in *L'Indépendance tonkinoise* of 10 January 1891: "If we abandon Tonkin, do you know what will happen to our missionaries? Well! They will be condemned to a slow death. They will cut off their heads!"

Within Vietnam, opinions were obviously different. Opposition to colonialism from within the milieu itself was marginal, but there was a progressive trend that dared to oppose the system. Sometimes this current was voiced, which enraged the die-hard colonists; but often it remained mute in the underground of the colonial world. One of these progressives was Antoine de Lanessan. Elected in 1881 as deputy of the fifth arrondissement in Paris as a member of the extreme Left, de Lanessan later moved closer to the Republicans. He had a lot of experience in colonial issues, having spent several years in Africa and then in Cochin China as a medical aide. When appointed governor-general of Tonkin in 1891, he was welcomed symbolically to his post by a cannon shot fired from the port of Haiphong. His Masonic brothers in the Tonkin Fraternity marked his promotion by a banquet in his honor, under the leadership of Mr. Fellonneau, grand master of the Masonic Lodge. That same year, during the reception at the governor's palace for the sixty-three graduate-laureates of the examination of Nam Dinh, de Lanessan made this subtle pronouncement: "I congratulate you on the success that you have just received, and I want to assure you of my respect for the elevated philosophy of Confucius which has been instilled in you. I know that this philosophy teaches you the respect of authority and of the family, that it teaches you about the duties of the Mandarin towards citizens, as well as his duties as citizen towards his leaders."[22]

Still others took their function to heart and tried to reconcile the two cultures, like the French *résident supérieur* of Thai Binh, Monsieur Peret. He committed suicide in 1926 after not having been able to save his constituents from a devastating flood. The latter then elevated him to the rank of "spirit" and built a temple for him. The French Socialist Ernest Babut, who has today been all but forgotten, took the side of the Vietnamese in their fight against colonialism. He used his clout as a journalist to raise critical issues in his bilingual newspaper, *Librement socialiste*. In 1936, he wrote an article in the feminist journal *Dan ba moi* [New woman] (created by Mrs. Thuy An), denouncing the vote-catching gimmicks used by candidates in local elections. Other members of the colonial section of the French Socialist Party, many of them journalists and teachers, also contributed to the blossoming of new ideas of social progress. The League for Human Rights (a French equivalent of the American Civil Liberties Union in the United States) was very active at one point and intervened to arrange the release from prison of Phan Chu Trinh, an aging patriot who had been arrested for sedition before World War I. The colonial consensus wanted him to be repatriated to France, but he was allowed to return to his native Vietnam in 1925, where he died of cancer one year later.

After the victory of the Left in the legislative elections in France, everyone hoped that the situation in the colonies would be improved with the formation of the new Popular Front government. Justin Godart was put in charge of a "Mission of Information" to analyze public opinion in all French colonies and make a report upon his return to France. After stopovers in Cochin China, Cambodia, and Laos, he arrived in Hanoi on 2 February 1937. The organization committee for the reception had been arranged by political groups—including one that represented *Le Travail* [Labor], a newspaper run by the Communists—and other representatives of the population. Some 30,000 people were to congregate at the train station to welcome the delegate of the Popular Front; but the date of his arrival in the capital had been kept secret by the authorities until the last minute. The night before, the chief of the Sûreté, Mr. Arnoux, had called in the press and announced that Godart would arrive on 1 February. He corrected this the next day but still did not give the exact time of arrival. On the day of Godart's arrival, some "overzealous policemen" intervened, probably out of fear that the situation would turn against the government. Eventually, Mr. Arnoux himself went to the rally with the intention of turning back some of the demonstrators with the help of native guards, to "impress" them at the *résidence supérieure*. But the audience became indignant and dispersed of its own accord, leaving Godart without the grand reception that had been planned for him all along. This political blunder on the part of the authorities hardly surprised the delegate from France—which only proved right the organizers of the demonstration.

In 1936–37, strikes broke out again, now even stronger than those of a few years earlier. They spread over the whole territory, from north to south, and struck French businesses as well as those run by Vietnamese. To cite only one example, 300 workers at the Hanoi sawmills went on strike, and at the end of a week (19–26 October 1936) they won their case and got a 40 percent pay raise. A Vietnamese foreman, "detained pending legal inquiry," was found hanged, the victim of a suicide, before the resolution of the conflict. But the arrival of Godart was hardly enough to spark big changes, for colonial opinion was more or less hostile to the ideas incarnated by the Popular Front. Raymond Delmas, president of the local section of the Association for the Intellectual and Moral Formation of the Annamites, gave a speech on 15 February 1937 at the reception for Godart. In his speech in front of 100 members of the Hanoi section of the League for Human Rights, he alluded to two factors:

> European proletariats cannot form an accurate picture of the abject misery of these poor men. . . . Public opinion in this country—by that I mean "that of the French" in this country—is not by any means favorable to the ideal of the *Rassemblement Populaire*. The French press has its share of responsibility for this state of affairs. In certain papers, the news is always presented in a tendentious and unfavorable light.[23]

Despite such attitudes, some measures were put into effect: a decree of 13 October 1936 reduced the work day to eight hours, cut back on night work by women and children, and prescribed annual vacations; moreover, many political prisoners were liberated. A decree of 30 December stated that the French work code was to be applied in Indochina as well. The Vietnamese wrote up other requests and put them to the delegate, concerning a variety of freedoms: of politics, unions, meetings, association, opinion, travel, and so forth. But they would have to be patient, for in Paris their demands were placed on a very distant back burner. In the end, the question of independence was never officially brought up by the Vietnamese, for conditions were not favorable at that time. Only the outbreak of World War II would reanimate these aspirations and bring them out into the open. Then all hopes were finally allowed, especially one contained in a small but magical word: *doc lap*, independence.

Notes

1. *Translator's note:* Built by the French at the end of the nineteenth century, the Municipal Theater would eventually be the site of many of the key events of the Vietnamese revolution.

2. *Translator's note:* Paul Doumer was the first governor-general of French Indochina and later became president of France.

3. The pagoda was the tomb of a rich Hanoi businessman and was built in the mid–nineteenth century.

4. *Translator's note:* The *résident supérieur* was the highest French official in the Protectorate of Tonkin, stationed, of course, at the *résidence supérieure*.

5. See the article by Christian Pédelahore, "Hanoi, miroir de l'architecture indochinoise," in *Architecture française d'outre-mer* (Liège: Pierre Mardaga, 1992).

6. *Translator's note:* Haussmann was the city planner who redesigned the streets of Paris and put in the grand boulevards during the reign of Louis-Napoléon in the 1850s.

7. *Translator's note:* The École française d'Extrême-Orient was an institute that trained scholars and led research in Indochinese archaeology and history.

8. *Translator's note:* The Association for the Intellectual and Moral Formation of the Annamites was sponsored by the French to indoctrinate Vietnamese elites in French rules of behavior.

9. Quynh was editor-in-chief of the pro-French journal *Nam Phong* [Wind from the south] (1917–34) and then minister in the cabinet of Bao Dai before being assassinated by the Vietminh in 1945.

10. Bobillot was a military engineer who played an important role during the siege of Tuyen Quang, a fortress in Tonkin that fell into the hands of the Chinese in February 1885.

11. Kim is the author of, among other things, *Viet Nam su luoc* [The abridged history of Vietnam], published in the 1920s. It was the first work on the subject written in *quoc ngu*.

12. *Translator's note:* The Indochinese Congress was to be formed in conjunction with

the visit of a French inspection team to Indochina. The trip was cancelled, however, and the congress was never held.

13. *Translator's note:* Nguyen Van Huyen had a doctorate in both literature and law and worked at the École française d'Extrême-Orient. Hoang Xuan Han was the first Vietnamese graduate of the École Polytechnique in Paris and was first a professor at the School of the Protectorate and then minister of National Education in the government of Tran Trong Kim in 1945. He died in Paris in March 1996 at the age of eighty-eight.

14. *Translator's note:* In Vietnamese, *congaï* signifies "girl." The term has since taken on a pejorative sense.

15. *L'Éveil économique de l'Indochine* 398 (25 January 1925).

16. *Mao len* is a loose transcription of the Vietnamese *mau len,* which in this case signifies "faster."

17. Hoai Thanh and Hoai Chan, *Thi nhan Viet Nam* [Vietnamese poets] (Hue, 1942).

18. Vu Trong Phung, *Ky nghe lay Tay* (Hanoi, 1936).

19. *Translator's note:* Con Son Island, a small island off the coast of South Vietnam, was transformed into a penitentiary during the French colonial regime and renamed Poulo Condore. The extremely harsh conditions and "tiger cages" earned the prison a reputation for being a "school of Bolshevism," for many prisoners, hardened by their brutal treatment, were confirmed Communists by the time they left.

20. The entire passage is in French in the text.

21. Chau was an important nationalist who had opposed the colonial regime in the early twentieth century.

22. *L'Indépendance tonkinoise,* 19 December 1891.

23. Justin Godart, *Rapport de mission en Indochine January–March 1937,* ed. François Bilange, Charles Fourniau, and Alain Ruscio (Paris: L'Harmattan, 1994), 72–76.

PART TWO

HISTORY AND ITS SECRETS

CHAPTER THREE

1945: Under the Red Flag

Georges Boudarel

In 1945 the city on the banks of the Red River continued to suffer under the yoke of colonialism. Hanoi was still the capital of a supposedly French Indochina, but for more than four years it had been occupied by the Japanese. The colors of the French flag waved above the city, but they could not mask the atrocities of the famine that ravaged the nation. Under Japanese orders, farmers had replaced their rice paddies with jute, and peasants flocked to the city only to die of starvation in the streets. World War II also left in its wake a groundswell of nationalism, which had seen years of preparation and repression throughout the colonies. The French leaders of Vietnam, however, did not seem to be aware of this growing threat to their power.

In mid-1944, General Mordant became head of the French Resistance in Indochina and sent a message to Hoang Xuan Han (then minister of National Education in the government of Tran Trong Kim) that he wanted to meet with him to discuss Vietnamese aspirations. Han spoke frankly and told him what he thought: "We have to completely change the government, but it won't be easy. All the best men are in prisons or penal colonies, in places like Son La and Lao Bao." This frankness shocked Mordant, who had expected the usual Vietnamese reserve. "Can't we work with anyone else?" Mordant asked. "Impossible. They have all become servile from too many years of enslavement," answered Han. He did agree, though, to consult with his comrades and write up a list of Vietnamese aspirations.

He wrote that they desired the abdication of the emperor, which would lead to autonomy and then independence, whereby Vietnam would become a republic. Han learned of General de Gaulle's plan to set up a French protectorate and deemed it totally inadequate, knowing that London had already promised independence to India and Burma. Although the prospect of independence for Vietnam seemed far away, Han knew that they first had to get out of this impasse. Han describes the situation thus:

My words provoked a frankly hostile reaction from Mordant, who must have had other contacts because he told me that the Communists were asking for much less. The general thought that we were trying to balance a pyramid by standing it on its head. Mordant was convinced that after the catastrophic defeat of the Japanese fleet at Leyte Gulf, in the Philippines on October 1944, the Japanese wouldn't dare touch the French government of Indochina. I was convinced of the contrary, but it was in vain that I told him that the Vietnamese people would rather be granted their independence by the French than by the Japanese.[1]

The Japanese coup of 9 March 1945 brought an end to French rule and led to the spurious independence of a puppet Vietnamese state under Emperor Bao Dai. The treaty of the protectorate was rendered obsolete, but it would be May before a new government was created under the leadership of Prime Minister Tran Trong Kim. The pro-Japanese views of Kim and of the Dai Viet Party (which had hitherto been clandestine) were counterbalanced by intellectuals who were members of the nationalist groups Thanh Nghi (Discussion) and Tri Tan (New Thinking).

Hanoi was once again the principal site for these new power struggles, but the situation was far from stable as the corpses continued to mount. Novelist Nguyen Hong published harrowing accounts of the famine, which were later published as *Dia nguc vo lo lua* [Hell and the inferno]. According to some recent studies, there were some two million deaths in Tonkin alone.[2]

During this time, a handful of Communist militants began to weave links among nascent resistance forces, rural revolutionary groups that sent peasants out to find hidden depots of rice, and Ho Chi Minh, who had gone secretly to China to contact the American secret services of the Office of Strategic Services in Kunming. Forty years later, Han reflected that Ho had shrewdly taken full advantage of the situation with very little military strength. His propaganda was irresistible and his slogan was highly effective: "The Americans are with us!" A French colonist confirms:

On August 22, American parachutists were released over Gia Lam. That very evening we learned that 25 rooms had been reserved for them at the Hotel Metropole. This news had an enormous impact on the colonial milieu, which quickly lost its illusions. It soon became apparent, even to the staunchest American supporter, that those we had believed were coming to "save" us were in reality helping the Annamites! And at our expense![3]

A Nonviolent Revolution

If there is one pivotal date in the history of Hanoi, it is without a doubt that of the nonviolent revolution in the last days of August 1945. Without a single exchange of gunfire, everything changed. History rarely sees such an explosion that has such an effect without causing a single death. It also says a lot about the leaders who laid the fuse and lit the spark. In his work *Vietnam 1945: Quest for Power*, David Marr writes: "Even as I dug deeper among Vietnamese materials, I realized that it was impossible to fathom developments in 1945 by treating them as an exclusively Vietnamese affair."[4]

Of course, it is tempting to say that the whole world was implicated in this extraordinary entanglement: from the warring nations like Japan and the United States to China, France, and Great Britain, and of course the USSR, which was a strong presence even though it remained behind the scenes. But in reality we know that fundamentally it was a Vietnamese problem and that it is in Vietnam that we must search for the roots. General Giap, one of the most important actors on the scene, states the problem clearly: "Most often, it is only after the fact that we learn how a possibility became reality. And then we are tempted to say that it had to happen that way."[5]

Regardless of the external circumstances, real credit must go to the plotters of this radical and nonviolent transformation, which was achieved in just several days—perhaps even twenty-four hours. These masters of revolution were Ho Chi Minh, Truong Chinh, and Vo Nguyen Giap, as well as other members of the party Politburo. But one must not forget the local agents, whose role has been well documented by official histories in Hanoi.

On 15 August, news spread that the Japanese had issued an unconditional surrender. Almost immediately, Nguyen Khang, secretary of the local committee of the Indochinese Communist Party, called a meeting in the village of Van Phuc in the suburbs of Hanoi. The few men present, sitting cross-legged next to an old weaving loom, were about to decide the fate of the city—and of the entire nation. The Central Committee was far away, and a quick decision had to be made; but the men already had directives that guided their decisions. The aim was to overthrow the Japanese. As they could not do it by force, they chose to "neutralize" them.

For months they had organized political agitation: impromptu speeches in the marketplace, arms trafficking, and hunting down informers who were then cruelly and theatrically executed. A young party member, Tran Do, who had been imprisoned at Son La just a short time before, received an arms shipment on the shores of the Red River. In some suburbs, entire villages were practically under the command of their liberation committees. In one of these villages, Vuong Thua Vu, future commander of the regiment of Hanoi, carried out military training using wooden rifles. He soon had a motley group of new soldiers and sent some 800 men into the city.

The Association of Employees of the Pro-Japanese Government soon provided them with a springboard for action by calling for a demonstration on 17 August. It was then that people first started singing "Tien quan ca" [Soldiers arise], the song that Van Cao had just composed that would become the national anthem. Nationalist Doan Them came to the demonstration to cheer Tran Trong Kim, prime minister of the pro-Japanese government in Hue, but was stunned to hear voices crying out, "Long live the Vietminh!" The cheers increased as the march progressed toward the square in front of the Municipal Theater after the meeting. Them writes:

> As we reached the intersection at the South Gate (Cua Nam), a group of men from the outskirts—shabbily dressed in black jackets and pants, certainly not government workers—burst through our ranks, running and waving red flags with a gold star in the middle. One of them, brandishing a weapon that wasn't very common at the time, fired several pistol shots into the air for effect and everyone started to shout: "Long live the Liberation Front!" Did they do so out of fear? The fact is that some government workers ended up yelling cheers simply by reflex. The policemen posted on the sidewalk couldn't believe their eyes, and stood wondering what to do without intervening; even though a number of other groups held hands and gave a rather fascist, Italian-style salute in honor of an organization that the government workers knew nothing about.[6]

In the next forty-eight hours everything started to move very quickly. Several days before, Phan Ke An had put his father, Viceroy of Tonkin Phan Ke Toai, in contact with the Vietminh. By the evening of 17 August, Toai had gone to the side of the revolution. On 19 August, a new meeting was called in the square in front of the Municipal Theater. A crowd of Vietminh supporters from the outskirts invaded the center, while the Japanese, who had been secretly notified and were tired of conflict, did not intervene. Hardly had a government official taken the floor when Nguyen Khang, who had hung a red flag on the façade of the theater, grabbed the microphone and started to sway the crowd in favor of the Vietminh. Led by Le Trong

Nghia, they stormed the imperial viceroy's palace by scaling the gate, just steps away from the rally.

By evening, the crowd and the Vietminh were in control of the capital. However, the most important leaders of the organization were absent. They were still at their base at Tan Trao, about 100 kilometers (sixty miles) away to the northwest. It is at this point that a forgotten figure emerged, a master of disguises famous for his work in the revolution from its inception. He was the best testament and symbol they could have asked for: Vu Dinh Huynh.

A Master of Secrecy: Vu Dinh Huynh (1904–91)

It is difficult to sketch out the portrait of Vu Dinh Huynh. His photo may be found in the French press of 1946, when he served as aide-de-camp for Ho Chi Minh during an official visit. We know that in the early 1920s, at age sixteen, he joined the Association of Revolutionary Comrades, run from Canton by Nguyen Ai Quoc (one of Ho Chi Minh's aliases, 1919–45). He then became a member of the Communist Party at its inception in 1930, opting to fight in an unusual way: he went underground and "disappeared" into total incognito. Radically allergic to the colonial government, he preferred the shadowy milieu of the business world, figuring that the Vietnam of tomorrow would need more business people than bureaucrats—who were already too numerous.

His wife, who was both progressive and active in politics, was also quite extraordinary. She organized the first public track and field races for girls who, to the shock of many in society, ran in shorts that revealed their bare thighs. An ultraconservative journalist wrote a vitriolic account of the race in his newspaper, and Huynh's wife was afraid that his polemic would have an ill effect on her project. So she burst into the editing session of the paper and, in the middle of the meeting, slapped the culprit, putting a definitive end to all discussion.

As for Huynh, he continued his clandestine activities in a variety of business ventures, but his outspokenness got him fired several times. A well-connected brother then set him up in another venture, but it is not clear exactly what he was doing. The party directed him toward the intellectual milieu, in which he was highly appreciated despite not being well educated, but his activities remained so vague that even today certain well-informed journalists deny that he ever was a member of the Communist Party.[7] The

Sûreté, which had contacts everywhere, arrested him in 1939 and deported him to Son La, where he suffered alongside several key leaders. After his release in 1941, he resumed his activities as a business traveler, which allowed him to organize clandestine party meetings.

Vu Dinh Huynh's activities of that summer are not recorded anywhere, except in one article, which miraculously appeared in 1990 under his name in Ho Chi Minh City, that evokes the burning "Summer of '45" in Hanoi:

In the midst of the chaos, the political prisoners at the Central Prison escaped one after the other, jumping over the wall or going through the sewers. My little house at 65 rue Sergeant Larrivé (formerly rue de la Distillerie, today rue Nguyen Cong Tru) became a quiet but hectic way-station. Hectic, since so many old comrades arrived at the same time. . . . Discussions and plans of action were the order of the day. The revolution needed all the arms it could find—but without making too much noise. My wife had to continually call to order those who got carried away in their discussions or laughed out loud, making them lower their voices.

First we had to find clothes for all of them, something adapted to their character so they could pass unnoticed. We dressed them as workers, teachers, and students. A greater problem turned out to be feeding them, both the shopping as well as the cooking. This task we completely handed over to Mrs. Tuong, who helped us with housework. She was a fervent Catholic who prayed every day and went to mass every Sunday, but spent most of her time helping Communists who believed neither in god nor in the devil; she kept away the informers and the spies, and even arranged their liaisons. She would later be decorated for services rendered to the revolution.

The biggest problem was passing unnoticed in front of the informers who were sent to spy on everyone. Sao Do (pseudonym of Nguyen Luong Bang, a member of the Politburo who had just escaped from prison) forgot that he had a price on his head of 10,000 piasters and walked up and down the street in his big black cardigan with all the confidence of a respected businessman. . . .

The ranks of the pro-Japanese government started to thin out seriously. A number of well-informed figures came over to the side of the revolution, including the man whom the Japanese had trusted and named viceroy. Later research indicated that his son, Phan Ke An, was a militant in the student and teachers' movement. When the Kempeitai [the Japanese equivalent of the Sûreté] found out, they refrained from arresting him, but wrote to his father to warn him against this movement "at the heart of which we have the regret of finding your honorable son." The father couldn't help laughing when he read this message, which he passed on immediately to his son who was sitting right there with him. What would these men have said had they known that while he was still governor of Thai Binh in 1943, the future head of the puppet government of 1945 had offered the Vietminh a contribution of 500 piasters? . . .

Ha Ba Cang (alias of Hoang Quoc Viet, a prominent Party member and labor organizer) had asked me to find a radio at all costs so that we could follow the news of the war, in particular that coming from the Soviet front—which was of crucial importance to the Party. I managed to find a Dutch-made Philips radio. Every evening we would stay up late, sometimes working in shifts to be able to tune into broadcasts that were barely audible, beamed half way across the world. We couldn't risk turning up the sound: to get identified by the Japs was as dangerous as having weapons at one's house. At the time all radio receivers had to be registered so that they could remove the short-wave capability. We mere mortals could only listen to the longer frequencies and their local news.

I can't begin to describe our joy when we learned, on May 2, of the entrance of the Red army into Berlin. Our youngest member jumped onto his bicycle to go bring the news to his father, Tran Huy Lieu, who was running *Cuu Quoc*, the Party's daily newspaper. And on May 8, when Nazi Germany fell, we all celebrated.[8]

In early August 1945, Sao Do went to see Vu Dinh Huynh, with whom he had been imprisoned, to set up a meeting with an eye toward insurrection. This important congress is still much talked about today and remains much of a mystery for lack of direct and uncensored accounts. As far as we know, the only report of this decisive assembly is that of Tran Huy Lieu, published in 1960.[9] This account reveals a fundamental point: all the Communists who attended this national congress did so using pseudonyms to hide their true colors. They were often representatives of recently created democratic parties, which they had joined in order to infiltrate them. Lieu, who had recently escaped from Nghia Lo prison, came to the congress with Xuan Thuy and other militants. They sang out revolutionary poems without knowing that their author, Lieu, was right there in their midst.

At Dinh Bang, in Bac Ninh Province, Lieu found himself face to face with a comrade who would later become known as Hoang Minh Chinh. Without thinking, he called him by his real name, "Nghiem!" and immediately realized his error. The latter said quietly, "From now on, call me Chinh." It was under this name that he appeared at the meeting, with other members of the Democratic Party. At that time, the departing revolutionaries did not even know where they were going. One by one they arrived in a small village inhabited by ethnic minorities, recently chosen by General Giap as a rear military base and renamed Tan Trao.

According to Hoang Van Hoan, whose memoirs were published after his exile in China, there were about sixty people present on the opening day of the congress, 16 August. Ho Chi Minh was there and talked very clearly about the negotiations he planned to hold with France. Hoan writes: "Later, all material dealing with Tan Trao avoided mentioning this fact. I believe that it should be clearly noted, however, because it was a very prescient program, based on a grand and profound vision of both our opponents and ourselves."[10] The only other account of this event is that of Vu Dinh Huynh. When Sao Do asked him in highest secrecy to prepare for this decisive assembly, he specified that flags and banners covered with slogans be provided, as well as French wines and aperitifs. They had to do things right, after all, seeing as there were foreign guests expected. Huynh had champagne sent to Hanoi, some Dubonnet and other good bottles; and with that accomplished, he returned to the road.

What follows (sidebar, "A Peasant from Nghe Tinh Conquers Hanoi") is an important account that reveals the disagreements at the heart of the party apparatus. The author, Vu Dinh Huynh, was at the time a social leper, politically dead for almost twenty-five years. Years later, after Le Duan and Le Duc Tho took action to remove Ho from power, Huynh was part of the group of militants who were thrown into prison in 1967.

The information revealed by Vu Dinh Huynh in the next sidebar ("Uncle Ho Visits the Central Prison") confirms the remarks of Tran Van Chuong, former minister of Tran Trong Kim.[11] During an interview at his home in Washington, D.C., in 1978, Chuong declared:

> I saw Giap in November 1945, when I was arrested by the Sûreté and spent four days in prison in its headquarters on Avenue Gambetta. I said to Giap, "The revolution will take twenty years to become stable. Our primary problem is to defend ourselves against France. Why did you replace the government with committees, when you know what we need most is unity?" He didn't answer me, perhaps out of generosity. He set me free immediately. After that he welcomed me to the *résidence supérieure* [then the seat of Ho's government].[12]

This account by Vu Dinh Huynh is shocking, so much does its portrait diverge from those painted by Ho's usual sycophants. Although this account brings up a number of new questions, there is still one that is never pronounced: the fate of the Trotskyites (who were "eliminated" by the Communists after World War II).[13] The opening of the archives in Hanoi will finally allow us to answer with the seriousness the question deserves.

A Versatile Actor Takes History's Stage

Vu Dinh Huynh's revelations about Ho's concerns during the summer of 1945 raise historical and political questions that remain topical today. One

A Peasant from Nghe Tinh Conquers Hanoi

Vu Dinh Huynh

It was as if someone had given me wings. The words "general insurrection" rang inside my head like a haunting refrain, and I suddenly felt drunk. I got a taxi to Bac Ninh. As soon as we crossed the Canal of the Rapids and hit Hiep Hoa, only eight kilometers from Hanoi, we were on our soil, the land of independence and freedom. Throughout the countryside I heard children singing what would become our national anthem, *Soldiers Arise!*, by Van Cao. In the distance I could see red flags flying. I had tears in my eyes. When my young guide noticed, I told him I had gotten dust in my eyes. It's hard, sometimes, to say the truth. That's just the way we are.

Ho Chi Minh at Tan Trao

At Tan Trao I again met up with Sao Do. We were the first to arrive to organize the preparations. We were housed with the resident "Ong Cou" (Honorable Elder) in a little hut away from the others. For a very small handful of militants sworn to secrecy, Ong Cou was the very respectful name we had given to Nguyen Ai Quoc. To others, he was a character shrouded in mystery, a certain Ho Chi Minh. I had never met Nguyen Ai Quoc before. But for years—and I wasn't alone in this—he had become a myth for me, the very symbol of the Vietnamese revolution. On my way to Tan Trao I had hoped to be able to meet this mythic figure. Hardly had I entered Sao Do's hut than he said to me, "Just a few moments ago, Ong Cou asked me a bunch of questions about intellectuals and other important figures from Hanoi and the North. I told him that I wasn't up on those things, but that another comrade would go to answer all of his questions. Now that you're here, why don't you go right over and see him."

We entered the forest and came to his hut, where we found Ong Cou immersed in a paperback book. Emaciated like a hermit, with his tiny goatee, but solid, with a lively expression, he welcomed us simply and warmly. He spoke seriously and from the heart, and first asked me some questions about myself as a formality—then asked me straight out to tell him all I knew about the nation's intellectuals.

Beginning with the movement for the restoration of the monarchy at the end of the nineteenth century, I spoke of the Dong Kinh Nghia Thuc [Tonkin Free School] of 1906, the dead and the survivors; I told him about the Phuc Viet,[a] the group of intellectuals of Thanh Nghi [Discussion], the Tu Luc Van Doan, *Ngay nay*, etc., and each of their attitudes with respect to Vietnam and the Revolution. He listened attentively, interrupting every now and then to find out more about one point or another.

"Tell me about Mr. Huynh Thuc Khang. Why are people spreading the word that he is collaborating with the French?"

"It's nothing," I replied. "Upon his return from the penal colony of Poulo Condore, he began the newspaper *Tieng dan* [Voice of the people]. Not knowing exactly how to handle the situation, the *Tays* thought about buying him,[b] so promoted him to the head of the Assembly of People's Delegates in Central Vietnam. At that time, I went to Hue to interview him. I remarked that he still had the attitude of a scholar and a patriot, a friend of the people—not at all an opportunist. The *Tays* who wanted to take advantage of his prestige were fooling themselves. They'll be waiting a long time."

Uncle Ho nodded. He seemed satisfied with the information I had given him. Though it was our first meeting, he was warm and friendly, as well as direct. I called him "Cou" as he instructed us,[c] even though he was only fifty-five years old. As for me, I referred to myself simply as "I" or "me."[d] It was like that in all the years we were together, even though later on I used the term "Bac" (uncle), meaning the elder brother of one's father, responsible for the cult of the ancestors. Everyone called him that.

In July the Americans had sent parachutists down on Tan Trao, under the orders of Lieutenant-Colonel Thomas [the OSS "Deer Team"]. Their first contact with the Vietnamese revolutionary forces filled them with enthusiasm. For my part, I had several meetings with Thomas that were both direct and upbeat. I had the impression that at that moment the Americans didn't care if we were communists or not. The only thing they cared about was fighting the Japanese. This young colonel and his men were flabbergasted when our guerillas brought them a wad of dollars that had fallen out during the parachute jump. They were literally stunned. All the more so because they knew that this restitution wasn't the work of primitive savages who knew nothing about the price of things, but from Resistance forces schooled in a number of languages and thus perfectly aware of the value of what had fallen from the sky.

Ho Chi Minh Discovers Hanoi

At the end of the Congress, after all the farewells, Truong Chinh (Dang Xuan Khu), Vo Nguyen Giap, and I returned to the capital, via Thai Nguyen. Pham Van Dong was assigned to remain on the base to reinforce it. At that time, we weren't entirely sure of having a total victory, so we thought it indispensable to keep a fallback position in the southern resistance zones. Dong wanted me to stay back with him, but I refused. "I know Hanoi like the back of my hand," I told him. "I will be more useful there." I was dying to go back to the city, which I loved dearly and where I feared there would be more bitter struggles.

At the Bridge of the Rapids, I proposed that we all get out and go visit a teacher and sympathizer of the revolution who helped in the propagating of *quoc ngu*. I borrowed a bicycle from him to go directly to Hanoi, leaving Truong Chinh and Giap there. I was anxious to go off and scout around, to first get a good idea of the situation *de visu* and *de auditu*, and then go and welcome them. For who knows?

. . . How was I to know I would find Gia Lam awash in a sea of red flags? Once I crossed the Paul Doumer Bridge, I headed down Rice Market Street to Nghiem Tu Trinh's house. I barely had time to say, "What's going on? Are we ready to bring in Truong Chinh and Giap?" when he answered, eyes large with surprise, "We have already taken power! You'll find them all at the governor's palace!" I jumped on my bike again and took off to find them. I arrived at the palace and saw that the flag flying above the black stone at the top of the façade was ours, as were the guards in front of the door. . . .

I went to find Truong Chinh, who was delegating tasks. He put himself in charge of supervising the whole affair until the arrival of Ong Cou. Giap and I were in charge of contacting intellectuals and key figures, to start forming the government once Ho had arrived. We went first to the house of Dang Thai Mai, who had just returned to Hanoi with Tran Minh Viet, who had gone up to Thanh Hoa to get him. At the same time, Le Trong Nghia contacted Tran Duy Hung to invite him to help us. The man who would later become Hanoi's long-time mayor merely asked one question: "Who will be in charge of this whole thing?" Once he learned who it would be, he was satisfied. Dang Thai Mai, who arrived at that moment, told us that Hoang Minh Giam, Nguyen Xien, and their companions had sent a telegram to the last descendent of the Nguyen Dynasty to demand his abdication. I then drove Giap to see Nguyen Xien. They had first met when they were both teachers at the Thang Long school, but Giap had never been to his house.

After that we went to see Ho Huu Tuong. Then Ta Quang Buu, Nguyen Manh Tuong, Hoang Xuan Han. . . . Everywhere people were celebrating the victory, the bloodless taking of power. Everyone wanted to contribute something to the cause. We really had a marvelous group of intellectuals, and we were very proud.

Sao Do proposed to get me exempted from other work so that I could be placed close to Ho as his assistant. During my clandestine activities I had traveled all around the country; I knew the provinces well and had contacts with all sorts of people from all walks of life. Ho, who had come from abroad, needed someone like me at his side to keep him informed. Sao Do's proposal was accepted.

An old print-laborer went to pick up Uncle Ho, who stopped first in a village on the other side of the river. Truong Chinh went there immediately to give his report. On August 24, in my capacity as personal secretary, I drove Ho to the house of an important bourgeois from the capital, Trinh Van Bo, who held sympathies for the revolution. He and his wife had supported our militants long before our taking power. Although my wife was a relative of his wife, I had never wondered about the motives that brought them close to our organization. For us, it was completely natural. Since early August, their case was not unusual. Every Vietnamese felt patriotic, and wanted to do, or offer, something. It's hard to say who gave the most. Those that had nothing but their wedding bands gave them up during "Gold Week," during which the Bo's gave 117 taels [gold coins, worth a fortune]. I had chosen their house because I trusted them. No one ever said a word about it. They welcomed our militants into their home without any fuss, and it's not an exaggeration to say that their house literally became our caravansary.

The car that came to pick up Ho crossed the Paul Doumer Bridge, then went straight down Street of Potatoes to get to the Street of the Cantonese by the big market of Dong Xuan. They had just lit the street lamps, and children were playing noisily in the streets. We saw a group of people marching, yelling slogans and holding a banner. On another street corner, people stood in a circle around a militant who was laying out the ten-point program of the Vietminh. . . . The whole capital was bathed in a festive air.

Before getting into the car, Ho had asked me, "Where are you taking me?" "The comrades have chosen the best possible place," I answered with a tone of profound respect, knowing his natural caution.

When we were on the bridge, he leaned out the window and looked down at the streaming torrent below, with an attentive and surprised air. I wondered: could this be the first time he has seen the river? Is it possible that he has never set foot on Thang Long, that he has never seen the river that was so appreciated by King Ly . . . nor so many other sites inscribed in the pages of our history? The question ran through my head, though I didn't dare give it voice. Just as we were about to arrive at the other side of the bridge he said simply, "What a lot of water!" It wasn't until we had passed the market that he finally said, "I still have never set foot in Hanoi." I answered "yes," in a very deferent tone, but with a thought that stung my heart: to think that this man had known Paris, Berlin, Moscow, but has never seen Hanoi.

He entered the capital in his rustic indigo-blue suit, the kind worn by the peasants of the highlands when they go to their fields or the market. The next morning, he asked me to give him an even more detailed analysis of our intellectuals and key figures. I was surprised by the close attention he paid to the problem of religion, especially the Catholics. He took notes in his notebook, using Chinese characters, which he used like a form of short-hand. On the basis of these more than sketchy notes, he would later elaborate his plan for setting up the government of the Democratic Republic of Vietnam.

Each morning he would go to the presidential palace to work. After several days at 48 Street of the Cantonese, he moved into the house of the former President of the Tribunal, 8 rue Bonchamps, only returning to the Street of the Cantonese to eat. Every morning Mrs. Trinh Van Bo ordered two meals from a famous Chinese chef down on the Street of Sails, which were delivered at the appointed hour. We also had to think about making a wardrobe for Ho—and quickly—, since he only had two suits in his possession, one indigo and the other brown, and cloth sandals. I wanted to buy him a pair of leather shoes, at the Street of Sails, but he refused. He shook his head, and said, "I am not used to them, let me just keep my sandals."

When I spoke to him of a tie, he answered with a categorical "no":

"I have never knotted one of those around my neck."

"But what about when you were in France?" I objected.

"Not even there."

Things weren't any better for the rest of the suit. Faced with my unfathomable perplexity,[e] Ho came to my aid and explained: "Make me anything, but make sure it is very simple. No wool, no leather. Make it simple and easy, practical; and especially not expensive or elegant." I ended up basing the suit on what Stalin wore in photographs. Mrs. Bo chose the fabric. And that was what he wore, on September 2, when he proclaimed the nation's independence from atop the platform that had been built in forty-eight hours by the leader of the Association for the Propagation of *Quoc Ngu*, Nguyen Huu Dang.[f]

During these busy days working with Ho (whom we had started to call "Bac" to create a more relaxed atmosphere), I spent my time meeting with famous figures, most of them older, like Nguyen Van To, Pham Ba Truc, and Bui Bang Doan, former minister at the court of Hue.[g] I will never forget my meeting with Nguyen Van To, from the École française d'Extrême-Orient, to whom I had just offered a place in the government. After inviting me in for tea, he voiced his refusal: "I am not a revolutionary. I know a bit about history, but nothing about politics. You could find someone much better than me!"

Modest by nature, he expressed himself very frankly. But when he found out that Ho was actually Nguyen Ai Quoc, he said, "How can I refuse? I will give you what little I can." In 1947, when the French parachuted into Bac Can, where our government was, he was struck down like a common soldier. The presidency organized his funeral with the participation of Uncle Ho.

Notes

[a]The Restoration of Vietnam or Annamese Independence Party was created in 1926 in Paris by Nguyen The Truyen. A friend of Nguyen Ai Quoc, Truyen disagreed with the latter by his opposition to Communism. See his biography in Vietnamese by Dang Huu Thu (Melun, 1993). We hear from Nguyen The Truyen again in 1954. The organization referred to by Huynh, Phuc Viet, seems different. Born in Tonkin around the same time, it lasted until 1945.

[b]*Tays* means Westerners; it is a fairly pejorative term designating the French.

[c]*Cou* is a very respectful term meaning grandfather. The Vietnamese language, of a very informal tone, plays as much on the waves of respect and sympathy as on those of disdain. See Phan Thi Dac, *Situation de la personne au Viet-nam* (Paris: Editions du CNRS, 1966).

[d]He does not use terms for a lower relative but, rather, ones more deferent, like *chau*, son, grandson, nephew.

[e]These reflections must have stunned Vu Dinh Huynh, whose impeccable dress—three-piece suit and tie—was well known. This sartorial concern would have negative repercussions later, as it grated on some who played at being peasants.

[f]A member of the Indochinese Communist Party, Nguyen Huu Dang had convinced the famed Orientalist Nguyen Van To to patronize this movement. He later became the head of the dissident paper *Nhan Van* in late 1956.

[g]Bui Bang Doan, former minister of Rites for Bao Dai, would become president of the National Assembly. He is the father of dissident Colonel Bui Tin.

Uncle Ho Visits the Central Prison
Vu Dinh Huynh

One morning Ho said to me, "I want to go to Hoa Lo [the Central Prison].[a] Come with me." I phoned Le Gian, one of our militants whom the colonial authorities had deported to Madagascar, where he was liberated by the allies and sent back to Vietnam, after having been put through a training program. He parachuted into Ha Dong with a radio and supplies, then found his way back into contact with our party, and joined up with the resistance forces in the South. After our entry in Hanoi, Ho had named him Director of the Sûreté, since he had received training in the area of Information.

"What does he want to see at Hoa Lo?" Gian asked me.

"I can't tell you. He didn't tell me anything either."

Le Gian and the Chief of Police of Hanoi, Chu Dinh Xuong, were waiting for us at the entrance to welcome Ho, who asked to see the cells of the political prisoners. At each door, Chu Ding Xuong opened the grill so that Ho could have a look. He asked questions about the food and hygiene conditions, and seemed satisfied with the answers.

As we went along, I told Ho what I knew about certain prisoners. In the past, I had tried to dissuade one of them from collaborating with the Japanese. We later ran into each other several times but never brought up the subject again. But he never denounced me to the Japs. Then, when Ho asked me questions about the diminutive Dr. Chuong, barely knee-high to a grasshopper, I said that he couldn't care less about politics. If he had attached himself to the pro-Japanese it was only in the hopes of making a buck. Several days after this visit Ho gave the order to liberate both my friend and the doctor. As for a third prisoner whom I knew, Cung Dinh Van, Ho merely said, "When someone has committed a crime somewhere, he must be brought back to be judged by the people."

Ho had used the word "someone." This way of speaking was very Vietnamese, human, correct. I never heard him refer to someone as "that rotten guy" or "that bastard," even when referring to an enemy. It is too bad that these denigrating expressions have slipped into current usage, to the point where they are the norm in the press and other writings.

One of these former prisoners continued his wayward activities in the French-occupied zone, where he accepted a post as governor in Bao Dai's government. He only came to his senses when Ngo Dinh Diem came to power,[b] at which point he refused to participate in the government. And since I have brought up Diem, I shall mention the fact that his destiny would have been completely different had he not met Ho. For it was Ho himself, and no one else, who made the decision to liberate Ngo Dinh Diem, at the time imprisoned in Hanoi.

Ngo Dinh Diem Liberated

Hardly anyone in Ho's entourage approved of this decision. We spoke amongst ourselves, but no one dared express this disagreement openly, less out of fear than out of confidence in Ho. We had all known occasions in the past when decisions that first appeared incomprehensible turned out to be wise as time passed. Only Bui Lam dared to charge into Ho's office to proclaim loudly, "Why are you liberating such a dangerous man? If he were in your place, he would never let you go."

Having known Ho since the time they were both in Paris, Bui Lam was the only one of us who addressed him with the informal "you" or sometimes "comrade."[c] Lam was just like that, bald head and all. Without beating around the bush, he would throw out whatever he thought needed to be said, without worrying about the repercussions. This directness ruffled many feathers, with the exception of Ho, who greatly appreciated Lam.

"If the Imperialists didn't have this Ngo Dinh Diem at hand, they would simply create another," said Ho, without missing a beat. "If we want to achieve national unity, what good does it do to multiply the number of arrests?"

"But he is an exceptionally dangerous case," responded Lam. "He hates the Communists more than anything in the world."

"I hope you know what kind of man his father was," Ho said. "He has become a proverb in Central Vietnam: 'To deport the king, get rid of Kha; to open his tomb, get rid of Bai.' When the French sent King Duy Tan into exile, they ran into Diem's father, Ngo Dinh Kha, who refused to be implicated in this nasty affair. The memory of such a father prevents us from laying a hand on the son."

Once he was liberated, Diem took refuge in the bishopric. And everyone knows the rest. At the time, I was one of those who didn't approve of Diem's liberation. When he became president of the Republic of Vietnam and struck out at the Communists and massacred so many patriots, I didn't dare let myself think that we had been right and Ho wrong. His clemency and his humanity were part of something larger than contemporary notions of right and wrong.

Notes

[a]*Translator's note:* This prison later became known as the "Hanoi Hilton," where many American prisoners of war were incarcerated during the war. It has since been torn down, though parts have been preserved as a monument to the Vietnamese who were kept there by the French during the Indochinese war.

[b]Ngo Dinh Diem would in the future become president of the Republic of South Vietnam.

[c]*Translator's note:* The Vietnamese language has many forms of address to indicate one's social status with respect to others. In this case, Bui Lam would have addressed Ho as an equal.

fact stands out that has not been sufficiently explored: the man who was about to found the Democratic Republic of Vietnam planned to achieve a national revival through methods that were more political than military—even if it meant endangering the social revolution.

On 30 August 1945, Cu Huy Can and Tran Huy Lieu went to demand Bao Dai's abdication in Hue; but the latter (now living under the name Vinh Thuy) still remained an important adviser in the government, along with the bishop of Phat Diem, Monsignor Le Huu Tu. During the declaration of independence, on 2 September, seminarians and cassocked priests formed an imposing, highly visible, black mass in the crowd.

The persona now projected by the chief of state is much closer to Gandhi than to Lenin or Stalin (even if his clothes were modeled on the uniform of the latter), and Gandhi of course brings to mind nonviolence. One day as Ho was going to meet the head of a Chinese division, he noticed that one of the members of his entourage was wearing sandals, just as he was. He told him to go put on shoes, adding: "When we go to meet people, let me dress as I see fit. But you, my friends, you need proper clothes."[14] Apparently only heads of state have the right to go barefoot.

Change of scene: 21 October. In the presence of his chief adviser, Prince Vinh Thuy, and a number of high-ranking Chinese officers, Ho presided over a solemn ceremony in honor of Confucius. He performed it in the traditional style, in the most appropriate setting in the capital: the Temple of Literature, built in 1070 in a style taken from the Middle Kingdom. A preliminary Buddhist rite was eliminated, as well as the old ceremonial garb with its dragon-fly-wing hats; the prostrations on the ground were replaced by slight bows, and the names of the last two emperors were replaced by that of the Democratic Republic. In the aromatic smoke of the incense sticks, Ho played at being the old scholar turned religious dignitary of a laic cult, claiming lineage back to the old dynasties to completely erase the image of the famous Communist Nguyen Ai Quoc.[15]

The president based his platform on two issues: the nation and democracy. If the first had to be Asian and Confucian, the second was to follow the American model, as the new declaration of independence openly stated. Under the aegis of Prince Vinh Thuy and General Gallagher (the senior U.S. military representative in Hanoi), the American–Vietnamese Association was created on 17 October 1945; its periodical appeared on the shelves in December. On 2 November, Ho wrote to President Truman to try to get his support.

Meanwhile, the ever widening scope of the political spectrum was fiercely debated behind closed doors, resulting in the formation of a coalition government on 1 January 1946. This caused difficulties on all levels. General Giap notes: "Some of our comrades were not in agreement with this solution." The primary objection concerned the naming of Nguyen Hai Than (a well-known Communist Nationalist—an old acquaintance of Ho's but a rival as well) to an important post, and many vainly made their views known to Ho.[16] Negotiations with France, which had resumed in the month of August, resulted in the return of the French Army under the orders of General Leclerc on 6 March 1946. On the eve of this event, according to Bao Dai, Ho told him in the morning that he was putting him back in charge of the government, then announced that evening that he had changed his mind and would remain head of state himself.[17] It would be fascinating to know what was being discussed at the heart of this organization, which formally did not exist anymore.

Ho's political game during these three months was both subtle and complex, achieving a delicate balance between three volatile areas: international relations, internal politics, and the internal workings of the Communist Party. If the mysteries of the first two have been well investigated, the third is still shrouded in fog.

In November 1945, Ho Chi Minh made a decision that many considered political suicide: he dissolved the Communist Party. The decision was very clearly taken on his own initiative, for his actions were condemned by both Moscow and the French Communist Party.[18] Nevertheless, the entire apparatus was now completely maintained in secret. He thus achieved a first of this type: a clandestine organization at the heart of the regime it controls. These political machinations at times resemble a farce, which is understandable given that, to some degree, every politician must be both actor and director on history's stage. But in the drama of history, who writes the story, and who reads from the script? Was there unanimity from the start at the heart of this apparently suicidal Communist Party? The few remarks written by Giap lead one to think that this was not the case.

But why, then, do the contents of these debates still remain unknown? The question needs to be asked, for the response (or absence of one) would provide the key to understanding the system that Ho wanted. The existence of divergent views as well as the silence about their nature and their proponents appears from then on as a characteristic of this organization—as both its strength and its weakness, as we will see.

Notes

1. Conference at the Institut d'histoire du temps présent, Paris, 8 November 1982.

2. This statistic is put forth in the study by Van Tao and Japanese historian Furuta Motoo, whose research is based on *Tuoi Tre chu nhat*, November 1995: 34.

3. Françoise Martin, *Heures tragiques du Tonkin* (Nancy: Berger-Levrault, 1948), 153–54.

4. David Marr, *Vietnam 1945: The Quest for Power* (Berkeley: University of California Press, 1995), xxiii.

5. Vo Nguyen Giap, *Des journées inoubliables* (Hanoi: ELE, 1975), 68.

6. Doan Them, *Nhung ngay chua quen* [Unforgettable days], vols. 1–2 (Saigon: Dai Nam, 1967–69), 47–48.

7. See Mo Ba's story in *Phu nu dien dan*, no. 104 (September 1992): 16–20.

8. Vu Dinh Huynh, "L'oncle Ho de Tan Trao à Hanoi. Souvenirs," *Van* [Letters], no. 8 (March 1990): 6–25.

9. Tran Huy Lieu, "Voyage à Tan Trao pour le Congrès national," *Nghiem cuu lich su* [Historical studies], no. 17 (1960–68): 35–43. In a much later account, Hoang Dao Thuy does not mention Vu Dinh Huynh but gives the names of two other future "political ghosts": Ung Van Khiem, from the South, and Dao Duy Ky, a Hanoi writer known for his frankness. Cf. Hoang Dao Thuy, "Lin chien Khu" [Toward the combat zone], *Xua va nay* [Then and now] 2, no. 3 (May 1994): 16–17.

10. Hoang Van Hoan, *Giot nuoc, trong bien ca* (1986), 257.

11. Kim was the father of the famous Madame Nhu, sister-in-law of President Ngo Dinh Diem.

12. Interview by the author, Washington, D.C., October 1978.

13. See Ngo Van, *Le Viet-nam de 1920 à 1945. Révolution et contre-révolution sous la domination coloniale* (Paris: l'Insomniaque, 1995); and Nguyen Van Thiet, "J'ai vu mourir Ta Thu Thau" (July 1949), *Inprecor*, December 1995: 30–32.

14. Giap, *Des journées inoubliables*, 99.

15. Cuu Quoc, "22 October 1945," *Xua nay*, July 1995: 7.

16. Giap, *Des journées inoubliables*, 113.

17. Though he does not give a date, this fact is confirmed by Joe Nordman in *Aux vents de l'histoire* (Arles: Actes Sud, 1996), 269–70.

18. See my chapter in William S. Turley, ed., *Vietnamese Communism in Comparative Perspective* (Boulder: Westview Press, 1980), 141–42; and my *Autobiographie* (Paris: Jacques Bertoin, 1991), 89–91.

CHAPTER FOUR

1946: In the Footsteps of the Colonial Sûreté

Georges Boudarel

When Ho Chi Minh went to France on 27 May 1946, the Nationalist Party (Viet Nam Quoc Dan Dang or VNQDD) planned an operation that would prove to be its undoing and threaten the future of the entire nation. It shattered the fragile union that had just been established between North and South and prompted accusations and blame from all sides.

According to Nationalist Hoang Van Dao, it was "on that day that Giap began his attack on the VNQDD, after first meeting with Colonel Crépin, acting High Commissioner of France. The latter supposedly was convinced that the ultra-nationalists were deliberately sabotaging Franco-Vietnamese cooperation. He agreed to provide specialists in heavy artillery and committed himself to helping Giap whenever he needed it."[1] Word was then spread that the VNQDD was going to hold a demonstration on 14 July (the French national holiday) during the review of the troops and that members of the government would be assassinated. On 12 July, Vietminh agents burst into the headquarters of the VNQDD, 7 rue Bonifacy (On Nhu Hau), donned their uniforms, and occupied the offices. The government police then entered, rooted out important documents, and even dug up corpses. Hoang Van Dao disputes this account and admits that while the VNQDD sometimes had to kidnap people and kill them, it never would have executed seven people and then buried them right inside party headquarters. He added that "it would have been easier to tie a big stone around their necks and throw them into Lake Halais, just two steps away."[2]

95

The Vietminh displayed the bodies before the public, and on 13 July Giap gave the order to raze all VNQDD offices throughout the country. The bulk of VNQDD forces, which had set up an army base at Vinh Yen, withdrew up the Red River Valley to Yunnan Province, in southern China. An account of this retreat can be found in a work by Nguyen Tuong Bach, the brother of Nguyen Tuong Tam, who is today living in exile in southern China.[3] This account came to us thanks to a refugee from Canada, with the consent of Beijing.

According to one of the Vietminh documents seized by the French on 19 December 1946 and reproduced by Henri Azeau in *Ho Chi Minh, dernière chance* [Ho Chi Minh, last chance], "the VNQDD were planning a series of assassinations of French figures from July 10–17, 1946—exactly during the Fontainebleau conference. Their primary goal was to destroy the stupid directives" of the Ho Chi Minh government regarding diplomatic relations, which they saw as pro-French. This document was only discovered by the French six months after the fact, during a search of the house of the mayor of Hanoi (Vietminh). Giap, however, had known about the plan much earlier, and it was with full knowledge of their plan that he struck out at the VNQDD in July 1946.[4]

This VNQDD plan had announced the creation of a "special service" using assassinations and abductions, aimed at "French soldiers outside the citadel," preferably high-ranking officers. While waiting for access to these officers, members were encouraged to "assassinate any and all military personnel, and to kidnap French women and children within the city of Hanoi." This initiative weighed heavily on ensuing events, dealing a fatal blow to Ho Chi Minh's line, as is described in the account of Vu Dinh Huynh. There were some who resisted, for example, the group led by Nguyen Van Xuan, who joined the Vietminh on July 19. Unfortunately, they rallied only a small number to join them.[5]

Xuan's revelations about the VNQDD plans only strengthened Communist hard-liners, who advocated similar methods. On 29 September, Truong Chinh wrote a pamphlet on the August Revolution in which he especially stresses the "lack of firmness in our repression of counter-revolutionary elements":

Once in place, the revolutionary leadership did not crack down on traitors, nor did they take stringent measures against the French colonists and their lackeys. Only a few regions have shown strength, like Quang Ngai for example, where insurgents applied the politics of "sweeping away the reactionaries"—but in an excessive manner. Everywhere else we have shown ourselves to be conciliatory to the point of weakness, forgetting that "any power that dominates is a dictatorial power."[6]

In setting off these mutual killings between revolutionary forces, the Nationalists had unwittingly committed political suicide. They forced the Marxists to organize their own killings—though they were not all in favor of it—and Leninism then offered an excellent opportunity for instituting at the same time a program of propaganda and secret operations.

Despite the lack of archival materials, it is clear that the source of this violence lay in the colonial heritage itself. Every revolutionary group, regardless of political affiliation, was haunted by the memory of the Mat Tham, the colonial Sûreté. "Indochina is far away, which makes it hard to hear the screams," writes André Malraux in 1935, in his preface to Andrée Viollis's *Indochine S.O.S.*[7] Viollis, a French journalist, gives a gripping description of what she saw and learned while traveling through Indochina in the 1930s: men and women detained, haggard and frightened; eighteen-year-old boys "trembling and ready to talk"; arms traffickers willing to sell out revolutionaries; prisoners who had been selected for interrogation—in other words, who would be subjected to a method that would soon become known as "brainwashing." She denounces the brutality of the interrogators, who used such atrocious tortures as *lon me ga* ("turning the gizzard inside-out"). These atrocities were also criticized by Justin Godart in 1937.[8] Viollis's account does not focus much on Hanoi. For her, the capital was reduced to the central headquarters of the political Sûreté, whose members were eager to have her tour their operations. She writes:

> They are quite large and perfectly organized. They have 20,000 political dossiers and 50,000 files, all stored in a vast library which is staffed by a large number of zealous employees. Some people spend their time decoding telegrams from China and other countries, while others inspect letters which are opened, photocopied, and then expertly re-glued. Swarms of informers enter, buzz around, accomplish their pestilential tasks, then leave.
>
> In an annex that is used as a prison, they keep the "stool pigeons": those who "talk" spontaneously or those who must be made to talk, i.e., betray their comrades. They choose the leaders that they think might weaken under pressure. But it is no longer a question of leg-irons or torture. They are shut away in well-lit rooms with good ventilation and receive whatever food they want; they are spoiled and fawned upon.

After this visit, the leader accompanying Viollis launched into a diatribe against the regime, which strikes out "blindly, unjustly. . . . There were unforgivable errors that should have been severely punished, but which instead were covered up. That whole secret group is sticking together, based on solidarity in incompetence and negligence, even chaos." Not to mention, she continues, the politics of bureaucrats who "traffic, misappropriate funds, and commit the worst crimes" under the protection of France. Then, according to Viollis, "this well-informed government official ended with these words, so completely prescient even with respect to the dates: 'In fifteen years maybe, the French won't be in Indochina anymore, and it will be our own fault!' "[9]

The system they were using at the time aimed essentially at using Vietnamese against Vietnamese for policing and for drawing out confessions and especially denunciations that would provoke acts of vengeance. Louis Marty, head of the colonial Sûreté, was its principle organizer.[10] However, even if the Sûreté managed to find out important information through these methods, it showed considerable weakness in its ability to analyze it.

There were, of course, some French groups that advocated reforms in the way of civil freedoms—groups from the very heart of the colonial milieu, like the Masons, the Socialists, or the League for Human Rights. And it was an astute French militarist, General Pennequin, who saw that the only possible way to save the situation was to create a complete Annamite army, a "yellow army." This implied a move toward decolonization, though the word was still unknown and never uttered.

Despite the presence of these groups, however, the only political options that were considered were those resting on brute force. This was clear during the events of 1930, which saw the violent suppression of the Yen Bay uprising and the "Soviets" of Nghe Tinh—neither of which the Deuxième Bureau (the "second bureau," more commonly known as the Sûreté) had foreseen. The Legionnaires who massacred innocent people were acquitted, and their brothers-in-arms were decorated, congratulated, and financially rewarded. Justice was harsh, however, on the insurgents who committed the crime of acting on the frustrations of the Vietnamese people.[11]

In 1937, during the period of détente opened by the Popular Front,[12] a government employee wrote in the Hanoi paper *La Tribune républicaine*:

We have lost time and energy trying to hide reality from the natives, that is, the fact that we came to power through force and that it is by force that we remain. . . . If I could speak my mind, I would tell these anti-French rebels: "Read whatever you want, go and see whomever you want, even indoctrinate whomever you want. If the result is that you feel you can then venture out into the streets by the hundreds or thousands, you must know that we will be posted in various places, and we will be ready for you. We will say to you, 'Disperse, at the count of three.' And we will count: one, two, three. If at three you are still there, some of you will soon find yourselves six feet under, and the rest of you will hurry back to your homes and won't venture out again in a hurry."[13]

Words like this create a disturbing echo with certain recent events, such as the government crackdown on the demonstrators in Tiananmen Square. This theme is again taken up in 1945, in the words of Lucien Bodard: "Alessandri is a friend of Pignon, and thinks like he does: that the only way to flush out Vietnamese agents, to destroy them, is to throw them into the hands of men like them, of the same race."[14] The same mode of thinking emerges from the South in 1954: "If you want to beat the Communists, you have to behave exactly like they do; such was the extremely wayward program of the Minister of Information at the time of Tran Chanh Thanh and Tran Thuc Linh," writes Cao The Dung: "The cult of president Ngo based on the model of Uncle Ho only trivialized and weakened his image."[15]

This violence, far from being limited to the Communists, was just as commonplace with the Nationalists, who were firm admirers of Chiang Kaishek and the Japanese Kempeitai. The root of this evil clearly resides in the very nature of colonialism, no matter what medals it chose to award itself. When the colonial administration stopped relying on brute force, it turned to fear, thanks to two time-tested techniques: the use of informers and the maintenance of files on the population. Barred from open political or legal action, all groups that supported independence were thus forced into creating secret organizations. Moreover, most of them turned to violence by getting support from foreign powers: Japan, China, or the USSR. Every party established its own espionage service and assassination committee (ban am sat). Because historical records have revealed next to nothing about this secret drama, we must once again seek proof through Vietnam's novelists.

The "Roman Vérité" of Nhat Linh

Literary fiction often sheds light on areas that have been kept in darkness by the silence of official rhetoric. Constantin Melnik, former head of the Secret Services of Michel Debré during the French war in Algeria, created a genre called the "true-false" novel.[16] Obviously he had no idea that a key figure in modern Vietnamese literature had already dared to break that ground, in the middle of the Diem period in Saigon (1961), while secrecy raged all around

him.[17] Like Melnik, Nhat Linh was an authority on the subject. He was first
head of the VNQDD in exile and then (under his real name, Nguyen Tuong
Tam) minister of Foreign Affairs under Ho Chi Minh in 1946. Driven to
China by Giap's offensive against ultranationalists, he later returned to Vietnam, as a semiclandestine official this time, to the South of Ngo Dinh Diem.

In 1961, two years before he was driven to the brink of suicide, Linh wrote
a novel called *Dong song Thanh Thuy* [The course of the Thanh Thuy River].
The novel is both a political sketch and a love story, in which the hero,
Ngoc, flees to Yunnan after the death of the girl he loved. In exile, he leads
the life of a militant, and his heart is torn between two young Vietnamese
women: the sister of a comrade and Thanh, the owner of a small boutique.
The latter had also fled to Yunnan with a friend, intending never to return to
Vietnam, where she too had suffered a painful love affair. Their relationship
progresses in the tense atmosphere of a passion that must be repressed, where
a direct openness alternates with vague metaphors about politics. Very soon
both have to leave on top secret missions, assigned to them by the two opposing parties they both belong to. Ngoc, a member of the VNQDD, is ordered
to assassinate Thanh, a member of the Vietminh; and she, in turn, is ordered
to kill him. United by love, they realize that they are now caught up in the
wheels of the political machine.

The term *guong may*, or this political machinery, reappears as a leitmotif
to describe the revolutionary apparatus. Beneath everything lurks the
unyielding force of violence and war, which pushes everything to extremes.
This violence without limits, unrealizable on the field of a military operation,
is the psychological matrix of totalitarianism.

In Linh's novel, the weapon of choice is the most discreet: a deadly poison
served to the condemned in an equally strong cup of coffee. Ngoc thus "liqui-
dates" two members of the Vietminh up in the mountains and then throws
their bodies to the bottom of a gorge cut by a raging river. He reveals these
operational secrets to Thanh. He refuses to let her come with him, afraid for
her security, and tells her that he has to accompany two Vietminh spies who
had infiltrated the Nationalists, with orders to kill them on the way: "They
could be suspicious, and might try to kill me first. That's the risk. You
decide."[18]

Ngoc manages to get Thanh integrated into the network of his party and
starts to call her "comrade," but she still is not very convinced in her own
mind. She ends up going on a mission with him all the way to the border
province of Ha Giang, where he has to check out the state of the Nationalist
movement, which is very strong in that area. Because of her connection with

the Vietminh, she is an excellent guide for him. Passing near the gorge into which Ngoc had thrown the two Vietminh one year before, Thanh insists on going to the site and sees their bones, which lay bleached at the bottom of the precipice. She tells Ngoc that she is also a member of the Vietminh. He responds that he already knew. To test him, she reveals all the information she knows about the Nationalists and dares him to kill her. He takes out his revolver but merely places it on her heart. After a long silence, seeing that she does not make a move to grab the gun, he says simply: "I'll wait for you. . . ."

Both of them enter Ha Giang Province, and Thanh contacts the members of her network. Seeing that all the Nationalist camps have been destroyed and that she herself has been unmasked, she insists that Ngoc return to Chinese soil. The local Vietminh leader soon hears of their approach on the other side of the river and, accompanied by two guards, opens fire on them in the night. They are both hit, and the story ends with this dialogue:

> "If we manage to survive, what will we do?" asks Thanh.
>
> "We'll be sucked back into the political machinery *(guong may).*"
>
> "And if there is no more machinery, I will build one where we could both work together."[19]

Linh leaves us with an ambiguous ending, especially for 1961, but is clear about one thing: the key role of assassination committees, from 1945 on, in every revolutionary party. His story reveals the climate of intense violence that, despite the efforts of Ho Chi Minh, had become the living reality of revolutionary politics in Indochina.

From Siege to Explosion

From June to August 1946, Ho Chi Minh and Jean Sainteny tried to reach an agreement at the Fontainebleau Conference. By September, however, they were at an impasse. Not ready for war, Ho Chi Minh signed the modus vivendi of 6 September in a desperate act to postpone the inevitable; but a number of events soon led to open hostilities. Philippe Devilliers unearthed provocative acts on the part of the French, which only added fuel to the fire.[20] And even today we still do not know exactly what the reactions were on the part of the various factions of the Vietminh.

Fearing a surprise attack by the French Expeditionary Forces (FEF), the Democratic Republic took precautions. The government evacuated public buildings and withdrew secretly to the countryside. Trenches were dug in the streets, and communications were established between houses through holes in the walls. These defensive maneuvers were meant to allow the Vietnamese to retaliate through street fighting.

On 18 December in Hanoi, French troops occupied the offices of the finance minister. The next day, General Morlière, commander of the garrison, demanded that the *tu ve*, the self-defense forces of the Ho Chi Minh government, lay down their arms. That very evening, at 8 p.m., the Vietnamese retaliated, and the next day Ho Chi Minh launched an appeal for resistance throughout the nation: "In the interests of peace, we have made concessions. But the more we do, the more the colonialists trample on our rights. . . . Join the struggle any way you can, with rifles or knives if you have to. Or even with pickaxes or clubs."[21]

The wide avenues of the city and the mobility of the FEF made it quite obvious that the residential areas would be destroyed rapidly. Indeed, on 22 December the *tu ve* found themselves encircled in the old section of the city, where a part of the population was still living. The narrow streets facilitated a stubborn resistance by Vuong Thua Vu's capital regiment, which had been created to allow the government to set up its operations in the countryside. Vu had expected 500 volunteers, but there were at least 1,200, including 200 women and 100 children.

On 14 February, after fierce combat, French forces occupied the Grand Market at the north end of the old city. The noose was tightening dangerously, and evacuation was finally decided on as the only option. Two ideas were rejected: a departure in small combat groups and a march to the outskirts through sewers. The column would instead slip quietly under the metal spans of the Paul Doumer Bridge and then cross the river a bit farther upstream, between two French checkpoints. The key to success lay in absolute secrecy.

At 6 p.m. on 17 February, the order to evacuate was finally given to the combatants, who had been told that morning to be ready for action. Before leaving, they managed to scrawl on the ruined walls with bricks or charred pieces of wood: "We'll be back!" Drizzle covered the city in a veil of mist. Visibility was zero. At 9 p.m., the phantom column left formation without being noticed. In public buildings, incense sticks sat atop stacks of mattresses that had been doused with gasoline and slowly burned. In a few hours they would start fires all over the city. At 4 a.m., the combatants began loading into some twenty boats, and they continued until 9:00. "We will continue the fight," proclaimed General Giap in his order of the day. "We will fight

for ten years, or more if necessary." Hanoi was left in ruins, as were all metro-
politan areas of the center and the North, where residents had applied the
"scorched earth policy" and sabotaged buildings with picks and axes when
they had no explosives.

Both the old city and the colonial city exploded, sending thousands of
small groups out into the rice fields, jungles, and forests. As a few nascent
clandestine groups remained within the city limits, two new sites took over
from the capital: Gray Hanoi, in the jungles of the northern mountains on
the Chinese border, where Ho Chi Minh and his central services had relocated; and Sunny Hanoi, in Thanh Hoa Province, now the refuge of intellectuals who worked in the universities that had already been moved to the
countryside. Even today the political discussions continue in these cities of
bamboo, sometimes revealing profound differences of opinion, but all united
under the banner of national unification. If the intensity of the conflict
silenced them, the return of peace in reunification at the time of the global
crisis in the Socialist bloc rekindled the debates.

Although it was not openly known until 1993, one of Ho's primary concerns at this time was to try to make contact with the United States. In early
1947, he sent his personal adviser, Dr. Pham Ngoc Thach, on a diplomatic
mission to Bangkok. Thach met with the U.S. ambassador to Thailand,
Edwin F. Stanton, and stressed the nationalistic aims of the government and
how Communist ministers "favored the development of a capitalist economy
and called upon foreign funding to reconstruct the country."[22] On 8 May,
Minister of Foreign Affairs Hoang Minh Giam sent a similar message to President Truman. Friendly overtures were even made to the Nationalist government of China in Nanjing. But Ho's effort at diplomacy was thwarted by U.S.
diplomats who seemed to dismiss the possibility that Ho Chi Minh could be
another Tito, who had been able to create a rather nonthreatening brand of
socialism in Yugoslavia.

At the same time, a small pamphlet was published in the northern jungles
by a certain "XYZ," whom every militant immediately recognized as Ho himself.[23] The pamphlet borrows heavily from Mao, even as far as the title, *Sua
doi loi lam viec* [To correct the style of work], although its message was quite
the opposite of Mao's. While Ho attacks individualism and subjectivism like
his Chinese counterpart, he refrains from attacking intellectuals, whom Mao
criticized for having only "book learning." Ho also takes up Stalin's formula,
"Cadres decide everything," and exalts revolutionary virtue in affected and
rather old-fashioned terms. Mao's scathing attack had announced a radical
change in policy and became the spark for the purge known as the Campaign

Uncle Ho planning strategy in the countryside, 1950.

of Rectification (*cheng feng*) begun in Yennan on 1 February 1942. Ho's text, on the other hand, exalts gradual change within continuity. He praises Marx, painting him in solid peasant colors cut from the most rustic of Confucian cloth. The five great revolutionary virtues are renamed "humanity" (*nhan*), "sense of duty" (*nghia*), "intelligence" (*tri*), "courage" (*dung*), and "honesty" (*liem*); their opposites are "misappropriation of public funds" (*tham o*) and "waste" (*lang phi*).

Meanwhile, deep within the City of Bamboo in the malaria-infested jungles, Truong Chinh had something else in mind when he put out his own pamphlet. Chinh took his title from Mao, *The Resistance Will Win*, and, with only a minor difference—the acknowledgment of the possibility of negotiation with the opposition during the hostilities—takes up the exact thesis of the Great Helmsman on the people's war and its successive phases.[24]

In early 1950, Ho went to Beijing and then to Moscow to seek diplomatic recognition of the DRV. He was successful on both counts, but Stalin remained suspicious of Ho's ideological unorthodoxy and apparently delighted in humiliating him. On one occasion he agreed to autograph a magazine on the USSR that was lying on the table. But the next night he had the KGB take it away, so that Ho could not make his own use of it upon his return.[25]

The victory of the Chinese Communists in 1949 not only led to a significant increase in Chinese assistance to the Vietminh movement, it opened up brilliant strategic perspectives as well. In fall 1950, Vietminh units trained in South China and armed with captured U.S. and Japanese weapons attacked French posts along the border. The French withdrew to the delta, and the entire frontier region came under Vietminh control in a matter of days. This opened up new avenues for Sino-Vietnamese assistance. This new relationship with China had an ideological component as well. In early 1951, the once-dissolved Indochinese Communist Party was resuscitated and renamed the Vietnamese Worker's Party, under the guidance of Chinese mentors. It then threw itself into two large-scale campaigns for the class struggle: agrarian reform, a plan that was as impressive as it was tragic, and internal purges of the Marxist organization, which supposedly was infiltrated by reactionaries. Freedom of expression in arts and literature was then assailed by Marxist jargon, which imposed its static black-and-white vision of the world on the entire nation. Militants fell under the bullets of their comrades, raising their fists and crying, "Long Live the Revolution!" persuaded that they were face to face with the henchmen of colonial repression.

Violence and Rupture

By 1951, the leaden atmosphere induced by Maoist sectarianism that hung over the Vietnamese underground caused many intellectuals and artists to return to Hanoi. They were capable of withstanding food shortages and the absence of comforts but not the weight of a permanent state of censorship that was heavily organized and severely imposed. In that same year, the famous composer Pham Duy abandoned the Vietminh, the very day after he was asked to adhere to the Communist Party and go on stage in Moscow to toe the party line. A few days spent in prison ("offered" by the French authorities in Cochin China in autumn 1945) helped him to understand the importance and the tenacity of militants who had served time, but the total conformity and "correct thinking" demanded by his party only destroyed what was left of his illusions.[26]

In February 1951, Nationalist leaders such as Nguyen Tuong Tam and Nguyen Huu Tri returned to Vietnam from Kunming and Hong Kong—leaders who were hostile to both the Vietminh and Bao Dai. To those who "came back" (dinh te), Hanoi looked lost and without prospects. Put off by the brutality of the FEF, contemptuous of an ex-emperor safely tucked away on the French Riviera, and disappointed by the intransigent dogmatism of the hard-line resistance, these intellectuals were cast to the margins of history.

The Other Road

Such a Manichean vision of the conflict cannot adequately describe the situation at the heart of the Vietminh Front, which was much more diverse in composition than is usually perceived. Even if the machinations of the Deuxième Bureau often led to widespread arrests, not everyone in charge of the Sûreté's Vietminh counterpart, the Cong An, was in favor of blind repression. We learn today that a highly placed cadre like former printer Tran Dang Ninh, one of Ho Chi Minh's most astute military commanders, managed to thwart one of these "brainwashing" sessions, which had sent many militants of the resistance to prison.[27]

Today we can also read about the extraordinary fate of Hanoi native Nguyen Son (1908–56), whose story was totally eclipsed for decades by the official censors. At the end of 1995 a historical colloquium was even dedicated to Son with the participation of General Giap.[28] At age seventeen, Son left the École Normale in Paris to join Nguyen Ai Quoc in Canton, where he entered the Chinese military academy on Whampoa Island. Excluded from the Chinese Communist Party in 1930 because of his opposition to growing leftism, he was later readmitted. He then became a journalist, poet, playwright, and actor in the "red zones" (zones occupied by the Vietminh) and was the only foreigner to go on the Chinese Long March from start to finish before returning to Vietnam to fight in 1945. He was put in charge of the Southern Front, then Zone IV, where his command post at Thanh Hoa became a center of attraction. This colorful militant left vivid memories in intellectual, literary, and artistic circles, including those who went back to the French Zone. Pham Quynh's son-in-law, Nguyen Tien Lang (1909–76), was Son's personal secretary and speaks highly of him (under the pseudonym of "General Ton") in a book published in France in 1953.[29]

The Hanoi colloquium of 1995, however, leaves the reader hungry for more. One wonders, for example, what difference of opinion—political or operational—caused Son to leave Vietnam for China in 1951 and then return again to his home, where he died in 1956. Much still remains to be said about this interesting figure who represented a great liberalism in the world of arts and culture. His ideas appear in stark contrast to the tortured ideological debates of party hacks that raged in the mountains of Viet Bac (the site of Vietminh headquarters after 1946).

Other party members, like General Giap himself and a number of senior Army officers, also felt put off by the new Maoist line. A former cadre in the Hanoi regime, now living in exile in France, writes with respect to this:

> I won't spend much time on the Agrarian Reform Campaign or the purges of the Party, about which much has been said. I will mention something less well known, that is, the use in 1952 of brainwashing sessions and accusations in a number of civil and military groups. In 1953–54, at the preparatory school in Thanh Hoa, political courses in connection with the Agrarian Reform Campaign forced the students from exploitative families (or merely thought to be) to write self-criticisms and accusations. Some were even subjected to *danh dap* (physical correction). In 1952, in the artillery regiment of Tot Thang (Certain Victory), there were strange results: in certain companies, the number of those who confessed to having been enemy agents was as high as fifty percent. Luckily, the higher echelon judged this result absurd, and began a "mini-operation" of rectification of errors. They burned all of the self-criticisms and then restored calm in people's minds, which permitted the men to distinguish themselves at Dien Bien Phu.[30]

"A large number of those who lived in the French zone," he continues, "weren't supporters of the colonists, but rather opposed to the Communists. Others joined the Resistance but came back to the city under pressure of errors committed somewhere along the way, as was the case with my parents." It was the same, he believes, for a large number of those who went to the South in 1954.[31]

It is against this paradoxical background, where patriotism worked in favor of the Vietminh, that the latter won its victories. The victories were also due in part to the astuteness of General Giap, who, with Ho's support, refused to follow the misguided advice of his Chinese military advisers. Already during the border campaign in autumn 1950, against the advice of experts from the North, he believed that a conventional attack on the city of Cao Bang would lead to a French victory, while the retreat of the garrison would allow its destruction at the time of its withdrawal, which was the case. In 1954, he deemed that a frontal attack to try to capture Dien Bien Phu in several days would end in a fiasco, and he did all he could to institute a long siege, which would end by gradually taking over their bases one by one.[32]

Throughout this period, Ho insisted on openness on the political front, which is clearly illustrated by Dang Huu Thu in his biography of Nguyen The Truyen. Ho and Truyen were friends in Paris in the 1920s, but they drifted apart after Ho left for Moscow in 1924 and Truyen rejoined the Nationalist camp.[33] At the 1953 municipal elections in Hanoi, Truyen won the majority of the votes (11,763) ahead of Dr. Tran Trung Dung (8,643).

In early August 1954, Ho sent a letter to Nguyen The Truyen recalling their lifelong friendship and offering him the post of vice president of the republic. In reply, Truyen thanked him for the offer but noted that "each of us [has] chosen to serve the country in his own way."[34] One can only wonder whether his presence in the government would have helped reduce the number of errors committed, especially if France had acted on new information transmitted via the French Information Services. On 13 November 1954,

The One Pillar Pagoda: built in 1049, destroyed by the French, and subsequently rebuilt.

one month after the arrival of the Vietminh army in Hanoi, a top secret note was addressed to President Mendès-France: "One trustworthy piece of information will establish that Ho Chi Minh always follows the lead of Moscow but never that of Beijing. My informant believes that the leaders of the Democratic Republic are indeed Communists, but that the regime could very well stabilize, especially after reunification with the South, with half of its institutions from the free world and half from the communist world."[35]

In fact, official DRV sources disclose that party leaders had given consideration to a policy declaring that the government would be bourgeois democratic in form and people's democratic in substance. This platform, which was never mentioned in the party's newspaper, *Nhan dan* [The people], testifies to the diverging views that continually clashed in heated discussions.

Of course, there is a limit to second-guessing what could have altered the course of history. If Ho wanted to play the card of peaceful coexistence in order to obtain the reunification of the country two years later in general elections, it was not the same in the opposing camp. Shortly before the departure of Franco-Vietnamese forces from the capital, a senseless act of French sabotage blew up the monument most dear to Vietnamese, the One Pillar Pagoda, made famous by stamps from the colonial era.

Notes

1. Hoang Van Dao, *Viet Nam Quoc Dan Dang, 1927–1954* (Saigon, 1965), 278–79.

2. Dao, *Viet Nam Quoc Dan Dang*, 280.

3. Nguyen Tuong Bach, *Viet Nam, nhung ngay lich su* [Vietnam, historic days] (Montreal: Groupe vietnamien de recherche sur l'histoire et la géographie, 1981), 160.

4. Henri Azeau, *Ho Chi Minh, dernière chance* (Paris: Flammarion, 1968), 88–91, 281–85.

5. Philippe Devillers, *Histoire du Vietnam de 1940 à 1952* (Paris: Le Seuil, 1952), 278–80.

6. Truong Chinh, *La Révolution d'août* (Hanoi, 1958), 9, 39. Ho's minister of finance, Le Van Hien, was to have been executed in Quang Ngai, which he reveals in his memoirs.

7. André Malraux, "Preface," in Andrée Viollis, *Indochine S.O.S.* (Paris: Gallimard "NRF," 1935), ix, 21. "What is the only country where the mandarinate still exists? Not China, not Japan, but Annam. . . . Ah! What a paradise the colonies would be if the West had to build hospitals for all those it has killed, and gardens for all those it has deported!" Malraux writes in his article "Orient and Occident," *Le Crapouillot, Expéditions coloniales*, January 1936: 63.

8. Justin Godart, *Rapport de mission en Indochine, 1er janvier–14 mars 1937* (Paris: L'Harmattan, 1994), 81–82.

9. Viollis, *Indochine S.O.S.*, 127–28.

10. Following the reports of Louis Marty, all police services were unified on 7 February 1917. Cf. Patrice Morlat, *Les Affaires politiques de l'Indochine (1895–1923)* (Paris: L'Harmattan, 1995), 245.

11. Philippe Franchini, *Continental Saigon* (Paris: Métailié, 1976), 87 (reissued in 1995). For the clear-mindedness of certain French officers during this time, see "Tran Van Ba, Ba Dinh, Dien Bien Phu la stratégie du secret," 101–21, and "L'uniforme sous les tropiques," 108–17, both in *Tonkin 1873–1954* (Paris: Editions Autrement, 1994).

12. *Translator's note:* In 1935, Stalin called for all Communist nations to abandon their fight on colonialism and capitalism to unite against fascism—and to create "popular fronts" to stand up to the Germans and Japanese. This led to a more tolerant attitude on the part of the colonial government toward the Communist Party in Indochina—which hitherto had been illegal but was now tolerated.

13. Franchini, *Continental Saigon*, 93.

14. Lucien Bodard, *L'Humiliation* (Paris: Gallimard, 1973), 307.

15. Cao The Dung, *Viet Nam 30 nam mau lua* [Thirty years of blood and fire] (Alpha, 1991), 489.

16. Constantin Melnik, *L'Agence et le Comité* (Paris: Lattès, 1991).

17. Nhat Linh, *Dong song Thanh Thuy* [The course of the Thanh Thuy River], vol. 1: A walk for three; vol. 2: A cell for two; vol. 3: The lost country (Hanoi: Doi nay, 1961).

18. Linh, *Dong song Thanh Thuy*, vol. 1, 68.

19. Linh, *Dong song Thanh Thuy*, vol. 3, 210.

20. Philippe Devilliers, *Paris, Saigon, Hanoi. Les archives de la guerre, 1944–1947* (Paris: Gallimard, "Archives," 1989).

21. Ho Chi Minh, "Appel à la résistance nationale," in *Ecrits, 1920–1969*, 2nd ed. (1976), 66–67.

22. Jayne S. Werner and Luu Doan Huynh, eds., *The Vietnam War: Vietnamese and American Perspectives* (New York: M. E. Sharp, 1993), 6.

23. XYZ, *Sua doi loi lam viec* [To correct the style of work], 3rd ed. (1949), 136.

24. Truong Chinh, *The Resistance Will Win* (Hanoi, 1960).

25. This detail was revealed in 1991 in Khrushchev's memoirs and was confirmed by Giap in 1995. See Nikita Khrushchev, *Mémoires inédites* (Paris: Belfond, 1991), 194–95; Vo Nguyen Giap, *Chien dau trong vong vay* [Battle within the encirclement] (Hanoi: Editions Quan doi nhan dan [the People's Army]/Thanh Nien [Youth], 1995).

26. Pham Duy, *Hoi ky cach mang khang chien* [Memoirs, the revolution, the resistance] (1989), 319–29.

27. *Xua va nay* [Then and now] (Hanoi monthly), October 1995: 17–18.

28. *Tuong Nguyen Son* [General Nguyen Son] (Hanoi, 1995).

29. Nguyen Tien Lang, *Les Vietnamiens. I, Les Chemins de la révolte* (Paris: Amiot-Dumont, 1953), 103–6, 135–36.

30. Nguyen Ba Hao, "Dang cong san Viet Nam trong khang chien chong Phap va van de giai phong dan toc" [The Vietnamese Communist Party in the resistance against

France and the problem of national liberation], *Thong Luan* (monthly), no. 63 (September 1993): 20–21.

31. Hao, "Dang cong san Viet Nam trong khang chien chong Phap va van de giai phong dan toc," 21.

32. Georges Boudarel and F. Caviglioli, "Comment Giap a failli perdre la bataille de Dien Bien Phu," *Le Nouvel Observateur*, 8 April 1983: 83–98.

33. Dang Huu Thu, *Than the va su nghiep nha cach mang Nguyen The Truyen* [The life and revolutionary work of Nguyen The Truyen] (Melun, 1993), 350–52.

34. Roger Faligot and Pascal Kropp, *La Piscine. Les Services secrets français, 1944–1984* (Paris: Le Seuil, 1985), 135.

35. Faligot and Kropp, *La Piscine*, 135.

PART THREE

TOWARD LIBERATION

CHAPTER FIVE

1954: A Troubled Independence

Georges Boudarel

In October 1954, the People's Army entered the Radio Hanoi Building, but the soldiers stopped at the sight of the carpeting on the stairs. Most of them were of peasant origin and had grown up without even a blanket on winter nights, so they saw the old faded rugs as the height of luxury. They took off their sandals before daring to walk on them.

What a strange group of soldiers they were, these men who had won the war without ever having learned to march in step. They eventually did learn to march, for the procession past the presidential podium during the belated celebration, on 1 January 1955, of the taking of the capital. Even the people of Hanoi were brought out to train for the celebration and were made to practice marching behind the troops.

In May–July 1954 the Geneva Conference split the nation of Vietnam into two parts. The population was then given 300 days to move to one zone or the other, depending on what system of government they preferred to live under—Communist or democratic. A settlement was reached in two months, with the proviso that elections be held within two years. The French accepted quickly, having tired of war and wanting just to get out. The Americans were not completely happy with the outcome, however, believing that it gave away too much to the Communists. The Chinese accepted the settlement to avoid being sucked into a war with the United States. The Geneva Conference itself was held to reach a solution to the Korean War, with the last part of it devoted to the Vietnamese question.

Gradually Hanoi was emptied of the French presence, and it seemed to Western journalists to be a dead city. All machines, necessary supplies, files, and technical installations had been taken to the South, in defiance of the accords. When the last French troops left several months later, North Vietnam was literally stripped of everything, as described in a cable sent from the United Press Agency in Haiphong: "The French Air Force evacuated the base at Cat Bi yesterday, under the command of Captain Charper. The pilots took everything they could get their hands on, even toothpicks, 'to not leave a single thing for the Vietminh,' said Charper."

The French Expeditionary Forces and Ngo Dinh Diem's men may have taken away all they could, but their departure left the Vietnamese the most precious commodity of all: their independence. For the first time in eighty years, Hanoi was again concentrated in its "thirty-six neighborhoods." People returned to the old streets, whose names had been given centuries before according to the guilds that operated in them, like the streets of sugar, hemp, and medicine. They went back to their shantytowns, in whose winding and dead-end streets they could finally breathe again. Hanoi was no longer split into pieces and was ready to start a new life.

In the month following liberation, a new exhibition hall for painting was opened. Then a large amphitheater with room for 10,000 was set up on the old fairgrounds. A Festival of Dramatic Arts was organized, and performances were held every evening to a sold-out house. At the same time, new art forms had been brought back by the victors of Dien Bien Phu, like the unusual *muong* dance in which girls and boys hop between bamboo poles that are clapped together. From the South came melodies of the *édé* and the *banhar*,[1] with the melancholic air of the high plains of the Pleiku and Ban Me Thuot plateaus. Vietnam was finding itself again in all its diversity, while a few narrow-minded and hypocritical ideologues objected to topless women dancing with men in loincloths.

Along with this grand celebration of culture came a new people's university, where students from the former French zone took courses in political economics and Marxist ideology. All departments soon reopened, with all courses taught in Vietnamese. Students returned from Moscow, Beijing, and elsewhere and prepared to create new professorial chairs. In all senses, Hanoi was becoming Vietnamese again. And, contrary to pessimistic predictions, the greatest progress was in the domain of education; illiteracy was rapidly eradicated in the capital and its environs.

Only one Frenchman remained in this city where "long noses" had practically disappeared, his bust standing alone in the public square in front of the institute bearing his name: Louis Pasteur. All other plaques and monuments celebrating conquerors and colonists had been torn down. Pasteur's likeness was joined by just two others: the Swiss doctor Yersin, who had identified the germ that causes the bubonic plague and had a hospital named for him; and the former Governor-General Albert Sarraut, who had asked Pham Van Dong in Geneva not to change the name of the elite French school that bore his name.

The presence of Pasteur is symbolic, for Hanoi intended to turn the page on colonization but not on its friendship with France. On 1 October, a decree stated that collaborators with the opposition would not be punished and would be guaranteed all democratic freedoms. Peace talks were opened to persuade French companies to continue their activities and to normalize the status of the École française d'Extrême-Orient, the Cancer and Pasteur Institutes, and the Lycée Sarraut. Jean Sainteny, who had returned to Hanoi as senior French representative to the DRV (1945–46 and 1954–55), was an ardent supporter of such a collaboration and was backed up in France by the director of the Renault Corporation, a man named Lefaucheux. In December 1954, a draft agreement was signed to the effect that French businesses "would suffer no discriminatory measures." But the French high commissioner in Saigon, General Ély, was hardly in favor of such an agreement, and the business world remained reticent.

Despite a variety of other minor agreements, notably regarding the coal mines of Hongay, the indifference of the French government and French companies dragged Franco-Vietnamese economic relations to a standstill. "France must choose between Washington and Hanoi," declared Pham Van Dong in Le Monde on 1 January 1955. To his dismay, France chose Washington. In July 1955, Ho Chi Minh left to seek much needed financial and technical assistance in Moscow and other socialist countries. Paris thus missed its chance to play a pioneering role in a politics of coexistence, which would have been novel in the world of economics. Only later would it realize the importance of this missed opportunity.

There had been many opportunities, however, to make this kind of cooperation possible. Under the orders of Truong Chinh, the radio program Voice of Vietnam "censored part of Ho's speech, given at the meeting organized at the former racetrack, upon his return from Moscow." Chinh knew that Ho's softer approach to relations with France would not be pleasing to some of the more militant members of the party. Moreover, since the party's return to Hanoi, Vu Dinh Huynh was no longer Ho's personal secretary and was now busy with flower arrangements in his new role as chief of protocol at the Ministry of Foreign Affairs. Where he once may have been a voice of support for Ho's moderate impulses, he was now spending his time studying ideological tracts appropriate to one of the world's people's democracies. But, even while Maoism was slowly seeping into the roots of power, Communist Vietnam still managed to experience a surprising few months of relative freedom of expression. During this brief period, many questions were raised about political and human freedoms in a democratic society. Unfortunately, these pioneers were raising such issues thirty years too soon.[2]

One Hundred Flowers that Blossomed Too Soon

In the days following Dien Bien Phu, a young writer named Tran Dan found himself in the Army's Department of Culture on the orders of Commissioner Tran Do. Sent to China to write the screenplay for a film about the battle—in which he had personally taken part—he returned from his brief mission with only one project in mind: to create a work that would both express his own ideas and spark an evolution of cultural politics. In early 1955, his novel-exposé on the battle, entitled *Nguoi nguoi lop lop* [Wave upon wave of men] appeared in print. The book shows the complexity of the men who fought at Dien Bien Phu—neither trying to transform them into heroes nor depicting the war itself directly—and had brief commercial success.

During the winter of 1954–55, a group began to form around Tran Dan consisting of two composers, two poets, and a playwright, all of them in the military. Their goal was to appeal to higher authorities for a reorientation of party ideology. Their initiative found support among army intellectuals, many of whom wholeheartedly agreed to help them oppose the supervision of artistic creation by political commissars and try instead to grant greater autonomy to the army's writers and artists in their creative work.

Their project had an even wider scope, however, one that would have repercussions on the party's cultural line. In 1955, the group drew up a platform, and Tran Dan agreed to present it to the National Assembly, where he was sure to have the ear of the highest authorities. Unfortunately, we only know indirectly a few elements of this plan, here presented by Dan himself: "The revolution doesn't need sycophants who praise official programs to the skies, nor *a fortiori* of shamans who make a cult of them, who lie to us while striking their cymbals and chanting lamentable litanies. . . . Our literature today is full of artifice (and even hypocrisy), and also many simplistic stereotypes. The writer is compelled to put down his frame and make reality fit into it." After having sketched an ironic portrait of the standard "hero,"

Tran Dan continues: "Why don't we write about offices, for example? Or about love? . . . Why do we think that the only characters worthy of being written about are peasants or factory workers? Realism encourages a hundred schools to bloom, in form as well as in substance."

In February 1955, a campaign labeled the "Hundred Flowers" was being launched in the Department of Culture of the Vietnamese Army. It would be another year before a more famous movement of the same name was launched in China and almost two years before it was put into action in Vietnam, only to be rudely cut short in summer 1957. This initiative brought forth by a small circle of intellectuals and its abrupt end attest both to the dynamism of Hanoi's intellectual community and to the strictness of those leaders who suffocated it—despite the relative openness of some veteran party figures in the higher echelons.

The campaign foundered at the start, following the intervention of the director of the Political Commissioner of the Army, General Nguyen Chi Thanh, who thought that the demands of the army intellectuals were inspired by "bourgeois liberalism." A rift was thus opened that soon split the entire artistic community. Some rallied to the side of the official line, while others refused to give in and were put under strict arrest, after which they were sent off to the countryside as observers of the Agrarian Reform Campaign to be "reeducated."

The movement seemed to have been silenced, but on the eve of Tet 1956 an antiestablishment journal appeared, entitled *Giai pham mua xuan* [Beautiful works of springtime]. A poem by Tran Dan, *Nhat dinh thang* [We will win], depicts the malaise that prevailed in the North. This small volume was primarily the work of writers from the army—including Hoang Cam, Le Dat, and Tran Dan—but it was censored by civilians in charge of cultural matters at the heart of the party: To Huu, seconded by critic Hoai Thanh. A former supporter of "art for art's sake" who went over to the side of Socialist Realism after 1945, Huu was first in line to combat what he took to be the reactionary ideas of Tran Dan.

The atmosphere became even more strained as the conflict spread from the Army to the civilian world. Even though there was no real dialogue between these two factions, there was, paradoxically, at least a certain mutual respect—an attitude that soon disappeared. Was this relative tolerance due to support from powerful figures in the leadership? Giap's political commissar at the battle of Dien Bien Phu, Le Liem, leaned in favor of the reformers. General Tran Do, depicted in a favorable light by Tran Dan in his novel, played the role of mediator. Despite such support, however, in February 1956 the ideological services entered into battle against the protestors. In one meeting, a slew of inflamed criticism descended on Tran Dan, who had been thrown into prison. The situation quickly became more serious for the regime, however, because of the conjunction of two factors: the crisis in international Communism and the revelation of bloody errors committed during the past few years in internal politics.

The year 1956, in fact, had seen a chain of explosive events at the heart of the Communist bloc: Khrushchev's secret report on Stalin, on 24 February; the speech of Lu Dingyi on the Hundred Flowers in Beijing, on 26 May; the ferment of the Petőfi literary and artistic circles in Budapest; the demonstrations at Poznan in Poland, on 28 June; and finally the October Revolt in Hungary, which was crushed by Soviet intervention in early November. These events found even greater echo in Hanoi because they laid the ground for the gradual revelation of the crimes and social catastrophes caused by the blind acceptance of Maoism. The protesters soon criticized the systematic police control of the population and its displacements *(ho khau)*, the classification of people based on their social status *(ly lich)*,[3] and the awarding of literary prizes in 1955–56 to writers who toed the official line. During a turbulent assembly of artists and writers that took place 1–18 August 1956, the aspiration toward freedom was expressed with as much force as that for material concerns.

On 20 September, the first issue of an antiestablishment journal that clearly did not intend to mince words was published. It was called *Nhan van* [Humanism], a title that already revealed its political agenda. Five issues of this periodical were published between 20 September and 20 November; the sixth was banned and confiscated at the printer's even before it was put together, on 11 December. In this same spirit, *Giai pham mua xuan* reissued its first issue, which had been confiscated, and put out four more. The autumn had become a springtime for these periodicals, which all began to bloom: *Dat Moi* [New ground], published by students; *Tram Hoa* [One hundred flowers], from poet Nguyen Binh (it published ten issues between October and December); *Noi That* [Speaking openly], from Hoang Cong Khai; and *Tap San Phe binh* [Critical review], which lasted until the end of 1957.

This wave of free speech opened the floodgates that had previously been blocked by conformist journals. The daily *Hanoi moi* [New Hanoi] and the weekly *Van nghe* [Arts and letters], the official journal of the Writer's Union, even began to depart from orthodoxy. In January, *To quoc* [The nation] published a piece by Tran Dan (under a pseudonym) that makes fun of the Agrarian Reform Campaign while still celebrating it. In early November, the organ of the party, *Nhan dan* [The people], also began to publish articles that were nearly exempt from propaganda.

The editors of *Nhan van* were former resistants, many of whom came from the Army. Most of them sincerely adhered to the Communist Party despite periodic dissatisfaction with it and thoughts of abandoning their positions. The head and strategist of the team was the former youth secretary of Ho Chi Minh's first government, Nguyen Huu Dang, a Communist from the 1930s who had linked himself with Tran Thieu Bao, a collector of paintings and the owner of the publishing house Minh Duc. The group was in contact with intellectuals and bourgeois patriots who provided financial support. Phan Khoi, who was eminent in the fields of journalism and Vietnamese sinology, took over the management. Painter, caricaturist, and novelist Tran Duy took over the editing, while in the background the dissident writers of the army and of the party, Hoang Cam, Le Dat, and Tran Dan, took care of the essential work. The result was an explosive mix of talent, polemic, erudition, diplomacy, and outspokenness.

On top of this, four masters of Vietnamese thought invested their prestige into the enterprise: the father of lexicography and Vietnamese anthropology, Dao Duy Anh, who had joined the revolution in the 1920s; progressive lawyer Nguyen Manh Tuong, who wrote in French and had two doctorates (in literature and law); philosopher Tran Duc Thao, former Husserlian and now a Marxist, collaborator on the French newspaper *Les Temps Modernes* with Jean-Paul Sartre, and author of *Phénoménologie et matérialisme dialectique*; and biologist Dan Van Ngu, who helped the Vietminh develop makeshift antibiotics in the jungle. Mrs. Thuy An, former director of two women's magazines and author of an ethereal romance novel, became the driving force behind the group. Also included were Van Cao, a musician, painter, and author of the national anthem; and Trotskyite critic Truong Tuu, who first introduced psychoanalysis into Vietnam in 1943. These key figures formed a core group around which about forty other artists and authors gravitated.

Nhan van, at first tolerated, if not authorized, by the party, became known for its free expression. Chu Ngoc clearly affirms this fact: "We intend to follow only this method in our critiques: Speak openly, speak the truth, speak of everything." Such protestors did not object a priori to socialism but only to the form in which it presented itself in Vietnam. They refused to equate socialism with monolithism, or patriotism with totalitarianism, and sought to show that there are other possible paths. Sincerity, respect, and truth inspired their efforts as they took issue with the hypocritical attitudes they saw around them. This direct and open criticism went farther than the simi-

lar trend that was developing at the same time in the USSR. There the protest was only expressed behind the mask of fiction in works like *The Thaw*
by Ehrenbourg or *Not by Bread Alone* by Dudintsev. Vietnamese dissidents
demanded that the debates be made public. Tran Le Van writes: "If public
criticism in the population and in the press had been allowed before, with
everybody saying openly and honestly what he thought, the administration
would have been able to distinguish truth from falsehood, even in the execution of its politics, and many catastrophes could have been avoided."[4]

These Vietnamese authors wrote in defense of humanism and its values,
especially love, which goes hand in hand with democracy. They painted the
vices and errors of totalitarianism with a somber realism while still keeping
a corrosive humor. In *Monsieur Nam Chuot* [Mister Spittoon], Phan Khoi
describes this familiar receptacle, which is indispensable to betel chewers but
has the inconvenient characteristic of getting blocked up over time. When
it becomes unusable, it is seen as a little god that one puts on the altar or in
the wall of a pagoda. Khoi writes:

> I wrote this modest essay to explain these few lines of Le Dat:
>
> > "There are men who manage to live a century
> > Like spittoons
> > The longer they live, the more useless they become
> > The longer they live, the more they become blocked."[5]

The essence of their protest lay in a demand for certain freedoms, whose
implementation would only be sketched out decades later, in the 1980s: (1)
freedom and democracy; (2) justice, human rights, and the strengthening of
institutions; and (3) openness in all domains of thought and research. The
issue of democratic freedoms was a common refrain in every issue of *Nhan
van*. Claiming to be rooted in the Soviet Twentieth Party Congress, philosopher Tran Duc Thao broaches this problem in the 15 October issue. He
stresses that the errors that might accompany these first steps toward freedom
are nothing compared with those of the Agrarian Reform Campaign, for this
new trend "will take place through writings and dialogues without affecting
the lives of real human beings." For intellectuals, freedom is as indispensable
as the air they breathe. It is the natural right of every person.

Respect of justice and institutions is brought out by Nguyen Huu Dang in
his editorial in *Nhan van*'s fourth issue on 5 November: "Our disdain of bourgeois legality has gone to such extremes that for many of us it has become a
disdain of legality in general. Our long and hard resistance has made us

accustomed to solving problems behind closed doors and according to our whims. This lack of a sense of legality explains the arrests, executions, tortures and other abuses of the Agrarian Reform Campaign." Denouncing the excessive zeal of the police, the overly strict control of the population (*ho khau*), the opening of private mail, and censorship, Dang demands the application of the constitution (or its revision), the normal functioning of the National Assembly, and the establishment of a real judicial power.

This juridical perspective was more amply developed by lawyer Nguyen Manh Tuong. In his opinion, the errors of the Agrarian Reform Campaign originated in ignorance of four basic principles: the "statute of limitations on certain crimes; the individual nature of responsibility, which cannot extend to relatives; the burden of adequate proof of a crime; and the respect for the rights of the accused." This analysis led him to recommend three measures: the creation of authentic legal institutions, the realization of a real democracy, and the promulgation of a regime guaranteeing freedom of expression, of publishing, and of the press. The yoke of ideology hinders the natural sciences, but it is even more formidable in social sciences, according to Dao Duy Anh: "It is not unusual to see cadres without any experience outside of politics, or who pretend to be specialists, put in charge of a cultural or academic journal. . . . Their narrow-mindedness leads to a loss of professionalism which engenders superficial research; and only those ideas which conform to classical Marxist themes or to the speeches of our leaders have the right to be cited."

"Words of Shadow and Wind"

The reaction of the authorities, who had just been shaken by the public reaction to the severe methods of the Agrarian Reform Campaign, were mostly of an administrative nature: they rationed paper, raised its price, and finally proceeded to seizures and prohibitions. The length of the debates held by the authorities bear witness to their disarray. A clandestine faith had led them to stick closely to the Maoist line, for which they were now paying a dear price. The only leader not implicated directly in this fiasco was Vo Nguyen Giap. After a lengthy session of the Central Committee, he was assigned the delicate task of explaining the errors to the public and reinspiring their confidence. In front of 700 cadres, in Hanoi on 29 October, he spoke words that were certainly strongly weighed, as well as frank and courageous. In early November, governmental measures were taken to "correct the errors of the

Agrarian Reform Campaign and of the purge"—which was not the case in China.

The feeling of family at the heart of the party, however, was stronger than realism or pragmatism. Those who supported the latter may have been prestigious, but they constituted only a small minority. After the Soviets intervened to crush the Hungarian uprising, the tone in Vietnam changed rapidly. A campaign was orchestrated to gag the discordant voices. A complaint by print workers served as a pretext for seizures and prohibitions. The government refrained, however, from pushing its advantage too far. The Congress of Arts and Letters, in February 1957, although very strict on its line, appeared to adopt a compromise view.

The end result of these few months of intellectual freedom is not easy to determine. The public exposure of errors caused by Maoist-inspired politics led the administration to temper its utopianism and to put up safeguards. It split the government between the dogmatic majority and the pragmatic wing, now very much in the minority. On the intellectual level, even though serious debate ceased, there was not a total standstill. Newly authorized historical research into precolonial forms of patriotism, now liberated of certain leftist prejudices, provoked a new interest in archaeology and folklore and in the translation and publication of writings of Vietnamese scholars from the past. In the literary world, a number of Communist authors, notably Nguyen Ngoc and Chu Van, learned important lessons from this period of openness.

From then on, free expression was blocked, but the protesters continued to subtly pursue a dialogue that too often fell on deaf ears. They turned to metaphor, to "words of shadow and wind" (noi bong noi gio)—an art that many had mastered years before. At the same time, they practiced "entryism,"[6] which was that much easier because most of the Communist editors-in-chief shared their point of view.

On 10 May 1957, the administration launched a new weekly, entitled Van [Letters], but even this journal would be closed after thirty-seven issues for putting out work deemed too pessimistic or sentimental. The theoretical review of the party had started to criticize it in July, but the subeditor, Communist Nguyen Hong, refused to admit any wrongdoing and reproached the author of the party's critique for "his schematicism and his bureaucratic thinking." To the party's dismay, this warning only pushed the weekly to more fervently pursue the path of deviation. There were fewer and fewer articles that praised the party, while authors and artists of Nhan Van Giai Pham (Hundred Flowers movement) became more and more frequent contributors to Van. Almost every one of these dissidents found refuge in this new periodical, except the acknowledged father of them all, Phan Khoi, a thorn in the side of orthodox thinkers. He finally appeared in the pages of *Van*, on 10 January 1958, with a story that clearly has a double meaning. The story tells of a certain Monsieur Nam Chuot, a goldsmith who was both clever and boastful, who explained his secrets: "When one knows little about the question, one must listen and not intervene. I would not throw myself into literary theories with you, no more than you would come to teach me my profession." That was the last straw. One week later, the weekly ceased to exist.

This was not an isolated incident, however, as harsher winds were blowing from much farther away. The communal declaration of Communist parties issued in Moscow in December 1957 provoked a general toughening up of the whole Socialist bloc. The first steps toward freedom only ended in a renewed repression. In China, novelist Ding Ling was subjected to harsh criticism, despite his past history of service to the state. In the USSR, Boris Pasternak refused the Nobel Prize and was excluded from the Writer's Union. Meanwhile, on 17 June, Budapest announced the execution of Imre Nagy and his followers for "treason." According to the memoirs of Andrei Gromyko, published that same year, Mao had even proposed to the USSR to draw U.S. forces into the heart of China in order to decimate them with an atomic blast.

A False Trial

In Vietnam, Le Duan attacked this "revisionism" on 29 May, three weeks after Beijing had done the same. That summer, under the pseudonym Tran Luc, Ho Chi Minh praised the new Chinese experiment called the Great Leap Forward. In *Nhan dan*, on 16 September, he published an article entitled "Danh tan phai huu" [Break the Right], holding up as an example China's struggle against Ding Ling and other intellectuals who had severely criticized the party during their own "Hundred Flowers" movement. "The Right," he notes, "is a poisonous weed. But we are clever in politics. We will pull out the weed and make it into fertilizer to improve our rice fields." The article stresses the role of political reeducation classes and the need to exclude rightists from the Communist Party.

In January, the machinery was in place and starting to crack down on the dissension. To Huu began a campaign against "ideological and cultural saboteurs." Classes on ideological rectification gained momentum, attracting first 172 and then 304 participants. The movement affected both the literary and the artistic worlds, as well as universities.[7] For two months, a press campaign attacked the key figures of the protest, notably the thinkers Tran Duc Thao, Nguyen Manh Tuong, and Dao Duy Anh. The writers, too, were criticized and were forced to write ambiguous self-criticisms, which the authorities had to accept for lack of anything better. Accusations were made against Phan Khoi, Truong Tuu, Nguyen Huu Dang, and Thuy An, who refused to give up the fight.

In early July, To Huu expressed satisfaction at the results that had been obtained. During summer 1958, numerous groups of writers, artists, professors, and students were sent either to factories or to the countryside to "reinforce their ideological platform" through contact with workers and peasants. Although there are no precise and credible testimonials giving the details of their experiences, which obviously varied greatly depending on the case, a novel written a few years later suggests that the results were mixed. The novel, entitled *Vao doi* [First steps in life], was published in April 1963 after author Ha Minh Tuan had spent several long months working in a factory. The book sparked a considerable outcry from the official press, and, despite having a "happy ending" (the novel describes a bureaucratic administration that provokes a strike through its incompetence), it was eventually pulled from circulation.

The next several months were uneventful, but in early 1960 controversy resumed when an unannounced trial resulted in a verdict that would fall like an executioner's blade. On 21 January 1960, *Nhan dan* ran an article entitled "The Tribunal of Hanoi's Ruling on the Espionage Case of Nguyen Huu Dang–Thuy An" in which it tersely announces that "crimes of opinion" would from then on be placed under the jurisdiction of the police. Five people were sentenced to jail terms: Nguyen Huu Dang and novelist Thuy An (Luu Thi Yen) were condemned to fifteen years in prison, editor Minh Duc (Tran Thieu Bao) to ten years, and two of their collaborators got five years. Apparently, ideology had triumphed. In the index of a literary manual that came out in 1963, thirty-one works (critical works, novels, and short stories) were divided into the following categories: (1) poorly received, (2) very poorly received, and (3) clearly reactionary. The last category was only assigned to three texts, one of which was *Monsieur Nam Chuot* by Phan Khoi.

In summer 1964, the first U.S. aerial bombings of the North dragged the DRV directly into the war. American military intervention helped the ideologues to stifle the protesters even better than judicial repression had. The patriotic ideal once again took primary place in the intellectual life of the Communist North. Problems of daily life, no matter how serious, paled in comparison with the struggle against the enemy from abroad, which had once again become top priority.

Between the Tiger and the Bear

On the eve of the U.S. escalation, the debate within the senior ranks of the Vietnamese Worker's Party became even more tense; all decisions would now affect the entire territory and have both political and military repercussions. National and international affairs had become inextricably linked. The Soviet bear and the Chinese tiger entered into a war of words, which threatened to erupt into an actual conflict on the soil of their tenuous ally, Vietnam. But this bitter debate passed unnoticed, for secrecy was of utmost importance to military operations. Though few Vietnamese knew it at the time, it is now clear that by late 1963 the pressures of war that had silenced the intellectual and artistic worlds reached the highest levels of the government and the party.

As the Sino-Soviet conflict became increasingly virulent, Ho Chi Minh espoused a point of view regarding the dispute that was much more diplomatic and nationalistic than it was ideological: noninterference. The official journal of the party waited to hear Chinese and Soviet positions on various issues before publishing both texts side by side; both positions were carefully balanced with equal commentary and formatting.

In the early 1960s, some leading cadres held overtly pro-Soviet sympathies, provoking the label of "revisionist" in Beijing. Although they only represented a small minority at the heart of the Central Committee, many occupied highly visible positions in the government or in the intellectual milieu. They were often quite influential, if not within the party itself, at least within the administrative machine. Several were originally from Nam Ky (Cochin China) and had been militants prior to the Geneva Conference of 1954. The only spokesperson who dared to announce his convictions in public was Duong Bach Mai, former Communist municipal adviser in Saigon in the mid-1930s, now shunted off to the side to head the Vietnam–Soviet Friendship Association. But Mai died in early 1964.

Several important figures shared his views but were more discreet and more subtle in their remarks: Ung Van Khiem, a member of the party Central Committee, minister of foreign affairs until May 1963, and then minister of the interior until 1971; Bui Cong Trung, director of the Economics Institute; Le Liem, a former political commissar at the battle of Dien Bien Phu; and Minh Tranh, chief of publications of the Vietnamese Worker's Party.

On the other side was Le Duc Tho, a fervent admirer of Mao Zedong, who held the key post of chief of the Organizational Department in the party. Tho's ideological preferences conflicted with those of the untouchable Vo Nguyen Giap, whose own views were much closer to those of Ho Chi Minh. Nguyen Chi Thanh, a senior general and Giap's rival, was Tho's most solid supporter, despite a certain distance between their views on tactics and the theories of the Great Helmsman, Mao.

Such rifts, of course, exist in every government and are usually not insurmountable, even if hard-liners stubbornly push them toward confrontation. In Vietnam, the ideological split within the party was kept carefully hidden because of the hostilities in the South, but they were reflected in the pages of a Maoist-inspired document that was kept secret even at the heart of the party. It was eventually revealed to Communist leaders in the South, who of course were directly concerned. The Americans found out about it later, after a series of captures, victories, and arrests.

Without openly referring to the USSR, the document is severely critical of "modern revisionism" (a reference to the USSR). It puts the accent on armed struggle, stopping just short of openly recommending the intervention of the Chinese People's Liberation Army above the 17th parallel (which was in fact the result).[8] The truth about this document remained hidden for thirty years and only surfaced with the publication, on 2 September 1995—the Vietnamese national holiday—of *Viet cho me va Quoc Hoi* [Written for my mother and the National Assembly]. The author of the work was Nguyen Van Tran, a longtime Communist who joined the party around 1930 and was the deputy chief of the Municipal Committee in Saigon in 1945. The son of a wealthy family, Tran was now eighty and now returned to the Catholicism of his ancestors. He has given us a rare account of this affair.

Le Duc Tho Wanted to Remove Ho from Power

Written and printed on Tran's personal computer, the book was immediately criticized by the Politburo in a note written by ideologue Dao Duy Tung. The latter requested, however, that Tran not be openly persecuted because of his popularity in the South. Tran's top secret criticism quickly reached the West, where it was published in émigré journals.[9]

In this book, eventually published in the United States,[10] Nguyen Van Tran admits that he himself was not at the meeting but based his account on the bitter confidences of two well-known participants: the party's economic czar, Bui Cong Trung, and the former minister of Foreign Affairs, Ung Van Khiem. Citing these sources, Tran paints a somber picture of Le Duc Tho, grand organizer of the discussions that led to the Ninth Resolution. Tran writes, citing Bui Cong Trung,

> That bastard Tho (*thang Tho*) even planned to oust our dear Uncle Ho, and put Nguyen Chi Thanh in his place. Ho wouldn't have been more than a specialist confined to studying Marxism-Leninism, the State having passed into the hands of Thanh. As for the Party, *status quo* with Le Duan. It was very difficult to get rid of that strange fellow who took himself for Confucius. He had too many feats of arms to his credit in the South, where the women cherished him dearly.

And Ung Van Khiem, for his part, confided to the author: "Before the meeting, I managed to whisper to Ho that I wouldn't say a word about our joint declaration with Novotny; so he shouldn't be worried on that account. He had, in fact, added certain passages himself, and we all recognized his handwriting. This text, which didn't affect me one way or the other, could very well serve as chopping block for Sau Tho to smash Ho to pieces."[11] According to certain well-informed journalists traveling through Paris in 1970, Le Liem supposedly said that he asked Ho if he would authorize him to express his pro-Soviet views at the plenum. Ho encouraged him to voice his views—which Liem did, without a word of support from Ho, who sat silently at the meeting.

According to Nguyen Van Tran, more than ten members of the Central Committee, notably Ung Van Khiem, Nguyen Van Vinh, Bui Cong Trung, and Le Liem, abstained from voting on the Ninth Resolution. The general anti-Soviet tone of the document frustrated Ho Chi Minh so much that he left the conference hall to smoke a cigarette, thus avoiding taking part in the vote. General Giap, who was also pro-Soviet, shared this view and supposedly went to Do Son the next day, where he played the piano to calm his nerves. It has been rumored that he shared the views of General Nguyen Van Vinh while never making them openly known.[12] According to Nguyen Van Tran, the adoption of the Ninth Resolution unleashed a campaign of repression against those party leaders who had opposed it. The arrests were not made until 1967 and took place without a trial and by the authority of the party.

This Ninth Central Committee also decided to escalate the war in the South. President Ngo Dinh Diem had been deposed in November 1963, which led the party's Central Committee to decide to intensify its efforts to promote the overthrow of the Saigon regime—now under new military rulers—before the United States could decide to intervene. Viet Cong forces were to be strengthened, but no regular forces from the North were introduced.

General Nguyen Van Vinh, who was in charge of problems of reunification, published his own point of view in the Communist monthly in February 1964.[13] In the article he explains what he saw as three possible reactions to Hanoi's new policy from the United States: Washington would either withdraw its troops, send reinforcements south of the 17th parallel, or else directly intervene against North Vietnam.[14] In Hanoi, the year 1965 was in fact marked by bitter internal debates within the Vietnamese Worker's Party, which leaned in favor of the USSR after the "incidents" in the Gulf of Tonkin—when U.S. warplanes bombed North Vietnamese ports during summer 1964. In the meantime, Ho Chi Minh found other support for his own views. Hoang Xuan Han wrote an article entitled "Propositions pour la paix au Viet-nam," published in Combat on 24 September 1964, wherein he wished that the DRV were not in the hands of extremists, for it was supposed to be governed by an elected assembly. But in times of increasing crisis, militants and warmongers cared little for such wise talk of peace. Han was not alone in his views, however, and was soon seconded by Nguyen Manh Ha, a former Catholic minister of Ho Chi Minh's, in an article that was issued in Phnom Penh on 2 February 1965.

But the pro-Soviet wing had little influence both in the strategic debate and in the party apparatus, which had been forged in the bitter legacy of the Maoist school. It did, however, find sympathy among many specialists and intellectuals, as well as in the Army, a sector that was more technologically advanced than the rest of North Vietnamese society. Certain leaders shared these views, but they were punished for having maintained their point of view (bao luu y kien) by being removed from their posts, though they were not the object of sanctions.

Soviet influence, however, did not limit itself to this arena of ideas. As the conflict with Beijing continued, Moscow continued to try to win favor among the Vietnamese, whose point of view was becoming predominantly Maoist. In 1963–64, some interns who had been sent to the USSR for studies refused to return to Vietnam. Among them was a divisional political commissar, Le Vinh Quoc, who is still in Russia today because the authorities have refused to extradite him.

In 1965 Moscow made a number of spectacular gestures toward reinforcing its military aid to the DRV and added a propaganda effort to support a negotiated solution to the war in the South. In mid-1966, the Soviets felt that they had enough trump cards to leak the information that "North Vietnamese leaders are trying to put an end to the supremacy of the pro-Chinese faction" and that "the Soviet Union discreetly supports their efforts."[15] At the end of the summer of 1966, Radio Hanoi broadcast a report that was critical of ideas favoring political flexibility and "concessions aiming at avoiding bloodshed." In September, an editorial in the official review of the Worker's Party announced the general restructuring of the Theoretical Studies Services (run by Hoang Minh Chinh) and the creation of an ad hoc commission to reclaim this domain, which was "too inspired by abroad." At the same time, diplomats from Moscow did not hesitate to tell their interviewers that "the Soviet Union is not without influence in Hanoi" and claimed to be ready to serve as intermediary in negotiations with the United States, a role that they had always pretended to refuse up until then.

Notes

1. *Translator's note:* The *édé* and the *banhar* are two minority peoples from the mountains of South Vietnam.

2. For more details, see Georges Boudarel, *Cent fleurs écloses dans la nuit du Viêt-nam, 1954–56* (Paris: Jacques Bertoin, 1991).

3. Each citizen had to have a kind of identity card noting his or her social class.

4. *Nhan Van,* no. 2 (30 September 1956).

5. *Giai pham mua xuan* 2 (1956).

6. *Translator's note:* "Entryism" is infiltration into a political organization to change or subvert its policies or objectives.

7. *Bon Nhan Van Giai Pham truoc toa an du luan* [The "Nhan Van Giai Pham clique" in front of the tribunal of opinion] (Hanoi, 1959), 309–310, 335.

8. *Translator's note:* The document in question was drawn up at the Ninth Plenary Session of the Vietnamese Worker's Party held in Hanoi in December 1963 and is very critical of the USSR because Moscow was reluctant to support Hanoi in South Vietnam. Those party members who supported Moscow were criticized at the meeting by Maoists like Le Duc Tho and Nguyen Chi Tranh. Giap and Ho leaned toward the USSR and were obliquely criticized as well.

9. See *Phu nu dien dan* [Women's forum], October 1995.

10. Nguyen Van Tran, *Viet cho me va Quoc Hoi* [Written for my mother and the National Assembly] (Stanton, Calif.: Van Nghe, 1995), especially 322–31.

11. Tran, *Viet cho me va Quoc Hoi,* 328.

12. In fact, after Tran Van Tra's military operations in the South in early 1975, it was Giap who managed from Hanoi to deal the decisive blow to the army of Saigon.

13. R. B. Smith, *An International History of the Vietnam War. Vol. II: The Struggle for South-East Asia, 1961–65* (London: Macmillan, 1987), 220–21.

14. Smith, *An International History of the Vietnam War*, 224.

15. *China News Analysis* (Hong Kong), 9 September 1966.

CHAPTER SIX

1965–75: War or Peace

Georges Boudarel

With hindsight, we often think of wars in terms of how they could have been avoided, judging them through the lens of failed negotiations. One could also claim that politics and diplomacy often end up escalating conflict into war. In the case of the United States and the Democratic Republic of Vietnam, we now see that the choices made by both governments were not made easily and that the debates that raged on both sides reveal a profound divergence of views. In the East as in the West, the advocates of conciliation and compromise came up against stubborn obstacles and strong ideological bias.

The Failure of "Operation Pennsylvania"

Nearly thirty years after the beginning of hostilities, the memoirs of two key figures were published: those of Raymond Aubrac[1] and former U.S. Secretary of Defense Robert McNamara. This new information brought confirmation of what had always been suspected: that peace talks opened at that time could have brought an end to the Vietnam War.[2]

Everything began at a meeting of the Pugwash Movement, which since 1965 had brought together scientists working against the nuclear threat. It was through this channel that Henry Kissinger contacted two key figures who were very close to the Communists in Hanoi: Herbert Marcovich and Raymond Aubrac. These two men were to organize a secret operation, baptized "Pennsylvania," that would eventually lead to peace—a word that was not even pronounced, so incongruous did it seem at the time.

Washington proposed the unconditional cessation of bombing, based on a North Vietnamese agreement to adopt reciprocal measures. McNamara writes:

> Aubrac and Marcovich arrived in Hanoi on July 21. Ho was ill but agreed to see his old friend Aubrac. Aubrac and Marcovich then met with Premier Pham Van Dong for lengthy discussions. Following their presentation, the premier said, "We want an unconditional end of bombing and if that happens, there will be no further obstacles to negotiations." He appeared willing to maintain the channel, and suggested Aubrac and Marcovich send future messages to him through North Vietnam's Consul General in Paris, Mai Van Bo.[3]

The stakes were high. After decades of colonialism, there still was not the least bit of democracy in Vietnam. What they wanted, in fact, was the establishment of a democratic system that would give voice to the wide diversity of Vietnamese. This diversity was poorly concealed by the uniformity of the prevailing rhetoric, which had been forged in the 1920s and 1930s. Even Ho Chi Minh, despite his adhesion to the theoretically radical party line of the Communist Revolution, never ceased advocating a dialogue that would shed light on the contradictory nature of democracy. Washington, however, did not seem aware of the political diversity in Vietnam and bet on the hand of the rightist extremists from the South, from Ngo Dinh Diem to Nguyen Van Thieu. This is, at any rate, what emerges from reading McNamara's memoirs. There is no mention of enlightened or tolerant figures on the parliamentary scene, not even of Au Truong Thanh or Truong Dinh Dzu, both advocates of compromise.

The United States knew, however, that the only possible solution was through a compromise. McNamara now admits that he shared the point of view of Secretary of State Averell Harriman, to whom he said in 1967, "We must make up our minds that the only way to settle this is by having a coalition government. We cannot avoid that."[4] In July, then, it seemed that the first phase of Kissinger's top secret project was on track; but the results were minimal. After hesitation from Washington, the channel that had been opened was definitively shut on 20 October 1967, when Mai Van Bo refused to receive Aubrac and Marcovich: "There is nothing new to say. The situation is worsening. There is no reason to talk again."[5] That was the end of "Operation Pennsylvania." But the initiative had laid the ground for the negotiations of 1968.

This failure was undoubtedly due in part to errors on the part of the United States, but it was also due to variations and contradictions deep within the Hanoi party line that would have other repercussions, especially in terms of its strategic plan. The opening of peace talks on this date could have spared the Vietnamese one, even two or three, million deaths. How can this failure be explained? Though they are never openly acknowledged, some answers can be read clearly enough between the lines of writings published at the time. Further clues can be found today in the recent appearance of internal documents of the time, smuggled overseas and printed in dissident, anti-Communist Vietnamese periodicals.

Divergence and Silence

Between 1965 and 1968, two Communist generals were developing differing ideas regarding strategy, both under revealing pseudonyms. Tran Do, who went by the pseudonym Cuu Long (Mekong) stressed local guerrilla operations and political factors. Nguyen Chi Thanh, who chose the name Truong Son (the central mountain range in Vietnam), insisted above all on military confrontation—and this at the moment when, in the name of the Maoism he admired, he was preparing an armed coup against the Saigon regime in the style of the Bolshevik Revolution of October 1917. These writings appeared officially in various journals in Hanoi and were later assembled and published by an American researcher.[6] Nothing better communicates the reality of the political culture in Hanoi than the veiled terms in which the debate was carried on in the party press.

We learn from this debate that after the massive intervention by the United States in the South in 1965, Vo Nguyen Giap advocated a return to guerilla tactics. Conversely, Nguyen Chi Thanh called for full-scale offensives with the full support of the northern army. Thanh believed that going back to outdated models of struggle—as he accused Giap of doing—was a sign of defeatism. While in Hanoi the party line was being discussed behind closed doors, Tran Do and Nguyen Chi Thanh, who were far from agreeing, were both in the field preparing the famous 1968 Tet Offensive on Saigon. The latter became ill had to fall back to Hanoi, where he died on 6 July 1967 at age fifty-three, worn out by a life of fierce militancy. Tran Do, on the other hand, participated in the fighting and was—mistakenly—given up for dead.[7]

The Tet Offensive of 1968 was launched after insufficient preparation, leading to catastrophic losses among the revolutionary forces in the South, but had such profound repercussions that it led to the opening of negotiations in Paris. According to rumor, the decision to launch the offensive was made by the highest authority, by Van Tien Dung, Le Duan, and Nguyen

Chi Thanh. General Giap, however, had serious reservations about this operation, judging by the ambiguous remarks he made to Italian journalist Oriana
Fallaci in 1968. He claimed that the North had nothing to do with the military campaign, that it was organized by the front in the South. This state-
ment was not just propagandistic double-talk. Giap emphasized the political
aspect of the problem: "The war in Vietnam is not only a military affair."
His words were censored by the press, who gave the journalist an "official
text" of the interview. All of the half-formulated or implied reservations in
the dialogue were erased.[8]

The Hoang Affair or the Ho Affair?

In autumn 1967, two important events rocked Hanoi. It is no coincidence
that in the same month that Aubrac and Marcovich arrived in Hanoi, the
first arrests of key figures implicated in what is called the "Hoang Minh
Chinh Affair" took place. These arrests sent shock waves up to the highest
spheres of the party. Among the first to "disappear" were General Dang Kim
Giang, who had run the logistics of Dien Bien Phu before becoming secretary
of state for Collective Farms; Hoang Minh Chinh, director of the Institute
of Philosophy; Tran Minh Viet, vice secretary of the party in Hanoi; and
Colonel Le Trong Nghia, director of the Department of Military Information.

The disappearance of all of these eminent figures could not pass unnoticed, even though the arrests were made under cover of darkness. Rumors of
spying, of treason, and of a coup attempt quickly spread, creating a climate
of suspicion and fear that was all the more distressing because the purges
continued to take place. Two days prior to 20 October—the date when Mai
Van Bo refused to receive Aubrac and Marcovich in Paris—the police raided
the house of Vu Dinh Huynh, former personal secretary to Ho Chi Minh and
a man who had played a key role at Ho's side during the revolution. Huynh
was taken away in handcuffs. His wife could not believe what was happening
and went to the Central Prison at Hoa Lo, where she met with a guard who
told her to go and see the Department of Security and the Ministry of the
Interior. She did this the next day but could not obtain her husband's freedom. Then her son, Vu Thu Hien, was arrested on Christmas Eve. On that
Sunday, Hien was going out by bicycle and was met by a liaison agent whom
he did not recognize. The man told him to come at once to the editorial
offices at the monthly *Vietnam Pictorial* for an urgent mission. Hien wondered
who would need him at that hour when a command car pulled up next to

them. Two men got out and ordered him to get into the vehicle. The friendly liaison agent then traded an engaging smile for a scowl and shouted, "Come on! Move it! What are you waiting for?" They headed for the prison.

About thirty well-known, clearly identified figures were kidnapped by the Party Organization Department in the second half of 1967, without any warrants for their arrest. After passing through the Central Prison they were sent to special camps, notably Bat Bat at the foot of Mount Ba Vi, near Son Tay. No contact with the outside world was permitted—no visits, no exchange of messages, only interrogations and self-criticisms. After their liberation, around 1975, most were sent out to the provinces and placed under house arrest. It is quite possible that these "detainees" benefited from some discreet sympathy from the highest level.

One writer has speculated that this was part of a coup d'état on the part of General Giap, but there is no real evidence to support this claim.[9] More likely, the motives for the arrests are indirectly revealed by the new legislation that had been adopted on 30 October 1967. The president of the assembly, Truong Chinh, signed a "law for the repression of counter-revolutionary crimes," which was undeniably aimed at the information services of Socialist countries (as well as those, obviously, of imperialist countries). Article 3 defines "the crime of treason" in a very general sense as "contact with a foreign power with the aim of undermining independence and national sovereignty." The article regarding the crime of spying is even more explicit and mentions the "delivery of state or military secrets to the imperialists and their lackeys, or to the information services of a foreign power, as well as taking orders from a foreign country, the collecting and furnishing of information and of documents not necessarily dealing with state secrets but which permit a foreign country to undermine the interests of the Democratic Republic of Vietnam."

Articles 7 and 9 deal respectively with "subversion" and the crime of "defection." This law was adopted the day after the arrests, while plans were being made for the Tet Offensive of 1968, but the authorities waited until April of the following year to publish it in the theoretical journal of the party, *Hoc Tap*, where its appearance rang out like a pistol shot.

All of these prisoners resurfaced around 1975, but they were never rehabilitated, and they ended their days in the bitterness of total anonymity. Though they were never even placed on trial, their condemnation by Le Duc Tho turned out to be much harsher than if they had been judged by constitution or law. All that appeared in the press, and only for one day, were the names of the former supporters of General Giap, who cited them in connection with the anniversary of the battle of Dien Bien Phu. In this edition, under the direction of Bui Tin, Giap wrote an article entitled "The Most Difficult Decision to Make." He explains how, on 14 January 1954, he had dismissed the plan put forth by Chinese advisers who wanted to attack the citadel at Dien Bien Phu from the west in a wave of rapid assaults over a few days. Giap believed that this plan was destined to fail, as it had one year before in Nasan. He then named Le Liem to the post of political commissar. Dang Kim Giang would be head of Logistical Command, and Le Trong Nghia would be director of information.[10]

Since the end of the 1980s, articles about these events have multiplied in émigré journals, in particular in *Dien dan* [Forum] in Paris. Curiously, supporters of the ex-government of Saigon have given little importance to Giap's dissidence in his attempts to forestall hostilities by distancing himself from the Chinese. A success of this kind, however, could have saved their political allies by leading to a compromise that otherwise proved to be difficult to establish. Issue number 10 (1993) of *Forum* provides a detailed explanation of the views of this group, as well as a list of its twenty-seven members, in the context of a long message to Hoang Minh Chinh. It sheds light on the famous Ninth Resolution, which was passed in winter 1963–64 despite the opposition of ten participants and the abstention of Ho Chi Minh.

The ratified text was somewhat ambiguous, and Truong Chinh tried to clarify it to an audience of 400 people in January 1964: "The Ninth Resolution doesn't lay everything out in black and white. In a sense, it is something that can only be transmitted orally. Its basic message is that our party line is essentially the same as that of the Chinese State." Le Duc Tho then added this point: "We are leaving the fight against modern revisionism to the Chinese Communist Party, who can take care of it on the theoretical level. As for organization, we will deal with that ourselves." This entire issue has its source in Mao Zedong's opposition to the critique of Stalinism expressed by Khrushchev at the Twentieth Congress of the Soviet Communist Party in February 1956. Khrushchev believed in a peaceful passage to Socialism, while Mao saw this as "modern revisionism." The Great Helmsman saw war, even an atomic one, as unavoidable because of the global class struggle. The adoption of Maoist policies was, thus, a vote for armed confrontation over peace.

Hoang Minh Chinh has written much about this Sino-Soviet conflict—which today seems like an ancient debate—and with good reason. For having opposed the Maoist orientation of the Ninth Resolution, he was stripped of all of his duties and then interned in a special camp without a trial. All of these decisions were made by one individual, Le Duc Tho, head of the Department of Organization of the Party. In defiance of the constitution, Tho had Chinh locked away twice: first to prison for eleven years and then under house arrest for nine more for having dared protest against the injustice of his first incarceration. This merciless repression against Hoang Minh Chinh was in opposition to the policy of Ho Chi Minh, a fact that is corroborated by the testimony of Ho's personal secretary, Vu Dinh Huynh. On 28 November 1987, at eighty-three years of age, Vu talks about his ordeal in a letter to the secretary general of the party:

> Engaged in revolutionary action since 1923, member of the Association of Young Revolutionary Comrades since 1925, then of the Communist Party in 1930, I was arrested by the Colonialists, who interned me at Son La. After the National Congress of Tan Trao in August 1945, I became President Ho's Personal Secretary. After the return of peace, I was Chief of Protocol of the Minister of Foreign Affairs and the Government Control Commission, until my retirement in 1964. In October 1967 I was arrested, and subsequently [in 1972], excluded from the Party for having led "anti-party and pro-Soviet revisionism," and for this reason kept in detention until 1973, and then put under house arrest at Nam Dinh until 1976.[11]

After reminding the reader that he had *legally* opposed the adoption of Maoism in 1964, he adds: "The Sixth Congress conducted a severe evaluation of our internal and external politics, but without giving the least thought to the grave errors of the Ninth Resolution."

In conclusion, he demands the creation of a commission authorized to reexamine the whole affair. But this commission never saw the light of day. Vu's widow, Pham Thi Te, wrote a letter to a high party member on 19 May 1995 to carry on with her husband's defense. In the letter she confirms what Nguyen Van Tran writes in *Written for My Mother and the National Assembly*. Te writes: "Huyn knew too much about [Le Duc] Tho, and this was his downfall." She too, then, knew that Tho wanted to remove Ho Chi Minh from power. It seems now that the wave of arrests was aimed not so much at spies or plotters as at the militants who wanted to put into place Uncle Ho's strategic plan of a united struggle for independence. But Ho, for his part, really wished to find a compromise to put an end to a war that had already spilled too much blood.

After 1965, Ho Chi Minh's activities were curbed by poor health, but he remained clear minded. His perspicacious opinions were kept secret, in the name of "grand principles," the better to be discarded. When Moscow invaded Czechoslovakia in summer 1968, Hanoi gave its approval despite Uncle Ho's objectives. Reformist communist Jiri Pelikan explains:[12] "According to trustworthy sources, Ho Chi Minh was at that time bedridden, and thus didn't participate in the meetings of the Politburo, but supposedly recommended to the latter that they not take a position in this conflict." Secretary General Le Duan hid this recommendation, however, and succeeded in pushing through the pro-Soviet line despite resistance from certain members of the leadership: "This marked the beginning of a new orientation within the Party, which would lead to conflict with China and the occupation of Cambodia."[13]

Curiously, the Communist Party in Vietnam in this instance presents a paradoxical analogy to its counterpart in Bohemia, situated at opposite poles in all respects. In the land of Jean Hus, the official line is caricatured by an anecdote regarding the traffic jams around Prague:

Q: Why is it impossible to drive in the capital?
A: The answer is simple. To avoid contradictions, the Politburo came up with this brilliant idea: half of the cars will drive on the right, half on the left.

What is surprising, though, is that in spite of the problems inherited from the totalitarian system, Red Vietnam still managed to move south down the Ho Chi Minh Trail. But this was certainly less out of any political conviction than out of nationalism.

Marxist Jargon and the Poetry of Rupture

In his 1952 study of the intellectual in people's democracies, Czeslaw Milosz writes: "Many Party members hate the system but, as is the case with independents, they are subject to a kind of personality split which makes them unclassifiable by Western criteria. Whether we like it or not, we must get rid of Yes is Yes and No is No."[14] Vu Can understood this divorce between official rhetoric and psychological reality and voiced his frustration in a poem while editor-in-chief of the official propaganda journal in 1965. He called this collection of poems *puèmes* because they deal with everything that stinks (*puer* in French means "to stink"). The following lines, as bitter as they are prescient, explore this split personality without needing to turn to psychoanalysis:

Intoxication

How is it that there are two of me?
One who laughs
One who cries
How is it that there are two of me?
One who speaks
One who acts
How is it that there are two truths?
One gilt-edged
One starkly naked
Which is, quite simply, only the truth.[15]

Splitting of the self, tragedy, tearing apart—what words can describe this wound, which is all the more painful because it must be concealed? Among the so-called friends who came to the capital of the DRV in its darkest hours, no one felt this rift more than Susan Sontag; the central part of her *Trip to Hanoi* is dedicated to it:

> Clearly, they have a different way here of treating the guest, the stranger, the foreigner, not to mention the enemy. Also, I'm convinced, the Vietnamese have a different relation to language. The difference can't just be due to the fact that my sentences, already slowed down and simplified, more often than not have to be mediated by a translator. For even when I'm in conversation with someone who speaks English or French, it seems to me we're both talking baby talk. To all this add the constraint of being reduced to the status of a child: scheduled, led about, explained to, fussed over, pampered, kept under benign surveillance. Not only a child individually but, even more exasperating, one of a group of children. The four Vietnamese from the Peace Committee who are seeing us around act as our nurses, our teachers. I try to discover the differences between each of them, but can't; and I worry that they don't see what's different or special about me. All too often I catch myself trying to please them, to make a good impression—to get the best mark of the class.[16]

Further in her analysis, Sontag claims that the Vietnamese language itself is a hindrance to the revolution. By the end of the fifth day, she is so exasperated that she is tempted to give up trying to understand the Vietnamese. Although Sontag admires the Communist Party for its struggle, their savoir faire, and their tact, she is still disconcerted by its stilted rhetoric. In the end, her brief visit to Hanoi leaves her with some fundamental questions. After mentioning "the more notorious crimes committed by the present government: for example, the persecution of the Trotskyite faction and the execution of its leaders in 1946; and the forcible collectivization of agriculture in 1956, the brutalities and injustices of which high officials have recently been admitted," Sontag brings up the paradoxical situation of the people she met:

> Several Vietnamese I met themselves brought up the dangers of single-party rule. . . . Of course, this conception of the Party as a vast corps of skilled, ethically impeccable, mostly unpaid public servants, tutoring and working alongside people in all their activities, sharing their hardships, doesn't exempt the Vietnamese system from terrible abuses. But neither does it preclude the possibility that the present system functions humanely, with genuine substantive democracy, much of the time.
>
> In any case, I noticed that the word "democracy" was frequently invoked in Vietnam, far more often than in any other Communist country I've visited, including Cuba.[17]

A Monument without Foundation

Among the many secret operations in modern Vietnamese history, one of the worst was the falsification of Ho Chi Minh's last will and testament, which he began writing in 1965. We first learned of this with the 1989 publication of the memoirs of Vu Ky, Ho's personal secretary.[18]

Ho died at 9:47 a.m. on 2 September 1969—the same day as the DRV national holiday—but his death was "moved back" a day so as not to cast a shadow on the national anniversary. Nearly fifteen years would pass before the truth about Ho's testament was finally made public. The issue surfaced when the Maoist Hoang Van Hoan secretly defected to Beijing and publicly charged that "Le Duan has falsified Ho Chi Minh's testament."[19] Hoan reveals that the Politburo wanted to meet with Ho right before the death of the latter. Secretary General Le Duan rejected this idea, declaring that Ho was in a state of mental confusion and that his words were incoherent. "Once death had come," Hoan continues, "Duan brought out a three or four page text signed by Ho and himself, stating that it was Uncle Ho's testament, a text which was then published with just one signature—Ho's."

Hoan's article also accuses the secretary general of pro-Soviet revisionism, referring in passing to the famous Ninth Resolution of December 1963. However, by mentioning Ho's testament, he exposed an extremely delicate issue for the Hanoi leadership, which was then discussed behind closed doors at the highest levels of the party. By this time, however, Ho's body had already been embalmed by specialists from the USSR, and on 19 May 1970, a competition was announced to carry out exactly the opposite of Ho's last wishes: under the pretext of honoring him, they decided to build a great funerary monument. It was a project totally foreign to the Vietnamese character, although the party argued to the contrary in the hopes of sustaining an impossible illusion.

The inauguration of the new mausoleum was planned for 2 September 1975.[20] And still, in all that time, nothing was said about Ho's last wishes. It would take nearly fifteen years before we would learn the true content of Ho's testament. On 2 September 1989, the official party journal revealed that Ho had expressed the wish to be cremated and asked that his "ashes be placed in three ceramic urns," which would then be buried respectively in the north, the center, and the south of Vietnam on three hills planted with trees. He had also rejected the building of any tombstone or statue. If the Central Committee decided, on the contrary, to embalm the body and exhibit it in a mausoleum, it was so that "our compatriots and foreign friends have a chance to visit him."

In the testament, Ho had also requested that peasants be exempted from all agricultural taxes once the war against the regime in Saigon was finished. At the time, this request could not be granted because of the "lack of ade-

The Ho Chi Minh Mausoleum, erected against the wishes of Ho himself.

quate conditions," but, according to a communiqué from the Politburo published in *Nhan dan* on 19 August 1989, the proposal was still under consideration. To this day, however, no action has been taken. Certain people who were close to Ho, such as General Tran Do, felt that the government should begin implementing the last wishes of the founder of the Democratic Republic, but their voices apparently were not heard.

Nowadays many people speak about Uncle Ho's ideas in the wooden language of Marxist jargon or even in a Maoist framework. But this, too, would have rung with dissonance in the ears of such a pragmatist, who appealed as much to Eastern sensibilities as to Western rationalism. Now there is increasing talk of reconciliation between the Vietnamese, and this is obviously something that Ho Chi Minh always dreamed about—even if this dream was riddled with contradictions, both in his own mind and in his relationship with his comrades.

Education: One Step Forward, Two Steps Back

In 1945 Vietnamese higher education was still struggling to establish itself. Its three disciplines—law, medicine, and agriculture—were not very sophisticated, and courses were taught entirely in French. This system produced only 240 Vietnamese doctors and a handful of graduates in the areas of science, mathematics, and technology.[21] There were, however, scholars like Hoang Xuan Han, a graduate of France's prestigious École Polytechnique, who devoted himself entirely to editing a dictionary of scientific terms that permitted universities to offer courses in Vietnamese after 1945. In 1950, the first two schools using *quoc ngu* were opened in Vietminh territory: one for surgical medicine, on a tributary of the Claire River, and another for pedagogy nearby.

In Hanoi, the government tried to promote Vietnamese as the language of instruction with the help of new professors who had been trained in the USSR during World War II. On the old fairgrounds, people gathered to applaud both locally trained troops and soldiers from the Soviet Union, China, and Eastern Europe. Right next door, refurbished offices were turned into a new "people's university" to teach Marxism-Leninism, organize manual labor, and hold talks on agrarian reform. The public was excited by these new projects, carried away on a wave of enthusiasm for the class struggle. In the outskirts of town a whole academic world sprang up around a new specialized university with technical education *(bach khoa)* as the crown jewel. Foreign experts helped doctoral candidates organize their courses, all taught in *quoc ngu*. At the same time, worker-peasant schools were opened to allow underprivileged youths to earn higher degrees.

This university environment was not free of ideology, however, which permeated all areas of study, including mathematics. Beneath this apparent progress in the intellectual milieu lurked the absolute primacy of the class struggle. The primary criterion of admission into higher education was neither knowledge nor competence but, rather, politics: in this new system, the sons of the bourgeois were automatically shunted aside in favor of the children of manual laborers or revolutionaries.

Professor Le Van Thiem tried to curb this ideological contamination by supporting the appointment of a real scientist, Ta Quang Buu, as minister of higher education in 1965. But party leaders in charge of ideology, To Huu and his assistants Tran Quang Huy and Tran Tong, led the fight against "deviationist" mathematicians and won the first round of the fight by implementing a reorganization that removed officials holding a "bourgeois point of view." Ta Quang Buu intervened in 1965, which allowed academics to win the second round. Organizing the transfer of all institutions of higher education to the countryside to avoid U.S. bombing raids, Buu snubbed China's offer to set them up on its own soil. With the support of Pham Van Dong and Giap, Buu moved schools to the countryside, created additional ones, and extended the period of study by one year. Thanks to him, one dissident professor has written,

> Vietnam ranked as one of the top third-world countries in number of graduates, with a proportion comparable to that of industrialized countries. . . . Contrary to what happened in 1957–58, years which were dominated by Maoism, theoretical studies found numerous civil and military applications. Thanks to his studies on ultrasound, one doctor and his team destroyed American mines which had been blocking the re-supplying of Vietnam by sea. Schools of medicine worked on new treatments for the sick, while Professor Ton That Tung was invited to give lectures on a new, original method of liver surgery. Professor Le The Trung developed a treatment for the harmful effects of napalm.[22]

The election of To Huu to the Politburo in 1975, however, led to the removal of Ta Quang Buu from the Ministry of Higher Education and the creation of a more politically oriented staff. But this new straightjacket could not hamper the activities of certain daring individuals like Phan Dinh Dieu.

Dieu, a vocal member of the new Computer Science Institute, ventured at his own risk into dangerous territory far removed from his own professional domain. As deputy to the National Assembly, he apparently dared to call for the resignation of party chief Le Duan. It is no surprise that Dieu was not re-elected.

Soviet Watches and Chinese Moonlight

Upon Ho's death in September 1969, Viet Phuong, personal secretary of Pham Van Dong, wrote a poem in homage to Ho Chi Minh that bears close resemblance to Jacques Prévert's "Diner de têtes" [Dinner of heads]. This poem no longer refers to Ho with the honorific "Nguoi,"[23] which transformed him into the semidivine spirit of the nation. In so doing, Viet Phuong hoped to better exalt Ho's simplicity and extraordinary achievement as a real man. A month later, this poet from the high ranks of politics submitted a new collection of poems in the same style, titled *Cua Mo* [Open door], whose ideological and artistic nonconformity rocked the bureaucratic world.

As soon as *Open Door* (see pp. 147–48) was published, on Tet 1970, word quickly spread that "this collection caused problems." Eighteen years later, in 1988, one critic would write:

> *Cause problems*, this euphemism was usually the harbinger of terrible catastrophes. Anyone who dared to ask, "But where is the problem?" only received the vaguest of answers: "They're asking questions in high places." And who is that exactly? Some say A, and some B. Some are criticized for holding incorrect views, others for being too politically stilted; or others raise a *thac mac*, a grievance or misunderstanding, which asks, "What does all this nonsense mean?"[24]

Did Pham Van Dong share the views of his secretary? We have good reason to wonder, for he secretly defended him when pushed to the wall. Today no one knows what happened to this collection of poetry, which seems to have vanished without a trace. It was taken out of circulation and probably put through the shredder, just at the moment when two of its iconoclastic maxims were being transformed into proverbs by freethinking intellectuals of Hanoi:

- It is clear, Soviet watches are a hundred times better than Swiss ones.
- The moon in China is much rounder than in the USA.

Cua Mo [Open door]
Viet Phuong (1969)

"Our Lives as Beloved as Our Wives"

"Madly," "super," "ultra," that's what we were shouting at the top of our lungs.
We thought we were hard as iron. That was definitely the worst part.
We didn't know that a little piece of blue sky was better than a totally blue one.
Our common sense melted under the fire of a delirious enthusiasm.
To say "comrade" was enough to wipe out all the bastards,
In our ranks, only affection had a place.
Once the direction was established, nobody was left behind,
Moscow soared higher than any heaven,
It is clear, Soviet watches are a hundred times better than Swiss ones
That was our credo, our will, our pride,
The moon in China is much rounder than in the USA.
Our lyricism of the absolute rang with a strange naïveté.
Maybe after a quarter of a century we finally know
What it means to love, what it means to kill and to liquidate.
We discovered blemishes on the star of the moon
And found mud at the summit of our heights,
Our force, increased ten-fold in intoxication, rendered us so perspicacious
That we said coldly to the enemy:
"All the bad things that we carry around comes from you,
All the good things that you have, you owe to us."
To believe in it even more, we looked at life through rose-colored glasses.
Today, our thirst for faith no longer needs such pincers,
We have become used to the most stupefying surprises,
We have paid a high price; it opened our eyes.
We stumbled against obstacles and fell far short of our expectations
And not only on snakes hidden in a flower garden.
From being good to the point of spinelessness, good people are now nothing but
    garbage,
The sleeping viper lies coiled up deep in our hearts.
We have thought hard during eight thousand nights of battle
Crushing black ideas with the popping of corn.
Through the tangle of bombs, we have filtered our happiness,
Our hearts beating for a tomorrow which will sing forever.
We learned who made a mistake and who can still make mistakes,
In our Communist Self, the heart of humanity is a little bit richer.
In stripping the apparatus of the idol, we have exalted the heart of the man

In every sense, from the front, the back, the outside, and especially from the inside.
Quang Binh, Vinh Linh, our love fallen prey to flames,
We have seen the ultimate horror and we can't help smiling.
When, turning on the radio like opening a door to the outside,
We hear it insult us for our confidence in the future,
We suffer terribly, like a women giving birth.
We care about this life which links us together; it is our breath.
Our lives overflow with an explosive joy,
Our lives as beloved as our wives.

The author was not openly sanctioned but, rather, simply removed from his functions for a number of years. He was (poorly) paid to do nothing until the affair blew over, before being reintegrated into his job as high political adviser. In 1988, the reissue of his collection was accompanied by hushed rumors about the existence of other poems. As much as one would like to see them revived, the likelihood is low. They carry with them too much of a past and will probably remain hidden away at the bottom of a bureaucrat's desk drawer. The important thing, though, is that today Viet Phuong has regained his place in the government apparatus of Hanoi. His presence shines like a ray of hope, a reassuring critical mind in the obscurity that reigns behind the scenes.

Is it possible that the Communist Vietnam of tomorrow will head down the road to real change, to a profound transformation or a political turning? History is full of battles between hard-liner nomenclaturists, with their unrelenting persecutions; but it is the same everywhere in times of great change. The violence of Hanoi's revolution is no different than the destruction that so ravaged the England of Cromwell or France of 1789.

In his study Le Viet-nam entre deux mythes [Vietnam between two myths],[25] Claude Palazzoli recognized the problem: after raising North Vietnam too high, we then cast it too low. In totalitarian Hanoi, the wrenching violence that seemed to destroy everything always left a place—meager though it was—for self-expression in the fields of literature and politics. Poet Tran Dan, for example, managed to publish poems in the journal of the Communist Party in 1970, though only by pretending to be a worker named Ly Phuong Lien.

Notes

1. *Translator's note:* Raymond Aubrac was a French leftist and friend of Ho Chi Minh, who had opened his home to Ho during the Paris peace talks of 1946.

2. See Robert McNamara, with Brian Van De Mark, *In Retrospect: The Tragedy and Lessons of Vietnam* (New York: Random House, 1995); and Raymond Aubrac, *Où la mémoire s'attarde* (Paris: Odile Jacob, 1996).

3. McNamara with Van De Mark, *In Retrospect*, 297.

4. McNamara with Van De Mark, *In Retrospect*, 300.

5. McNamara with Van De Mark, *In Retrospect*, 302.

6. Patrick McGarvey, *Visions of Victory, Selected Vietnamese Communist Military Writings, 1964–1968* (Stanford, Calif.: Hoover Institute on War, Revolution, and Peace, 1969), 276. The work is based on the writings of these two authors, as well as those of Giap, Van Tien Dung, and Chien Binh.

7. *The Times* (London), 14 February 1968.

8. Oriana Fallaci, *Témoignage sur le Nord-Viet-nam* (Sablé-sur-Sarthe: Imprimerie Coconnier, 1969), 51–52, 61.

9. V. G. and J.-L. Arnaud, "Les deux coups d'Etat manqués du général Giap," *Le Matin*, 27–28 October 1979.

10. Vo Nguyen Giap, *Nhan Dan Chu Nhat* [People's daily] (Hanoi), 7 May 1989.

11. Letter addressed to the highest authorities in the legal system of the Socialist Republic of Vietnam, 27 August 1993. Complete French translation appears in *Forum*, no. 10 (December 1993): i–iv.

12. *Translator's note:* Jiri Pelikan was a Czech dissident opposed to the Soviet line.

13. Jiri Pelikan, "Connexion des Conséquences internationales du printemps de Prague," presented at a colloquium, 22–23 October 1981, 9.

14. *France-Asie*, no. 72 (May 1952): 144.

15. Vu Can, "Intoxication," clandestine edition, published by the author.

16. Susan Sontag, *Trip to Hanoi* (New York: Farrar, Straus, and Giroux, 1969), 12.

17. Sontag, *Trip to Hanoi*, 73–75.

18. Vu Ky, *Bac Ho viet di chuc* [Uncle Ho writes his testament] (Hanoi, 1989).

19. *Beijing Information*, no. 37 (14 September 1981): 12–14.

20. Nguyen Vinh Long, "Le mausolée du président Ho Chi Minh," *Courier du Vietnam*, no. 40 (September 1975): 10–11.

21. *Indo-China* (Naval Intelligence Division, 1943), 109.

22. B. H. Nguyen, "Engseignement supérieur et idéologique du Vietnam," *Églises d'Asie*, no. 153 (April 1993).

23. *Translator's note:* Nguoi simply means "he" in Vietnamese, but when capitalized it functions in the same way as the "He" that refers to the Christian god.

24. Hoang Minh Chau, *Van Nghe*, 17 December 1988.

25. Claude Palazzoli, *Le Viet-nam entre deux mythes* (Paris: Economica, 1981).

PART FOUR

VISIONS OF THE FUTURE

CHAPTER SEVEN

The Era of Renovation

Nguyen Van Ky

In the 1980s, after so many years of struggle and conflict, Vietnam was again thrust into war, this time with its neighbors. The Vietnamese then had to suffer the sanction of isolation. By this time power was once again solidly rooted in Hanoi, but the government found itself faced with a new problem: how to resolve the contradictions between ideological imperatives and the pressing realities of a modern nation. The solution can be summed up in one word: *doi moi*, or renovation. This primarily involved the transformation to a free market economy, but with it came a demand for political and economic freedoms that would shake the very foundations of power and compromise the country's future.

While the winds of change brought new materialism from abroad, changes were also taking place within the country. Many now felt the need for freer expression, which resulted in a blossoming of literary works. These works are marked by suffering but are also enlivened by a newfound critical sense. The nation's youth, however, were plunged into a new kind of crisis, faced with the uncertainties of both the present and the future.

Vietnam has always surprised foreign observers by its range of possibilities, even if many were questionable. Can we now predict what direction the country will take based on the example of other socialist countries that have traveled the same path? The answer may lie in the fact that Vietnam has always managed to bring together contrasting viewpoints and thus find moderate solutions between the extremes.

To Be Twenty in Hanoi

According to a reliable 1989 census, 18 percent of Vietnam's population (almost eleven million out of sixty million people) is between twenty and twenty-nine years old. This figure can also be applied to Hanoi, a city of more than two million people. Since the end of the war, the country's population has risen sharply while development has not been able to keep pace. Under such economic pressure, Hanoi is becoming the most expensive housing market in the nation. The illusion of easy money that comes from the tourist sector has created a proliferation of "mini hotels" that spring up in the urban landscape. These hotels push the inhabitants of the older buildings toward the periphery and encourage an alarming rise in promiscuity. Young people often find themselves in the streets, where public spaces have replaced the family home.

In the 1960s and 1970s, at the time when the *bao cap* (a policy to provide amenities to cadres) was still in place, an unmarried cadre had the right to an apartment in a collective building with an area no larger than twelve square meters (108 square feet); and one had to be a party member to be eligible. The less fortunate found themselves in four square meter (thirty-six square feet) rooms without any modern conveniences. Today the price of a square meter in a central neighborhood of Hanoi can cost the equivalent of a gold bar *(cay vang),*[1] while the average monthly salary of a young person is around 400,000 dong (about U.S.$40).

Several years ago the journal *Lao dong* ran a story that illustrates some of the hardships facing young people today.[2] It recounts the problems encountered by a young man from the provinces who went to Hanoi in the hopes of finding work. After having gotten his bachelor's degree in arts and letters in 1993, this young man—let us call him X—returned home to be among his own people. After a few months, however, he was full of dreams of adventure and went back to Hanoi where he stayed with friends. He did not find any work and so went up toward the Chinese border and returned two weeks later with a story about the widespread trafficking in that region. A magazine accepted his story, and he thought he had been taken on as a reporter. Full of excitement, X called his friends, and they invited him to share their apartment. But now his sister had been accepted to the university and had come to join him in the capital. He looked for a new place, with room for both him and his sister. After a frustrating search, he managed to find an apartment with running water and electricity for 200,000 dong (about U.S.$20) per month, a perfectly reasonable rent; but after a month the owner told him the room had been sold. X was back to square one. He started on a new search and learned that the university dormitories, built to house 300 students, must cope with 2,000 applicants. What he found is surreal: some students sleep on mats in the courtyard, and others, in the hallways or on the sidewalks, all the while hoping for a room. Then X's parents came all the way from their distant province to help the girl in her search, but they were increasingly distressed. X, in the meantime, found luxurious lodgings just waiting for tenants. The catch? Rent was $1,000 to $3,000 per month. The owners were obviously aiming at the foreign market: expatriates working in international organizations or foreign companies. On the other extreme, hundreds of huts have been set up on the waterfront to house the destitute for just ten cents per night, but even here one has to fight to get a place. In the end, it was there that X and his sister found a place to live.

In an attempt to catch up with other countries in the Association of Southeast Asian Nations, Vietnamese universities accept more and more students each year. But their infrastructure is poorly equipped to accommodate them all, and there is no employment policy to deal with the increasing number of graduates. *Lao dong* reports that at the beginning of the 1988–89 school year there were 15,000 students throughout the country; five years later, the number had risen to 40,000. Since 1988 more than one-half of Hanoi's 22,000 college graduates have not found work. In the space of four years, from 1988 to 1992, the unemployment rate among young graduates quadrupled, going from 10 percent to 41 percent. Broken down by school, 88 percent of graduates from the University of Hanoi were unemployed, as were 75 percent of those who studied at the School of Agronomy and 91 percent of young doctors. Some graduates even agree to work for free, as was the case with 200 young doctors who wanted to maintain their knowledge as well as familiarize themselves with real practice.

These new circumstances have forced the heads of educational institutions to revise their programs, especially in the area of foreign languages. Ten years ago Russian was still mandatory, while English and Chinese were optional. Today, English is at the head of the list, and Russian is not even offered. French is still offered, but its popularity is well below that of English. The young people of today have abandoned classical studies in favor of more lucrative areas like management, marketing, business, law, and computer science. According to a survey of 430 students conducted by the newspaper *Tuoi tre* [Youth] and reported on 26 March 1995, employment tops a list of concerns for 92.8 percent of students; next came friendship (85.8 percent), community service (66 percent), family (63.3 percent), and then money (52.7

percent). Even if this survey did not follow standard statistical methods, its results still reveal the current trends among young people. Interestingly, there is no sign of the ideals that motivated the political fervor of preceding generations. Born near the end of the war or at the time of reunification in 1976, today's youth have been spared the painful sacrifices that their parents had to endure. They throw themselves into life without looking toward the past. Social success and material comfort, accompanied by a little personal freedom, are their primary goals.

The society of consumption and the influx of Western lifestyles have rapidly transformed Vietnamese customs and standards of behavior. Previously guarded by strident taboos, sexuality has now come out into the open and is becoming a problem that worries many parents. The discussion about sexual education in *Tuoi tre* earlier that year only mentions the most conservative viewpoints, like abstinence, or vague suggestions concerning the introduction of sexual education programs in schools. The loosening of morals has resulted in a rise in young mothers and has driven some young girls to have abortions and still others to abandon their infants to traffickers who then sell them to Western couples looking to adopt. In Vietnam as a whole, 18–22 percent of abortions are performed on girls younger than eighteen, but in big cities like Hanoi and Saigon the number may be as high as 20–30 percent, according to *Van hoa* [Culture] (the weekly of the Ministry of Culture). One of these young girls told her story:

> It's like we're sliding from the top of a slippery slope. We ended up losing what we couldn't hold on to. In the heat of passion, they [boys] swore to us up and down; you would have thought they would sacrifice anything for us. But when "that thing" happened, they went crazy and invented all kinds of excuses and begged us to go and take care of it. But once it was taken care of, even though we weren't back on our feet again yet, they started in on us again to give them everything.[3]

In the absence of future prospects and in an attempt to alleviate their boredom, young people flock to karaoke bars, which have sprung up in every part of the city. But this current fad cannot hide the fact that Hanoi is sadly lacking adequate entertainment facilities. A city of more than two million people, it has only two or three cinemas, a couple of theaters—one built by the French at the turn of the century—a small stadium, and two public pools. Moreover, there are very few movies to choose from because of poor distribution and commercial relations with foreign countries, a situation made even worse by censorship. And in theaters, plays are only put on a few days per month.

Of course, economic openness has allowed a few people from Hanoi to rise to the top of the social ladder. These nouveau riche flaunt their wealth shamelessly. Their children now hang out in the discos at the chic hotels and have scrapped their Soviet or Czech motorcycles, like the Rochod, Minsk, or Samson, to acquire a Dream (a popular small motorcycle by Honda) or other more powerful machines. Some of them indulge in drag races after having blown out the brakes of their motorcycles, expressing their "lust for life" by taking tremendous risks. When they started in 1994–95, these motorcycle races only took place late at night, but nowadays this spectacle goes on in the middle of the afternoon. The route takes the racers down the widest avenue in Hanoi, Duong Hung Vuong, which happens to go past the mausoleum that houses the remains of Ho Chi Minh.

In May 1995 *Van hoa* reported on an event that had stunned both parents and teachers two months earlier. A group of high school students, both boys and girls, had tried to kill themselves by swallowing pills; thankfully, they were saved in time. According to the investigation, they had formed an "association" united by an oath of solidarity and loyalty. The statute stated that members had to live and die together. Upon learning this, the parents of one boy declared, "Let him die! Then we won't have to feed him anymore!"

The current generation of people in their twenties seems to have inherited the feelings of deception and disillusionment from the generation before—as if they unconsciously took over the burdens of their parents. Because of a blindness to current and past problems—whether they be political, cultural, economic, or pedagogical—the future of this group of young people remains precarious.

Renovation in the Literary World

Thanks to a number of recent translations, the English-speaking public now has access to the works of such authors as Duong Thu Huong, Bao Ninh, and Nguyen Huy Thiep. These three enfants terribles of Socialist Realism were all liberation fighters during the war with America before turning to the arts to express their feelings of disillusionment. Still others have been able to bring the past alive, with its unforgiving wall of repression, to finally exorcise its ghosts.

Duong Thu Huong and Her Paradise

For the first time since the Nhan Van Giai Pham affair of 1957, the Hanoi literary world—or at least its liberal and renovationist part—once again found its antiestablishment voice. The impetus was paradoxically given by the speech of Nguyen Van Linh, secretary general of the party, who in 1987 invited writers to "break their chains" and breathe new life into literature.[4] This rallying cry was an effort to enact the politics of *doi moi*, the Vietnamese version of Soviet perestroika that had been extolled the year before. Thus called on, many writers seized the chance to confront the past, even if some, like Duong Thu Huong, were skeptical about the chance for real democratization. The backlash was immediate, however, in the form of calls to order, threats, and incriminations. Progressive writers were once again banished by the regime. The Writer's Union that, since its creation in 1954, had served as a mouthpiece for government decisions, was careful not to take their part. Armed only with her courage, Hanoi author Duong Thu Huong had to pay the price for being outspoken, for standing up for human dignity, and for not submitting to a totalitarian regime. Her crime: she had just wanted to live "as a human being," according to her own terms. "No other Vietnamese author visiting France received as many shows of support and kindness, on the part of so many people, as Duong Thu Huong," writes an editor of *Dien dan* [Forum] about her visit in autumn 1995.[5] Curiously, this public appreciation and veneration left no impression on the French press, except for the newspaper *Libération*, which only briefly mentioned Huong's arrival in France.

Duong Thu Huong was born into a family of resistance fighters, but later her grandmother was condemned as a landowner during the Agrarian Reform Campaign. She studied the arts and became leader of a group of amateur artists who went to the front to support the troops. She devised the slogan "Tieng hat at tieng bom" [Sing to drown out the bombs] and also "carried the dead in her arms and dug up buried bodies" on the battlefield. Her works, such as *Novel without a Name*, explore the profound disenchantment that set in after unification in the generation that had once been dedicated to the war. Huong felt betrayed and wanted to become the spokesperson for the common person, whose "neck is too short and whose mouth is too tiny."[6] She dared tell, for example, of how the liberation forces could only take a plastic doll and a bicycle frame with them as recompense after the war, while whole truckloads were needed to transport the spoils amassed by certain generals for their wives up north. Witness to injustice, to discrimination, and to other abuses of power committed even before reunification, Huong long endured an inner revolt before finally giving voice to her bitterness.

Unlike many other novelists, she had no formal training in literary studies. It was only in 1979 that she sat in on talks about literature, philosophy, linguistics, and biology at the School for Writers (Nguyen Du) in Hanoi. A writer more by conviction than vocation, Huong began to write short stories in 1980. She came into the public eye in Hanoi in 1988 with the release of her book *Paradise of the Blind*. During a meeting of the Science and Technology Association in Hanoi on 9 February 1990, she explained why she had written this novel:

> While I was writing *Paradise of the Blind*, I found myself alone in front of the pages of a notebook; the images that had tormented my consciousness flooded back. I was nine years old when the Agrarian Reform Campaign began. I lived in Bac Ninh in a house along the highway, and the little garden where we grew our kohlrabi was next to the railroad tracks. One morning we awoke to find the body of a suicide victim, his head crushed on the tracks, his body lying on the edge of the garden. We found out that he was a member of the Party, a resident of the village of Dai Trang, who had been accused in denunciation sessions of being a landowner. Four days later, we found another body, this one hanging from a tree. Also a member of the Party, this village chief had previously been named to this post by the revolutionary organization for activist operations. As time passed I remembered other images. Condemned by popular justice, an accused man was executed; his body thrown into the rice field and delivered up to the thousands of people who came one by one to trample on him, to express their class hatred. . . . Then, from one morning to the next, we would find eviscerated bodies bearing hand-written signs reading "Traitor." . . . I believe that you cannot build a generous and just society on the ruins of one that is unjust, when human beings are themselves inhabited by cruelty and injustice.[7]

It is important to note that Duong Thu Huong was one of the only writers to deal with the taboo subject of the Agrarian Reform Campaign of the 1950s. This was tantamount to attacking the regime itself. The reaction of the authorities was swift in coming, and she was subjected to the whole range of party persuasion: threats, rehabilitation, intimidation, promises, and so forth. In the end, given her obstinacy and refusal to give up, she was simply thrown out of the party. Called an "antiparty whore" by the secretary general himself, the same man who had previously called on all artists to mobilize and give new life to the arts and letters, Huong realized that her doubts had been well founded.

This attack on Duong Thu Huong announced an increase in repression, resulting in a long period of silence. The public security police (Cong An) devised a plan to attack Huong, called the "Secret Documents Transmitted

Abroad" affair. They used a Vietnamese doctor living in the United States, Bui Duy Tam, who was traveling through Hanoi, to set up the whole affair. First he was arrested at the border for having—they said—information concerning state security, information transmitted by Huong, hidden in his bags. The police then circulated a pornographic video accusing Huong of having had sexual relations with this doctor, to discredit her, damage her reputation, and incriminate her politically. She was arrested and imprisoned in the outskirts of Hanoi.

This was in 1991, on the eve of the Seventh Party Congress. The intervention of Danielle Mitterand (president of France-Libertés) and Roland Dumas (French minister of foreign affairs), as well as the pressure exerted by Vietnamese communities abroad, finally forced the Vietnamese authorities to let her go. Her popularity became even greater. For many she represented the three elements of struggle: freedom of expression, the emancipation of Vietnamese women, and the defense of human rights. It is for this last reason that Jacques Toubon, French minister of culture, awarded her the Medal of the Chevalier des Arts et Lettres in December 1994. This mark of distinction subsequently gave rise to more suspicion on the part of the Vietnamese authorities, who unilaterally decided to freeze Franco-Vietnamese cultural relations for several months. Poet and bureaucrat Huy Can, president of the Association of Artists and Writers in Vietnam, called Toubon's actions "acultural" *(phi van hoa)*.[8] The work and reputation of Duong Thu Huong, however, were not affected.

The Price of War and Blindness

The literature of a country ravaged by decades of killing will obviously deal with the theme of war. But rarely are writings as powerful and upsetting as those of Bao Ninh, in particular *Noi buon chien tranh* [The sorrow of war], a work awarded the prize of the Writer's Association of Hanoi in 1991 along with two other novels.[9] The reactions it provoked caused the authorities to "suggest" that the title be changed to *Than phan tinh yeu* [The destiny of love]. The author and the award committee refused—but this, of course, did not stop copies of the book with this title from circulating in Hanoi.

Bao Ninh transports his readers into the nightmarish world of a war that destroys and crushes human lives. Suspended between dream and reality, the characters are caught up in the workings of the machine of destruction. They fall, one after the other, into the trenches and valleys, filling the Valley of Death with "screaming souls" who die so that others may live. One passage in the novel sheds light on the emotions of those who have skirted death:

Now it's all over. . . . And because we have won, naturally the just cause has won, and that truly is a great consolation. Nevertheless, one only has to reflect a little, to look at what is left of our lives, to look closely at this shameless peace, this country which has won: what does one come away with? Pain, bitterness, and above all sadness, an infinite sadness. . . . Justice won, human duty won; but evil, death, and violence against humanity also won.[10]

What chance has love in the face of this carnage? One scene illustrates this tragedy in an encounter between the two principle characters of the novel: Kien, the wounded combatant, and Phuong, the young woman from Hanoi whose youth was stolen by the war:

It was so long ago. An event before all other events of his life. . . . That night, after the attack which had immobilized it, the suicide train continued on its way. . . . The cars were blackened and crude, identical, with doors hermetically sealed. All of a sudden one of the doors cracked open, men jumped out of the car onto the ground. . . . There were yawns. Swearing. The smell of alcohol. Without knowing why, Kien was sure that the car they had come out of was the one he had been in with Phuong the night before. . . . What he saw, initially, had nothing surprising about it, nothing frightening. In a corner shrouded in darkness, Phuong was sitting down, sleeping maybe, leaning back on sacks of rice, her legs tucked up, her head resting on her bare arms which encircled her knees, hair scattered about her shoulders.

"Phuong. Is that you, Phuong?"

Kien trembled, incredulous. He called out to her quietly, his voice hoarse, and went closer. He felt his knees weaken, and was afraid he would collapse. Phuong raised her head. Her cheeks were emaciated and pale. Her face looked different, like that of a stranger. The buttons had all been ripped from her shirt. Her neck was chafed. . . .

Phuong let Kien hug her convulsively, she bit her pale, cracked lips, and looked at him silently. A fixed stare, indifferent, unsure, far away, as if she wanted to block Kien's questions and his emotions.

Horrified, Kien shook Phuong's shoulders:

"Don't be afraid, my darling, we'll get over this. But what has happened to you? What's wrong with you? What is it?"

Kien tried to close her shirt, but there wasn't a single button left. Her bra was also crooked, and one of the straps was hanging off of her. Trembling and afraid, Kien put it back in place with feverish hands. Phuong's chest was ice cold, glazed with beads of sweat.

He was seventeen years old. At that time, and at that age, you didn't know a lot about life. . . . But he was in pain, a pain apparently without cause. Tears rushed to his eyes, salty and bitter, and ran down his cheeks.[11]

The narrator tries to start a new life in a new place, different from what he had known in his youth. His quest takes him to Hanoi, a city coping with the aftermath of war, and he finds himself isolated from reality, a reality in which he struggles to find meaning. The allegory that runs through the novel symbolizes the destiny of human beings confronted with tragedies that crush both hope and the future, love and friendship—in short, all that is left of human feeling. Undoubtedly, with the arrival of peace, some writers felt the need to tackle unconventional themes. Duong Thu Huong, for example, felt the need to "repay the debt," referring to the missing whose names we have forgotten, victims of murderous frenzy or of the Maoist-inspired Agrarian Reform Campaign.

The two other authors celebrated at the same time as Bao Ninh each dealt in his own way with the tragedies of the Agrarian Reform Campaign. The most compelling work is Nguyen Khac Truong's *Manh dat lam nguoi nhieu ma* [Land of men and ghosts].[12] In this novel, Truong juxtaposes the arbitrariness of ideology and the fierce struggle for power that pits two rival clans from the same village against each other. The struggle degenerates into the desecration of tombs, the most reprehensible and horrific act against a Vietnamese family. Nguyen Khac Truong exposes the extremes of love and hate: "Sometimes man threatens ghosts, and sometimes he disguises himself as a ghost to terrorize others." In the decisive hour of vengeance, one of the protagonists stands in front of the tomb of his sworn enemy and calls on the gods as his witness:

> Venerable tutelary spirit,
> Venerable village chief,
> Venerable Merciful Quan An in Nirvana,
> Venerable Mistress of Hell,
> Permit me to bring you this:

> For generations the Vu clan has betrayed us out of spite and bitterness, they have passed off vultures as crows, millipedes as snakes, and have inflicted countless hardships on our clan, the Trinh. They have confiscated our rice fields, our heritage, our love, and our loyalty, causing us constant difficulties. Too much smoke for so small a fire. Too much trouble in our clan. The time has come to repay kindness with kindness and blow for blow. Oh! Oh! Oh! . . .

> Venerable tutelary spirit, permit me now to defile the body of a member of the Vu by turning him over in his grave, to bring back on this Earth the vengeance of karma.

> > Let their line become extinct in three generations,
> > Let the Vu have only girls and no boys,

Let there be birth but without life,
Let their wives give birth backwards,
Let their men die without graves,
Some in the west, some in the east,
And let the survivors wander in unhappiness.
Let their vegetables be transformed into weeds,
Their rice into reeds,
Their betel into pepper-plants,
Their eggplant into pepper.
Let them struggle, let them toil.
Without hope of surviving.
Oh! Oh! Oh![13]

Duong Huong, author of *Ben khong chong* [Quay of the spinsters], focuses on the destiny of Vietnamese women. At the price of physical and moral sacrifices, they are forced to keep silent to preserve the appearance of harmony behind the wall of bamboo. In this novel we find prejudice against women, superstitions that still thrive in the countryside, and the clannishness that destroys two families—in this case, the Nguyen and the Vu. The story covers a span of some thirty years and opens on the return of the main character, Van, as he comes from the battle of Dien Bien Phu:

In days past, our elders used to call this the "Quay of the Spinsters." Today we call it the "Quay of Love." . . .

On the very day when the Nguyen clan was celebrating the inauguration of the biggest temple in town, dedicated to its ancestors, the beautiful daughter of the village chief went down during the evening to the Quay of Love to bathe. She didn't know that the boys of the Vu clan were also there, upstream, to do the same. The suggestive romanticism of the river, mixed with the beauty of the female body troubled one of the boys who dove gracefully into the water and embraced the tender and fresh body of the girl. The young girl fainted into the arms of this boy lit up by desire, taking him for a tortoise, a great snake-like reptile, or the red-faced ghost come to rape her.

The next morning, they found her naked body at the foot of Da Bac Bridge, and an unprecedented bloody conflict was unloosed between the two clans.

The ancestor of the Nguyen then issued a curse upon the Vu clan.[14]

A novel by Le Luu, *Chuyen lang cuoi*,[15] also caused a stir in Hanoi in 1993 and was harshly criticized by the authorities.[16] However, to this day Le Luu's tale provides us with the most concrete details about the Agrarian Reform Campaign. The author realistically portrays the procedures used by the "reform brigade" (*doi cai cach*), indicating its composition and the role and name of each of its members. The redistribution of land, which in theory was to bring peace and happiness to the village, in practice translated into executions, accusations, humiliations, condemnations, betrayals, and destruction even between members of the same family. Sons turned against their fathers, and wives turned against their husbands, all under the inquisitional eye of the all-powerful brigade that dissolved the party apparatus at the communal level the minute it took power. Both former resistance fighters and party members became targets for these new comrades sent in from the outside. It was the time of the "people's tribunal," as orchestrated by the brigade. As the novel illustrates, everything was planned out in advance:

> We have thirty-six people who are ready to denounce, divided into the following groups: three will denounce the confiscation of lands; four, share-cropping; six, ill treatment; five, interest paid in kind [i.e., in grain]; one, rape; four, spying for the enemy; three, participation in the VNQDD; six, the exploitation of day-laborers; two, the plot to assassinate Bat to silence the witness; two, an anti-reform plot. If one of them falters, the tribunal will call upon someone from another group to respect the time that has been allotted to us. . . .
>
> Tomorrow, if a victim stammers or stumbles over a word, the other members of the group will have to help him finish, and the comrades in charge of propaganda will follow them closely, yelling through the loud-speakers: "Down with —! Down with —!" If someone forgets the reply, the others are forbidden to laugh. Anyone caught laughing will be considered a reactionary who brings down the spirit of the peasant struggle. When the victim is at a loss for words, people can go up and slap him, saying: "How dare you remain silent?" or else: "This landowning bastard must pay for his crimes!"[17]

The novel brings us to the eve of the people's verdict condemning a supposedly dangerous character. But the accused is none other than a former combatant at Dien Bien Phu, a Communist who still believed in the ideals of the revolution and in the soundness of his party. He wanted to alert the central authorities about these misguided actions that endangered the party but was prevented from doing so. When the order to stop the executions finally reached the village, the war veteran had just been shot a few seconds earlier.

Notes

1. A gold bar of 100 grams is the unit of currency for real estate transactions, with one bar equal to about U.S.$500.

2. *Translator's note:* Lao dong [Labor], the journal of the Federation of Unions, published this article in its 28 March 1995 issue.

3. *Van hoa,* 19 November 1995.

4. Reported by Duong Thu Huong to students in Vietnamese studies at the University of Paris VII–Jussieu, 7 November 1994.

5. *Dien dan* is a bilingual Franco-Vietnamese journal published in Paris. Since July 1995 it is only published in Vietnamese.

6. *Translator's note:* This phrase, "Thap co be hong," is a Vietnamese expression that refers to the average citizen who has no possibility of expressing him- or herself.

7. Cited in *Dat Moi* (April 1990), a monthly published by the Vietnamese community in Canada.

8. *Van Nghe* [Arts and letters], 24 December 1994.

9. The three books in question are the following: Bao Ninh, *The Sorrow of War,* trans. Phan Thanh Hao (New York: Pantheon, 1994); Duong Huong, *Ben khong chong* [Quay of the spinsters] (Hanoi: Writer's Association, 1991); and Nguyen Khac Truong, *Manh dat lam nguoi nhieu ma* [Land of men and ghosts] (Hanoi: Writer's Association, 1991).

10. Bao Ninh, *Le Chagrin de la guerre* [The sorrow of war], trans. Phan Huy Duong (Paris: Ed. Philippe Picquier, 1994), 207.

11. Ninh, *Le Chagrin de la guerre,* 219–21.

12. Translated into French as *Des fantômes et des hommes,* trans. Phan The Hong and Janine Gillon (La Tour d'Aigues: Editions de l'Aube, 1996).

13. Nguyen, *Des fantômes et des hommes.*

14. Huong, *Ben khong chong,* 13.

15. This can be roughly translated as "Stories of the Village of Liars." For Vietnamese society, "Cuoi" represents a legendary character who lies as easily as he breathes. There are even competitions in certain areas for telling lies.

16. See also the novel of Ngo Ngoc Boi, *The Nightmare,* which also deals with the ravages of the Agrarian Reform Campaign, discussed in Georges Boudarel, *Cent fleurs écloses dans la nuit du Viêt-nam, 1954–56* (Paris: Jacques Bertoin, 1991), 179–83.

17. Le Luu, *Chuyen lang Cuoi* [Stories of the village of liars] (Hanoi: Editions Hoi nha van, 1993).

CHAPTER EIGHT

A Capital for All Vietnamese

Georges Boudarel

No matter how the Vietnamese feel about their current situation, it is unlikely that they will express their frustration through violent revolt. They have suffered through so many years of war that all they really want now is peace. Moreover, the constant change of political systems has left the people depoliticized. The Communist Party is well aware of this desire for peace and so continually reassures the Vietnamese people that stability will remain a primary goal in all future decisions. After all, peace is a nonpartisan issue.

Recognizing the importance of public opinion is one of the most vital qualities of a good government. Until now, the only countries that have made a fairly smooth transition away from Communism are those that had already had previous regimes that were in touch with the will of the people. At the head of this short list, one could place Hungary, Poland, and especially the former Czechoslovakia, where Jan Hus championed freedom of expression in Europe long before Luther. Everywhere else, be it the former USSR or the former Yugoslavia, the transition led to civil wars that were perhaps already lurking beneath the surface. Regardless of the theoretical differences, one thing is certain: the violence of these conflicts strikes at all kinds of freedom. The only freedom that is not wounded by the bullets of a civil war is the freedom to kill.

As opposed to the turmoil in Russia or Yugoslavia, China's current situation exemplifies a calm and successful transition—at least on an economic level. On the political level, however, this transition has resulted in suffocation, contradiction, and immobility. The party apparatus is now full of ideologues who stay in power by aligning themselves with a new organization, one that is stripped of all political vision: the "Red Mafia."

Hanoi prudently remains at the crossroads of these intersecting currents, as it has for years. Although the decades of war could easily have led to totalitarian and bloody regimes, Hanoi has remained relatively stable. Such regimes have appeared instead in Vietnam's neighbors: from the Maoism of Beijing, to that of its acolyte in Pyongyang, to its direct descendant in the Khmer Rouge. Caught up in the turmoil of these pseudo-allies, Hanoi deserves credit for having been able to maintain a certain stability in such a dangerous environment. At a time when market economies are fashionable all over the world, Hanoi could serve as a model for remaining stable through a potentially rough transition.

Despite the seeming contradictions, this "socialist market economy" is not a novelty in the world of Marxism-Leninism. There is no need to go back to Lenin's New Economic Politics;[1] the real models can be found elsewhere. The concept is not new, in fact, and was not devised by economists on Wall Street but, rather, by Slavic dissidents in a cultural context. Over the years the official line has tried to make us forget such dissidents and their revolutionary ideas—men like the Czech Alexander Dubcek and his Economic Minister Ota Sik, or the Pole Wladyslaw Gomulka, who disappeared from memory despite his prescience, or economist Oskar Lange.

Today, when so many revolutionaries have a hard time keeping in step with the modern world, there are still some who can teach us something, for example, Hanoi philosopher Tran Duc Thao. Thao is as famous for his theoretical ideas as he is for his political disappointments. He tried to work within a system that first put him on the sidelines and then rehabilitated him, though without daring to say it openly.

In 1950, Thao found a Vietnamese editor in Paris to publish his work *Phénoménologie et matérialisme dialectique,* in which he returns to Marx by way of Husserl. Then he joined the Vietminh Resistance. After his participation in the antiestablishment wave of 1956, he was relegated to doing translations for thirty years and wandering alone through the streets of Hanoi, a city now blinded by fear. When a green light was finally—and surprisingly—given from above, he was able to disseminate his own ideas again, and in 1988 he found a Vietnamese publisher for his *The Problem of Man and the Philosophical Theory Eliminating the Individual Subject.* This scathing anti-Althusserian attack does away with the "theoretical practice" that wedded psychoanalysis and structuralism and does without a theory of the individual subject. Based on his own sad experience, Tran Duc Thao's account disturbed the Maoist intelligentsia who claimed to be leftist. But as many Asians have now admitted: "For more than twenty years, Althusser's theories on the general absence of the subject *(Khong con nguoi noi chung)* was Stalinist-Maoism's strongest bastion of defense, blocking every effort to rethink Marxist-Leninism. So much so that it ended up creating a monster: the genocidal theory of the Pol Pot–Ieng Sari clique which helped form the murderous fanaticism of the Khmer Rouge."[2]

Renovation: A Question of Life and Death

Tracking the movement of ideas in Communist Vietnam is a complex project, but a good figure to follow is Tran Do. At the heart of the party apparatus in the mid-1950s, he privately advocated renovationist ideas while still conforming to the official line in his public remarks. In the 1930s he had the chance to become assistant to writer-journalist Tran Mai Ninh (alias of Nguyen Thuong Khanh). He was interested in journalism and literature, but the demands of revolutionary activity led him elsewhere. He escaped from Son La prison, played a key role in Hanoi during the August Revolution of 1945, and then fought against the French in the 312th Division, which he accompanied all the way to Dien Bien Phu. After having been a moderating force amid the ideological fervor of 1956–58, he was promoted to the rank of lieutenant general of the army and sent to the South as assistant to the commander in chief.

According to Kiem Dat, a military chronicler from the South, Do's analyses take all factors into account, from the political, to the military, to the literary.[3] His comprehensiveness and objectivity made him one of the forerunners of Vietnamese glasnost—before the word was ever uttered in Moscow—from which he would later take inspiration. It is under his influence that novelist Nguyen Minh Chau revived the views of the dissidents of 1956 in an article entitled "Writing the War," published in 1978 in the literary review of the army.[4] In this article Chau attacks the propagandistic literature that exalts the ideal qualities of fictitious characters without taking into account the realities and complexities of real people.

Critic Hoang Nghe Hien denounced this same literature as propaganda that tries to "conform to the rule" *(phai dao)* but is only a drab "illustration" *(minh hoa)* of the official line. Tran Do, who was then minister of culture but still more or less on the sidelines, supported these iconoclasts, whose ideas had won him over during the Sixth Party Congress—the 1986 congress dedicated to the policy of *doi moi.* He believed, as a Communist and as a militarist, that this sort of critical openness was necessary for real democratization.[5] It is at this time that Truong Chinh, the hardest of the hard-liners, made this observation, which sounded strange coming from him: "Renovation is a question of life and death."

This turning point sparked a blossoming of news reports, short stories, and debates. These new "Red" writers did not mince words and were not afraid to tackle taboo subjects. One of the most famous, Nguyen Khai, went as far as rehabilitating the Nationalists and peasant entrepreneurs in a short novel dedicated to the former Nationalist Minister Vu Hong Khanh, who was liberated from an internment camp and ended his days in his native village.[6] At the same time, a party resolution recognized the right of every family to work their land, though the latter remained, in principle, the property of the collective. From then on, a secret property market was created. Everything seemed to be changing rapidly, but progress was soon halted. In 1989 Do was removed as head of the Department of Arts and Letters by the Central Committee, which cleverly accomplished this by simply fusing two commissions. He was not able to publish again until April 1990, in a nonconformist review located outside the capital called *Cua Viet*—an edition that was immediately seized.

Around the same time, the world witnessed the fall of the Berlin Wall, perceived as a complete failure of the so-called Socialist bloc and a menace on all fronts for Communist Vietnam. It caused a temporary halt to the movement toward openness, and Vietnam seemed to have fallen back into a somber conformity. In reality, however, the political activity behind the scenes continued discreetly, as people and ideas continued to clash.

At this time, an order was given from above that "convinced" the Socialist and Democratic Parties to disband, parties whose journals *To quoc* and *Doc lap* had opened their pages to the views of antiestablishment intellectuals. But this sectarian decision then deprived the Communists of an instrument through which to enact a quiet and stable transition toward a plurality of opinions and organizations. The clearest result of this crackdown was the appearance of illegal Vietnamese presses, whose success was encouraged by the growing number of photocopy shops. These antiestablishment texts were often the work of Marxists such as Nguyen Khac Vien, an ardent proponent of revolutionary ideas. Since 1980, he had spoken out for changes in the realm of information, even in the pages of the Communist daily.[7] Vietnam was on its way toward a real renovation.

Steps and Missteps in the Diaspora

The Hanoi leadership encouraged the return of the "boat people" for rather pragmatic reasons: these would-be émigrés were appreciated not only for their financial strength but also for their skills and sometimes even their ideas. A special periodical was even created to deal with the issue. This reversal of the official current would end up having serious repercussions in the émigré community, a powerful group of two to three million people spread over five continents, with some 250 periodicals.

Strong contacts soon developed among many of these émigré groups, even though many had been in opposition only a short time before. In June 1989, the minister of Foreign Affairs in Hanoi, Nguyen Co Thach, met with a diverse group of exiles in Paris, some of whom were with the CIA.[8] And in Washington, young Vietnamese were planning a colloquium in the halls of Congress for 27 July 1993 to help their country, which was foundering under the oppositional force of Chu Ba Anh.[9] Several months later, Stephen Young, an American lawyer married to a Vietnamese woman, planned to hold a colloquium on the reconstruction of Vietnam. It was to be held in Ho Chi Minh City on 27 November 1993 and would include former members of the Dai Viet Party—many of whom had been recently liberated thanks to Young and other Americans involved in the war, such as former CIA head William Colby and General Westmoreland. According to Young, the month-long preparations were encouraged by "liberal" leaders of the Communist Party in Hanoi. At the tribunal of the United Nations in October, Vice President Pham Van Khai called for "step-by-step renovation of the political system," saying that "all Vietnamese who wish for a prosperous and strong Vietnam . . . will find a place in the great unity of the nation even if they are of different political opinions."[10] This promising colloquium was banned at the last minute, quite possibly sparing Vietnam the risk of a bloody incident like the one in Beijing's Tiananmen Square.

In spite of these brusque shifts and reversals, the progression toward political change seems real. At the very least it has led to the exchange of confidential information that makes the opposition papers in Hanoi exciting sources of information for those abroad. One must, of course, read everything with a high degree of caution, for propaganda is not foreign to either side.

The Seventh Party Congress in 1991 definitively put a halt to progress, and preparations for the Eighth Party Congress in 1995–96 were marked by a bitter struggle between two oppositionist factions. Their writings, in theory still "internal and confidential," landed shortly thereafter in émigré journals. At the end of June 1996, the Eighth Congress opened in this tense atmosphere. Shortly before, however, Vo Van Kiet's group, which supported openness on all fronts, had seen a sudden victory: the elimination of two of his powerful adversaries, Nguyen Ha Phan and Dao Duy Tung, removed for reasons of politics or health.

In spite of these events, the congress stuck to the official renovationist line in language that was more wooden than ever. The foreign press hastily concluded that there had been no change; but this was far from the truth. Reading publications of the émigré community, one has the impression that the top secret "information" of the Politburo reaches them regularly, to the point at which one can see a subtle compromise between oppositional viewpoints.

The Catholic periodical *Tin nha* reprinted the interview given to Radio France Internationale by Hoang Minh Chinh, who had only recently been released from yet another year in prison. Taking up the views of Phan Dinh Dieu and the former leader of the Socialist Party, Nguyen Xien, Chinh calls for the organization of a roundtable that would reunite the Communist Party with intellectuals living both in the country and abroad in order to search for real solutions. The monthly *Thong luan,* initially an advocate of reconciliation based on cooperation, cites at length a text from Communist Nguyen Ho, who had been under house arrest for years. He calls for the unconditional support of Vo Van Kiet, an advocate of openness. *Dien dan* in Paris, once a strong supporter of Hanoi but now highly critical, adopted a similar position, citing another militant equally persecuted because of differences of opinion, Nguyen Kien Giang. The latter advocated simultaneous progression in four areas: the demilitarization of society and the establishment of a free market economy, of a legal system, and of an authentic democratic regime.

These many points of view, which manage to come together despite their differences, reflect an optimism not seen in the Western press. But no one knows what the future will bring. It largely depends on the attitude of the countries that claim to defend human rights. Will they give priority to short-term economic interests, to the construction of capitalism by a corrupt mafia that supposedly has its roots in a single-party system that claims to be building socialism? Or will they prefer to give a place to political debate that reinforces the play of economic factors in the long term? In the end, both Vietnamese and international opinions will judge by facts and not by discourse, no matter what the color of the rhetoric.

Notes

1. New Economic Politics (1921–28) was Lenin's attempt to delay collectivization and encourage capitalism in order to stimulate the economy and make money that was much needed for the recovery and development of the Soviet state.

2. Tran Duc Thao, *Van de con nguoi va chu nghia ly luan khong con nguoi* [The problem of man and the philosophical theory eliminating the individual subject] (Hanoi, 1989), 168.

3. Kiem Dat, *Chien tranh Viet Nam* [The war in Vietnam] (Los Angeles: Dai Nam, 1982), 85.

4. Nguyen Minh Chau, "Viet Ve Chien tranh" [Writing the war], *Van Nghe Quan Doi,* November 1978.

5. Tran Do, "Rénovation et démocratization," *Le Courier du Vietnam,* April 1988: 8–10.

6. Nguyen Khai, *Mot coi nhan gian be ti* [A microcosmos of the country].

7. Nguyen Khac Vien, "Améliorer l'information, le pouvoir, et les médias," *Nhan Dan,* 16 March 1980, cited in *Infoasie* (Paris), no. 3 (January 1981).

8. See Georges Boudarel, "La diaspora vietnamienne et les perspectives de réconciliation nationale," *Vietnam Review,* no. 1 (1996): 350–53.

9. See *Phu nu dien dan* [Woman's forum] (published in the United States), no. 116 (September 1993): 10–12.

10. Nayan Chanda and Murray Hiebert, "Hawks and Eagles," *Far-Eastern Economic Review,* 9 December 1993.

Selected Bibliography

Annault, Jacques, ed. "L'expérience vietnamienne: Du colonialisme au socialisme." *La Nouvelle Critique*, March 1962.

Aubrac, Raymond. *Où la mémoire s'attarde*. Paris: Odile Jacob, 1996.

Azeau, Henri. *Ho Chi Minh, dernière chance*. Paris: Flammarion, 1968.

Bao Ninh. *The Sorrow of War*. Trans. Phan Thanh Hao. New York: Pantheon, 1994.

Boudarel, Georges. *Cent fleurs écloses dans la nuit du Viêt-nam, 1954–56*. Paris: Jacques Bertoin, 1991.

Brocheux, Pierre, and Daniel Hémery. *Indochine: La colonisation ambiguë, 1858–1954*. Paris: La Découverte, 1994.

Bui Xuan Vao. *Naissance et évolution du roman vietnamien moderne, 1925–1945*. Paris: La Voie nouvelle.

Chanoff, David, and Doan Van Toai. *Portrait of the Enemy: The Other Side of the War in Vietnam*. New York: Random House, 1986.

Devilliers, Philippe. *Paris, Saigon, Hanoi. Les archives de la guerre, 1944–1947*. Paris: Gallimard, "Archives," 1989.

Duong Huong. *Ben khong chong* [Quay of the spinsters]. Hanoi: Writer's Association, 1991.

Duong Thu Huong. *Histoire d'amour racontée avant l'aube*. Trans. Kim Lefevre. La Tour d'Aigues: l'Aube, 1991.

———. *Paradise of the Blind*. Trans. Pham Huy Duong and Nina McPherson. New York: Penguin, 1994.

———. *Novel without a Name*. Trans. Pham Huy Duong and Nina McPherson. New York: Penguin, 1995.

Fallaci, Oriana. *Témoignage sur le Nord-Viet-nam*. Sablé-sur-Sarthe: Imprimerie Coconnier, 1969.

Godart, Justin. *Rapport de mission en Indochine, 1er janvier–14 mars 1937*. Ed. François Billange, Charles Fourniau, and Alain Ruscio. Paris: l'Harmattan, 1994.

"Littérature du Viet-nam." *Europe*, July–August 1961.

Mai Thu Van. *Viet-nam, un peuple des voix*. Paris: Pierre Horay, 1983.

Marr, David G. *Vietnam 1945: The Quest for Power*. Berkeley: University of California Press, 1995.

McGarvey, Patrick. *Visions of Victory, Selected Vietnamese Communist Military Writings, 1964–1968*. Stanford, Calif.: Hoover Institute on War, Revolution, and Peace, 1969.

McNamara, Robert, with Brian Van De Mark. *In Retrospect: The Tragedy and Lessons of Vietnam*. New York: Random House, 1995.

Ngo Van. *Viet-nam, 1920–1945. Révolution et contre-révolution sous la domination coloniale*. Paris: l'Insomniaque, 1995.

Nguyen Huy Thiep. *Un général à la retraite*. La Tour d'Aigues: l'Aube, 1990 (reissued 1994).

———. *Le Coeur du tigre*. La Tour d'Aigues: l'Aube, 1993 (reissued 1995).

———. *Les démons vivent parmi nous*. La Tour d'Aigues: l'Aube, 1996.

Nguyen Khac Huyen. *Rêves, souvenirs, commentaires*. Hanoi: The Gioi, 1993.

Nguyen Khac Truong. *Manh dat lam nguoi nhieu ma* [Land of men and ghosts]. Hanoi: Writer's Association, 1991.

Nguyen Manh Tuong. *Un excommunié. Hanoi 1954–1991: Procès d'un intellectuel*. Foreword by Vo Van Ai. Paris: Que Me, 1992.

Nguyen Tien Lang. *Les Vietnamiens. I, Les Chemins de la révolte*. Paris: Amiot-Dumont, 1953.

Nguyen Van Ky. *La Société vietnamienne face à la modernité. Le Tonkin de la fin du XIXe siècle à la Seconde Guerre mondiale*. Paris: l'Harmattan, 1995.

Palazzoli, Claude. *Le Viet-nam entre deux mythes*. Paris: Economica, 1981.

Patti, Archimedes. *Why Vietnam? Prelude to America Albatross*. Berkeley: University of California Press, 1980.

Pham Quynh. "Nécessité du nationalisme annamite." In *Nouveaux essais franco-annamites*, 457–64. Hue, 1938.

Pham Van Ky. *Frères du sang*. Paris: Le Seuil, 1947.

Quirielle, François de. *À Hanoi sous les bombes américaines. Journal d'un diplomate français 1966–1969*. Paris: Tallendier, 1992.

Ruscio, Alain. *Vivre au Viet-nam*. 1981.

Saaf, Abdallah. *Histoire d'Anh Ma*. Paris: l'Harmattan, 1996.

Salisbury, Harrison. *Un Américain à Hanoi, derrière les lignes viet-cong*. Paris: Presses de la Cité, 1967.

Schwartz, Laurent. *Un mathématicien aux prises avec le siècle*. Paris: Odile Jacob, 1997.

Smith, R. B. *An International History of the Vietnam War. Vol. II: The Struggle for South-East Asia, 1961–65*. London: Macmillan, 1987.

Sontag, Susan. *Trip to Hanoi*. New York: Farrar, Straus, and Giroux, 1969.

Thu-Trang, Gaspard. *Ho Chi Minh à Paris (1917–1923)*. Preface by Philippe Devillers. Paris: l'Harmattan, 1992.

Tonnesson, Stein. *The Vietnamese Revolution of 1945: Roosevelt, Ho Chi Minh and de Gaulle in a World at War*. London: Prio, 1991 (reissued 1993).

Tuchman, Barbara W. *The March of Folly: From Troy to Vietnam*. New York: Knopf, 1984.

Turley, William S., ed. *Vietnamese Communism in Comparative Perspective*. Boulder, Colo.: Westview, 1980.

Viet Tran. *Viet-nam, j'ai choisi l'exil*. Preface by Jean Lacouture. Paris: Le Seuil, 1979.

Viollis, Andrée. *Indochine S.O.S.* Preface by André Malraux. Paris: Gallimard, "NRF," 1935.

Vo Nguyen Giap. *La Guerre de libération nationale*. Hanoi: ELE, 1970–75.

———. *Unforgettable Days*. Hanoi: Foreign Languages Publishing House, 1975.

Vu Bao, et al. *Le Héros qui pissait dans son froc*. La Tour d'Aigues: l'Aube, 1995.

Vu Thu Hien. *Dem giua ban ngay*. Westminster, Calif.: Van Nghe, 1997.

Werner, Jayne S., and Luu Doan Huynh, eds. *The Vietnam War: Vietnamese and American Perspectives*. Armonk, N.Y.: M. E. Sharpe, 1993.

Yeager, Jack A. *The Vietnamese Novel in French: A Literary Response to Colonialism*. Hanover, N.H.: University Press of New England, 1987.

Suggested Reading

Bao Ninh. *The Sorrow of War*. Trans. Phan Thanh Hao. New York: Pantheon, 1994.

Duiker, William J. *Sacred War: Nationalism and Revolution in a Divided Vietnam*. New York: McGraw-Hill, 1995.

——. *Vietnam: Revolution in Transition*. Revised ed. Boulder, Colo.: Westview, 1996.

Duong Thu Huong. *Paradise of the Blind*. Trans. Pham Huy Duong and Nina McPherson. New York: Penguin, 1994.

——. *Novel without a Name*. Trans. Pham Huy Duong and Nina McPherson. New York: Penguin, 1995.

Harrison, James P. *The Endless War: Fifty Years of Struggle in Vietnam*. New York: The Free Press, 1982.

Hodgkin, Thomas. *Vietnam: The Revolutionary Path*. New York: St. Martin's, 1981.

Jamieson, Neil L. *Understanding Vietnam*. Berkeley: University of California Press, 1993.

Lockhart, Gregg. *Nation in Arms: Origins of the People's Army of Vietnam*. Wellington, New Zealand: Allen and Unwin, 1989.

Marr, David G. *Vietnamese Tradition on Trial*. Berkeley: University of California Press, 1985.

Nguyen Tien Hung. *Economic Development of Socialist Vietnam, 1955–1980*. New York: Praeger, 1977.

Porter, Gareth. *Vietnam: The Politics of Bureaucratic Socialism*. Ithaca, N.Y.: Cornell University Press, 1993.

Shaplen, Robert. *Bitter Victory*. New York: Harper and Row, 1986.

Sheehan, Neil. *After the War Was Over: Hanoi and Saigon*. New York: Vintage, 1992.

Thrift, Nigel, and Dean Forbes. *The Price of War: Urbanization in Vietnam, 1954–1985*. London: Allen and Unwin, 1986.

Turley, William S. *The Second Indochina War: A Short Political and Military History*. Boulder, Colo.: Westview, 1986.

Vietnamese Studies. *Hanoi: From the Origins to the 19th Century*, vol. 1. Vietnamese Studies, 48. Hanoi: Foreign Languages Press, 1977.

Young, Marilyn B. *The Vietnam Wars, 1945–1990*. New York: HarperCollins, 1991.

Index

About the Authors and Translator

Georges Boudarel is a professor and researcher at the Université à Paris VII. He has published numerous articles on Vietnamese history, as well as several books on the subject, including *La Bureaucratie au Viêt-nam* (Paris, 1983) and *Cent fleurs écloses dans la nuit du Viêt-nam, 1954–56* (Paris, 1991). He also worked as a professor in Saigon and was hostile to the war led by the French government against Indochina. Boudarel then joined the Vietnamese resistance, an action that would make him the subject of accusations and cause problems later with the French government, though he has now been acquitted. He brings to this book a profound knowledge of Vietnamese history, culture, and language. His analysis is based not only on experience, which gives him a vision of the interior of Hanoi, Vietnam, and the Communist Party, but also on unpublished documents of a nature to shed light on a period too often considered only from a Western standpoint.

Nguyen Van Ky has spent his career studying Indochinese history and has taken many trips to his homeland to study contemporary society. He currently lives in Paris and continues his research in Vietnamese history, especially Hanoi. His publications include *La Société vietnamienne face à la modernité: Le Tonkin de la fin du XIXe siècle à la Seconde Guerre mondiale* (Paris, 1995).

William J. Duiker is Liberal Arts Professor Emeritus at The Pennsylvania State University. His most recent book is Ho Chi Minh: A Life (2000).

Claire Duiker has a Ph.D. in comparative literature from the University of Texas at Austin. She has lived and worked in Asia and Europe and now resides in Italy.